CW01395275

A Woman's War

A WOMAN'S WAR

The exceptional life of Wilma Oram Young, AM

BARBARA ANGELL

NEW HOLLAND

First published in Australia in 2003 by
New Holland Publishers (Australia) Pty Ltd
Sydney • Auckland • London • Cape Town

14 Aquatic Drive Frenchs Forest NSW 2086 Australia
218 Lake Road Northcote Auckland New Zealand
86 Edgware Road London W2 2EA United Kingdom
80 McKenzie Street Cape Town 8001 South Africa

Copyright © 2003 text: Barbara Angell
Copyright © 2003 photographs: Dot Angell, Federal Capital Press, Rosemary Parrant-Todman,
the *West Australian* (as credited)

All rights reserved. No part of this publication may be reproduced,
stored in a retrieval system or transmitted, in any form or by any means,
electronic, mechanical, photocopying, recording or otherwise, without
the prior written permission of the publishers and copyright holders.

National Library of Australia Cataloguing-in-Publication Data:

Angell, Barbara.
A woman's war: the exceptional life of Wilma Oram Young, AM.

Bibliography.
Includes index.
ISBN 1 74110 012 7.

1. Young, Wilma. 2. Nurses—Australia—Biography.
3. Prisoners of war—Australia—Biography. 4. Prisoners of
war—Japan—Biography. 5. World War, 1939–1945—
Prisoners and prisons, Japanese. 6. World War, 1939–1945—
Participation, Australian. I. Title.

940.5476092

Publishing Manager: Robynne Millward
Commissioning Editor: Anouska Good
Project Editors: Sophie Church and Karen Gee
Designer: Karlman Roper
Production Controller: Jane Kirby
Printed in Australia by McPherson's Printing Group, Victoria

10 9 8 7 6 5 4 3 2 1

This book is typeset in Aldine401 BT 11pt.

Front cover: Wilma in her nurses' uniform (left); Wilma's official army photograph (middle);
Wilma in 1999 at the unveiling of the National Mermorial to Service Nurses, Canberra
(right, courtesy the *Canberra Times*).

About the Author

Barbara Angell was educated at PLC in Melbourne and studied music at the Melba Conservatorium. She began her acting career at Melbourne's Little Theatre, then worked as a dancer–comedian with the Tivoli Circuit for four years. During a visit to the UK in 1959–60 she was introduced to revue and wrote comedy sketches, music and lyrics. On returning to Australia she formed her own revue company and co-wrote and produced a series of successful stage shows, with many years of television and stage appearances following. She wrote for and starred in the satirical *Mavis Bramston Show* during its four years. The next twenty years were spent in the UK where she appeared on stage, in films and in television dramas and comedies.

Barbara's first book, *The Entertainment Machine,* was published by Horwitz in 1972 and her second, *Voyage To Port Phillip, 1803*, in 1983. Most of her prolific writing career, however, has been for television and the stage. She has also been involved with the Alzheimers Associations of both the UK and Australia, and has served as president of the New South Wales (1991–93) and national chapters (1993–94).

For Daniel, Lianne, Ben, Alexine,
Christine, Margaret, Alan and Kenneth

A proud heritage

CONTENTS

FOREWORD

A quiet achiever, Wilma Oram Young, AM, lived for many years in the shadow of her more famous nursing colleagues—Betty Jeffrey, OAM, and Vivian Bullwinkel Statham, AO, MBE, ARRC. Now it is Wilma's turn to have her own remarkable life recorded for posterity. It was indeed with great pleasure that I accepted the invitation to write the foreword to this biography of one of Australia's truly remarkable women.

I first met Wilma Oram Young in Canberra on Remembrance Day 1991, when I was Chair of the Council for the Australian War Memorial. Wilma and some of her prisoner of war nursing colleagues were in town for the dedication of a memorial plaque and garden seat in front of the Changi Chapel, which is situated in the grounds of Duntroon Military College. The plaque and seat were in memory of their nursing colleagues who had not survived the sinking of the SS *Vyner Brooke* as they tried to escape the fall of Singapore in February 1942; and in memory of the twenty-one nurses who were so brutally massacred by the Japanese on Bangka Island at this time; and the eight other nurses who had not survived three-and-a-half years of captivity in the camps on Bangka Island and on Sumatra. It is only a part of Wilma's life story, but I can remember thinking at the time of our meeting what a quiet and dignified person she was for someone who had suffered so much. There was an aura about her that, as I later discovered, reflected her inner strength of character and humanitarianism.

Because of our membership of both the RSL and the Liberal Party, our paths were to cross frequently over the years. The more I got to know Wilma the more remarkable her life story became. Here was a woman who, at the age of twenty-five, had experienced the brutality, deprivation and degradation of being a prisoner of war of the Japanese for three-and-a-half years; who, on her return to Australia, married a dairy farmer and had four children. Her husband had also been a prisoner of war in World War II, of the Germans, and their marriage is unique in that it is possibly the only recorded marriage between two Australian service personnel who had both been prisoners of war.

Because of her husband's postwar illnesses, Wilma can be seen to have raised her children and run the dairy farm almost single-handedly. Here was a woman who had also survived the tragic teenage death of her beloved daughter Chrissie in a motorcycle accident and the early death of her husband Alan, yet she was 'still on her feet' and, until the time of her death in 2001, was constantly looking to help others in need—especially returned service men and women.

Some of us who are blessed to have heard Wilma speak about her experiences have been given an added bonus. Her philosophy has given us all the strength and courage to endure whatever hardships life might present us with. Perhaps those who read this biography will also be inspired and reap the benefit of her wisdom.

Vale Wilma Oram Young, AM; you have left us with a tremendous legacy.

Dame Beryl Beaurepaire, AC, DBE
Former Chair, Council for the Australian War Memorial
Convener, The National Women's Advisory Council

PROLOGUE: THE LAST POST

A funeral took place on Friday, 1 June 2001 at St James's Anglican Church in the small Gippsland town of Pakenham, Victoria. The community was gratified and maybe a little bemused by the attendance of no less than 500 people of all shapes, sizes, ages, colours and religions. The crowd spilled out onto the street. Among the mourners were some of the most powerful politicians, public figures, medical and military personnel in the land. There were representatives, too, of just about every major charitable organisation.

This ceremony was clearly in honour of an important person. No doubt, had she been able to, Wilma Young would have been writhing with embarrassment, saying, 'Don't, it's too much!' But there was no way that this particular lady would be allowed to leave without a big send-off. The occasion was only a little short of a state funeral but, for all its pomp, there was that warm feeling of a shared and real grief at the passing of a friend.

Pakenham is the sort of place where almost a full page might be devoted in the local *Gazette* to the fact that an episode of the long running television series 'Neighbours' is being filmed nearby. There are vast areas around Pakenham where you cannot see a house for kilometres across wide, flat expanses of scrubby land. Here it is still safe to go out and leave your door open. You can say to tradesmen, 'Go in and leave it on the table,' and Wilma did that constantly. She told friends where they could find the key to the guest annexe and come to stay any time for as long as they liked: 'It's there, you might as well use it, even if I'm not here.'

The most interesting feature of this most interesting funeral was the attendance of a group of 'bikies' in black leather jackets with bold emblems on their backs. They wanted to accompany the hearse and the family was willing. The bikies followed Wilma's remains, solemnly gunning their Harleys in salute—or attempting to, as the cortège moved too slowly through the town's main shopping precinct to make this mechanically possible. Nevertheless the noise was loud and people stared, as well they might.

'Could this be *our* Mrs Young's funeral, that kind old white-haired lady, the one with the quiet and dignified manner?'

'Yes, she did something in World War II.'

'Ah, *that* war …'

Wilma did do something in that war and far beyond it, and Pakenham took pride in these activities. They continued right up to the moment when she was wheeled into the operating theatre for a heart bypass operation, which was to put her on her feet again but was destined, eventually, to knock her off them for that final time. But what were bikies doing at Wilma's funeral? And what was the significance of the Harley–Davidson tricycle that followed her coffin, alone, immediately behind the hearse?

PART ONE:
REVEILLE

CHILDHOOD

Wilma Elizabeth Forster Oram was born on 17 August 1916 at Glenorchy in the rich wheat-growing Wimmera district of western Victoria. She was to be the middle child of five born to farmer Alf Oram and his wife Jane.

The Orams came from a little place called Joel Joel. Alf was born John Alfred Oram on a farm outside Stawell on the road to Landsborough. He was the second son of Joseph Oram and Elizabeth Oram née Olney. Alf was one of ten children, eight boys and two girls; that part of Victoria is still home to many Orams.

'The farm was probably wheat and sheep,' Wilma said of her grand-parents' property. 'The house had the kitchen separate from the bed-rooms, and I think it had an earth floor. We didn't go there very often. Transport wasn't easy and we lived a fair way from them. I didn't see a great deal of my grandparents.'

This was partly because Alf did not get along with his father. He managed to pass his Merit Certificate at the age of eleven and promptly left school. After working on the farm for a while he went shearing, as they did then, with his swag on his back. He moved from place to place wherever he could find work. His philosophy was 'God helps those who help themselves.' He was practical and down-to-earth, a good farmer, but with little economic sense.

Alf already had a soft spot for one of the local girls before he left home. As soon as he settled into a steady job, managing a property in

Western Australia, he received an ultimatum from Jane Forster, who
was also from Joel Joel. 'Marry me now or this is it!' she told him. He
proposed; she accepted and the couple went to Western Australia,
where they wed on 27 July 1910 in St John's Church, Albany. Alf was
aged twenty-four and Jane twenty-eight.

Jane was quiet and dignified. People described her as erect and ladylike. Before she tied the knot with Alf she had been a piano teacher.
She also painted exquisitely, both in watercolour and oil. It must have
been a case of opposites attracting because Alf was a free spirit,
gregarious and jolly.

The Western Australian property at Pingelly, which Alf managed,
was home to a large indigenous population, the traditional owners of
the land. Jane found them frightening, especially when Alf was away
attending to business. With hindsight it seems inevitable that there
would have been some resentment. Alf and Jane were probably
regarded as interlopers. What there was not, and could not be at that
time, was mutual understanding.

When she became pregnant Jane insisted on returning to her family to
give birth. Alf stayed at Pingelly and was not present when their son John
(known as Jack) was born at Sale on 9 June 1911. Shortly afterwards, Jane
made the journey yet again—several days by train—to rejoin Alf. She
brought little Jack with her but their isolation proved too stressful, especially now that they had a baby, and Jane persuaded Alf to give up his job
and move back to Victoria. Before leaving, Alf made arrangements with
his boss for a position to be waiting for him at the other end, but when
the young couple returned to the Wimmera no job materialised.

By the time their second child, a daughter, put in an appearance, Alf
was farming a property called Minnaburra, not far from Stawell.
Phyllis Normand Oram was born at Joel Joel on 30 January 1914.
Later that same year, with the advent of World War I, Alf tried to enlist
but was rejected because of his varicose veins. When Wilma was born
in 1916 Alf was farming at Glenorchy.

All these locations are within the same small area of the Wimmera.
Folk tended to stay put around those parts. Alf was leasing; he had not

yet amassed enough capital to buy his own property, but that was his aim. Jane was instrumental in keeping her young husband focused. She was a person who was very sure of her views, and would not easily be led astray.

Shortly after Wilma had pushed her way into the world the whole family fell victim to the influenza epidemic that followed World War I. 'They were miles out from anywhere, no doctors,' said Wilma. 'I don't know how they managed to survive it. My mother told me she dragged herself around and she was breastfeeding me at the time, too. Goodness knows how, but they all survived.' Interestingly, although she was taking her nourishment from an infected mother, Wilma did not catch the bug. Even at that age she demonstrated an ability to overcome the odds that life stacked against her.

By now fully involved in the business of bringing up a family under tough circumstances, Jane no longer played the piano or painted. Such was the destiny of women in the early 20th century, but Jane did not complain. She was strongly religious, a Protestant stoic who believed in 'God's will'. It was probably this faith that empowered one so sheltered, who had never travelled far from home, to make that journey to Western Australia to marry her wandering Alf. She displayed a certain grit and determination in doing so.

In 1919 the family moved to Rupanyup where Alf developed a passion for the game of lawn bowls. 'He'd play anything,' Jack said of his father, 'but bowls had just started in the country, and he participated in a working bee making a bowling green in Rupanyup.'

Rupanyup was, and still is, a typical Australian farming town, barely changed in nearly a century. There is now a plantation growing down the centre of the wide main street that would, in Wilma's childhood, have been a broad thoroughfare for the easy passage of animals to and from market. The town is prosperous, despite the fact that most of its buildings are in a poor state of repair.

By the time Wilma was two years old Alf was doing well enough to lease a wheat farm halfway between Rupanyup and the nearby town of Murtoa, a property he later bought. This provided Jane with security and she was able now to enjoy raising her family and to commence the agreeable task of establishing a garden.

The road from Murtoa to Rupanyup is long and straight, the land flat on both sides. It is occupied by huge properties these days, mainly wheat-growing. Across the plains, in the far distance, are the Victorian mountains known as the Grampians, which seem to loom suddenly out of the ground. Apart from this awesome sight, the area is completely flat.

The old Oram homestead is still there, situated on one of only two slight doglegs in the otherwise straight road from Murtoa to Rupanyup, almost exactly halfway between the two towns. The fairly large building, which is set back about 200 metres from the road, is constructed of weatherboard, in the Australian vernacular style. It is surrounded by well-established trees, part of the garden originally planted by Jane Oram, and it nestles among sprawling expanses of wheat. The average block in Alf's time was 640 acres. Jack reckoned their farm was closer to 750 acres, which is not large by today's measurements but back then was a good manageable size from which to make a living. The land between Murtoa and Rupanyup was considered to be wonderful 'black' ground, excellent for wheat farming. Everybody on the farms had dams for watering the livestock, plus tanks for storing rainwater for drinking. The dams would have also supplied water for Jane's treasured garden.

Wilma was about three when a mild family scandal occurred that would change the little girl's life. Until then she did not have to share her mother. Both Jack and Phyllis were at school, so Wilma had Jane to herself during the daytime. Then one day her grandmother and aunt moved into the house; a day that Wilma was to remember always.

The scandal is one that will hardly go down in Australian history. It was yet another sad case of the husband dying and the son being given power of attorney, selling the property over his mother's head and leaving her with nothing and nowhere to go. Jane asked if the two refugees could become part of the Oram household. Easy-going Alf was amenable. Why not, when, with his mother-in-law and sister-in-law there to keep his wife happy, he could slip off to play bowls with a clear conscience? For Wilma, however, the prospect was not so attractive. The arrival of Grandma and Auntie Annie was not welcome to the child who, eighty years later, made a shame-faced confession that from that day onwards she resented them both.

As it happened, Wilma's resentment made no difference one way or another because, shortly afterwards, on 19 March 1919, a second son named Lancelot Clive Forster Oram was born to Alf and Jane. As a result of the lingering presence of Grandma and Auntie, Lance escaped Wilma's resentment for usurping her place in her mother's attention and the two were to become close. On the occasion of Lance's birth, which took place at home, Wilma remembered a stately figure who moved into the house dressed in 'funny clothes'. This was Wilma's first encounter with a midwife—an occupation that she would eventually pursue.

The Oram household was to develop a tradition of hospitality. Soon the local school teacher, Miss Tubb, moved in as a boarder, contributing a bit extra to the finances. Wilma's elder sister Phyllis formed a lifelong friendship with Gertie Jeitz,[1] who soon spent more of her time inside the Oram house than anywhere else apart from school. Being a youngest child with much older siblings, Gertie felt a need for company her own age. The Orams opened their collective arms to her. Gertie remembered Wilma, then six years old, as chubby with black curls. 'I would call Wilma placid, never argumentative. I don't remember that there were ever sisterly fights. She had a wry sense of humour and was easy to get on with.'

According to Gertie, Grandma and Auntie fitted in well. 'There was never any dissension that I could see,' she said, 'and they were methodical with their housekeeping. Every day Auntie did this or that. Everybody had their own particular job. Grandma used to sit on one side of the fireplace with her stick. I clearly remember that she would always say "My father was an Irish gentleman." They were sort of aristocrats. She brought her children up, I'm sure, with the idea that they were just a little bit out of the ordinary.' Jane always bore herself with aristocratic dignity and this was passed to her eldest daughter Phyllis, who, in adulthood, also carried herself with poise.

Wilma's personality slotted in somewhere between Jane's dignity and Alf's sense of adventure, but in a subtle way. Of all the children, the one who most resembled Alf was Lance. The Oram's fifth child, Pat, who was born at Murtoa on 2 October 1923, was different from the rest. A tomboy, she had her father's obstinacy and free spirit, but with no time for trivia. If one was to grade the Oram brood in steps from 'conservative' to 'spirited' the result would come out exactly in the order of their birth. All of Alf's and Jane's offspring inherited a warmth and generosity that drew people to them—a fine bunch, with Wilma placed exactly in the middle.

SCHOOL DAYS

Wilma started school at Murtoa Primary in 1922. On the same day little Kath Smith[2] was to commence her schooling. Kath Smith would eventually become Murtoa's town historian. She recalled that, on her first day, Wilma sat next to a child called Doris Slaughter while Kath sat in the back row with Dulcie Meek, but was promptly moved in order to accommodate the Methodist minister's daughter, Bertha Ivory, who was deemed to be socially superior.

Wilma travelled to school by horse and gig, leaving home at seven in the morning to get to school by nine. 'Jack and my sister Phyllis and myself would be driving in the horse and gig,' remembered Wilma. 'The road had a bit of metal on it for about two miles but the rest of it was unsealed. The mud was right up to the horse's belly in winter. We'd be covered in mud by the time we got to Murtoa. We'd wash it off when we got there.'

Kath continued: 'Wilma then left the horse and gig at the Harris's house and walked to school, about four blocks distance. After school, she had to pick up bread, then walk to the railway station and wait for the paper, before returning to the Harris's, again about four blocks away.'

'The trains didn't run on time,' Wilma said. 'Sometimes I used to wait at the station for up to an hour to get that paper. Then I'd collect a large loaf of bread, try to carry the paper and the bread in my school bag. It was boiling hot in the summer.' Much of Wilma's primary school life was spent looking at the rear end of a horse. 'We had this old horse that used to just plod along. On cold mornings we'd take it in turns to get out of the gig and run behind to keep warm. My mother would put hot bricks in the bottom of the gig.' One day, on their customary way home from school, a furniture truck tried to pass. 'The horse saw it and bolted, and we couldn't stop it,' Wilma said, 'The furniture truck people were concerned about it but, instead of going past, they stayed level with us. We got home in double quick time that day.'

Jack was attending Murtoa Higher Elementary School, which had just opened. Both the Primary and the Higher Elementary still flourish today. The latter is now called Murtoa College. When Wilma entered third grade, Jack went off to Melbourne's Scotch College, so she was no longer in close contact with her elder brother except during holidays.

At weekends, the Orams often went on family picnics, sitting around a cloth spread on the ground, or at a folding table, enjoying the change of scenery. They mostly went to the mountains. 'People didn't walk much in those days,' Gertie Jeitz said. 'The ladies were all trussed up, matronly. Mr and Mrs Oram were always there and most of us children. Jack was the oldest—he was more quiet and studious but I do remember him being there too.'

When there was no picnic, weekends on the farm often involved a family cricket game and always plenty of horse riding, 'I was among horses when I was growing up,' Wilma confirmed. 'My father was a mad horseman.'

As a child Wilma had an experience that might or might not have struck horses off her personal list of best friends. 'Phyllis sometimes used to ride a Shetland pony,' she said. 'I wanted to ride it too but Jack said no. Anyway I insisted, got on the horse, fell off and broke my leg. Well, Jack had to drag me into the gig and take me home. Nobody knew I'd broken my leg but, finally, they got the doctor. The leg was never X-rayed or anything, he just pulled it around and set it and put it on a splint, and I stayed in bed for six weeks. Then he took off the splint and said, "There you are, you're right now, you can walk."'

They bred them tough in the Wimmera, and this toughness was to stand Wilma in good stead. That nobody knew of the little girl's broken leg is an early indicator of Wilma's notable ability to bear pain.

During Wilma's third year at primary school, Alf decided to take early retirement and get rid of the farm. He read the economic signs as good for making a profit on his investment. Besides, the move would give him unlimited time to play bowls. The property was duly sold, probably under a mortgage arrangement through a bank, and the family bought a house in the town of Murtoa. It was a big house in Munro Street called 'Troon', with high sloping roofs and verandahs, which suited the climate. Surrounding the spacious block of land was a hedge of cypress. (Troon is still standing, as dignified as ever but minus the hedge, privately owned again after serving for a number of years as headquarters for the local Returned and Services League.)

Around the time of the move to Troon, Phyllis and Gertie started at the Higher Elementary School while Wilma continued her primary studies. These days she and Lance only had a short walk to school. Pat would soon start there too. Jack had been away for some time at Scotch College and Phyllis was to commence a year at Methodist Ladies College. Both of these are expensive private schools, so the financial status of the Orams was evidently strong. With both Grandma Forster and Jane Oram being pillars of the local church, the family's social status was never in doubt. The Orams belonged to the Church of England (as the Anglican Church of Australia was then known) and attended Holy Trinity in Murtoa.

In the sixth grade, under her favourite teacher Miss McDonnell, Wilma was close enough to a boy called Len Sprague for him to help her with her arithmetic. Len went on in 1939 to win the Stawell Gift—Australia's prestigious professional foot race, which has existed for more than 125 years. For Wilma, on the edge of puberty, this relationship probably marked a budding awareness of the opposite sex.

In 1928 Wilma went up to the Higher Elementary in a class that included Kath Smith and Len Sprague as well as at least one descendant of the pioneering Degenhardt family, who were among the early

German settlers at Murtoa. The original building is still in use, but in Wilma's day it was reached, as Kath Smith recalled, by 'a long walk out of town through a paddock that was often muddy.'

Life progressed typically at Troon. Gertie still visited regularly. Grandma still told anyone who would listen that her father was an Irish gentleman. Auntie Annie still cooked and did her share of the chores while keeping an otherwise low profile, possibly with the aim of staying out of everyone else's way. As the 'maiden aunt', she was socially considered to be 'on the shelf' (the contemporary terminology for unwed sisters) and she may have been wary of seeming to be a burden.

Jack worked for a year as a trainee municipal engineer after finishing school. During this time Jane gave accommodation to a visitor, who was the equivalent then of a careers officer. 'He was cruising around wanting to know everything about everybody,' said Jack, 'I was doing this correspondence course and he said to me, "Why don't you go to university?" And before I knew where I was, I was up at Ormond College.' The next four years for Jack were spent getting a degree in Civil Engineering at theUniversity of Melbourne.

Alf became president of the Bowling Club and also joined the Masonic Lodge. Jane resisted getting involved in the social side of these activities, preferring to absorb herself in church matters. However, when Alf rose to be Master of the Lodge it became impossible for Jane not to get involved. As the Master's consort, Jane had a clearly defined role to play and was required to help him plan his Installation Dinner. 'When he became the Master,' Wilma said, 'I remember that it was a big event, getting my mother ready to go to this great night.' Jane's embarrassment at being in the limelight can be imagined but, no doubt, with all her social graces, she carried the whole thing off perfectly.

Alf's business ventures expanded again when he bought himself a petrol station and workshop in Rupanyup. This might have been a better investment if he had spent any time there but, typically, he put in a manager. Wilma said: 'He used to do the books at home but he spent his time on the bowling green and let the garage run itself. With this other bloke in charge it was never going to be a success.' Alf preferred to go on bowling trips while the profits evaporated. Eventually he got rid of the garage; his financial fingers were again burned.

When he cared to apply himself to it, Alf's talent was farming. Soon he bought another property near Glenorchy. 'It was the one at Minnaburra, where they had originally lived,' said Wilma. 'He bought that and worked it from Murtoa. He had sheep on it. There was a little hut that he lived in down there. I used to go with him until I was seventeen. I was quite interested, I knew how to look after the sheep and I used to help him. But my mother always insisted that we came back. He used to go there for a couple of days at a time but she would never consent to me staying. He had to bring me home every night.' The family continued to live at Troon while Alf drove to and fro in his Singer automobile.

The three younger children connected with this farm. Alf kept horses there as well as sheep. 'There were always horses to ride,' Pat recalled. 'After Lance joined up I used to go down quite a bit. I helped Dad thatch a haystack at one stage, cut chaff, helped him with the horses.'

Lance grew into a boy who was full of fun and easy to get on with. He was soon showing an aptitude for farming and, after leaving school, took an agricultural course at the highly regarded Longerenong College, which was conveniently situated halfway between Murtoa and Horsham. (The campus is now part of the Institute of Land and Food Resources within the University of Melbourne.) Lance was to work on the Minnaburra property for a number of years.

On 21 September 1931, Wilma, along with Kath Smith and eight other girls, was confirmed by Bishop Crick. They were sweet young things, dressed from head to toe in virginal white, including white scarves bound tightly around their heads. No doubt the whole Oram family was present at the church to bear witness; perhaps a sentimental tear was shed by Jane, Grandma Forster and Auntie Annie.

In 1933 Grandma Forster died. 'They were all very upset and they rang for me to come and be with them,' Gertie recalled. 'I remember Lance coming out onto the verandah when I knocked, the tears streaming down his face, but telling me how glad he was to see me and pulling me inside.' In 1935, a brick sanctuary was added to Holy Trinity Church in memory of its first vicar and three windows were placed in the sanctuary directly behind the altar. Jane Oram arranged for the central stained glass window, depicting the Ascension, to be dedicated to her mother, Anne Forster. It is still in place.

Wilma was ambitious to matriculate, and as Murtoa Higher Elementary only went as far as Intermediate Level, which she had passed in 1932, she set out to do the course by correspondence. She concentrated on English, economics, French, history and trigonometry. 'But I gave up,' she admitted with regret. 'It was too hard by correspondence. I stayed home; I didn't know what I was going to do with myself. The Depression was with us.'

Like so many others, Alf Oram was to be touched by the Great Depression. His sale of the property on the Rupanyup road did not go according to plan. The buyer made an appeal to the Farmers' Debts Adjustment Board and as a result Alf did not get the rest of his money. 'Those people never did pay for that farm,' Wilma declared vehemently only a few weeks before she died, still smarting from the indignity of it. No matter how severely this financial setback hurt the Orams they were careful to hide the fact from the people of Murtoa. To outward appearances they were as prosperous as ever, far too proud to have it appear otherwise.

NURSING

Wilma's elder sister Phyllis returned home after leaving the Methodist Ladies College where she had completed a business course. Career opportunities for women in the 1930s were few. At the top, the most common paths led to teaching, secretarial work or nursing. There was also starting to be a number of female doctors, women who were forced to put up a tremendous fight for acceptance in a male-dominated profession. In the lower echelons were such occupations as seamstress, laundress, cook, and other forms of service including the more 'respectable' one of shop assistant.

In those difficult days of the Depression, the minister's wife, Mrs Bull, who had been a nurse at Warnambool Base Hospital, suggested to Jane that it would be good for Phyllis to go into nursing. Unknown to Mrs Bull, the Oram family rated nursing poorly as a profession. Alf, with his customary lack of restraint, declared that all nurses were prostitutes, so Phyllis declined the golden opportunity and in the meantime managed to land herself a secretarial job with the Shire Office at Rupanyup.

Unaware of developments within the Oram household, Mrs Bull went on trying to gain Phyllis a nursing post at a time when posts of any kind were all but impossible to get. Her efforts were rewarded when word came through that there was a place at Warrnambool (a large provincial city in southern Victoria) for Phyllis. Wilma recalled, 'When Mrs Bull came to tell us this, my mother said, "She's already got a job. We won't think about her going nursing."'

Wilma's next action was characteristic. 'I can remember the look of disappointment on Mrs Bull's face. I felt just terrible about it, so I said, "Look, I'll go" because I had nothing else in mind. She was so relieved that somebody would go and she said, "Oh, that'd be marvellous." I was only seventeen, so I had to wait till I turned eighteen in the coming August.' A nurse by accident and as a side effect of the Great Depression—how could this be an auspicious beginning?

Wilma started training at the Warrnambool Base Hospital in October 1934. 'And I couldn't have hated anything more,' she confessed. 'It was absolute slavery, that nursing, utter slavery.' The rules were tough, too. 'We had strong discipline, we weren't allowed out except at a certain time and then we had to report immediately to the night sister when we got back.'

As a student Wilma was thrown in at the deep end of practical nursing, immediately going onto the wards and picking up what she had to learn by observing those who knew more than she did. Trainees were expected to do the dirty jobs. Nurse Sheilah Jenkin[3] recalled, 'Local doctors used to come and give us our lectures and we hand-copied them. We didn't have training as a trainee does today, with everybody showing you everything. You more or less went in as an onlooker, and the next thing you were handing the doctor instruments. It was a different attitude.'

The hours were long. 'We started at six-thirty in the morning and worked through till perhaps two,' said Wilma. 'We were back again at five and worked through till nine or half-past, either that or we worked through till six-thirty in the evening.' The nurses had little time for meals, and if they were busy it was common for them not to eat. 'Lectures were given to us while we were on duty,' Wilma said. 'This meant extra hours to cope with all our work, because we had the same amount to do as the other nurses and we had to attend a lecture as well.'

Cooking was a required qualification for juniors, who had to prepare meals for the rest of the staff. 'On night duty, when we were doing our cooking lectures, we had to get up in the middle of the day, walk a mile and a half to the local school for those lectures, then back again and be on duty again at nine o'clock.' said Wilma. 'On at nine o'clock, off at seven in the morning. We did that for three months without a night off.'

Life was made even harder for Wilma because she was homesick. She detested her first year. Every letter to her mother contained an offer to come home, with the excuse of helping within the family. These letters were consistently replied to by Jane with strict instructions for Wilma to stay put and to stick at nursing.

But there was at least one compensation. On her first day, Wilma met a vivacious young nurse who was three years older but keen to initiate the newcomer. Her name was Mona Wilton and she came from a dairy farm called Bellbraes at Alansford, not far out of Warrnambool. Wilma and Mona were to become close friends. It was a case of opposites attracting. Madcap Mona led the way into mischief while reserved and dignified Wilma was an innocent though not unwilling partner in the mayhem. Mona had already an established friendship with Sheilah Jenkin and by the time Wilma joined the hospital these two were wreaking havoc in the nurses' quarters. Wilma found herself involved in escapades that would force this retiring young woman to blossom, though, according to Sheilah, Wilma preserved her dignity.

The first thing that mischievous Mona did was to take Wilma to meet her brother, who was confined to one of the wards with appendicitis. Tom Wilton was the same age as Wilma. 'I have a great memory of Wilma and Mona,' said Tom. 'Mona brought Wilma in the first day she had her uniform on. She was just in from northern Victoria and she was a little bit nervous. I was Wilma's first patient. That's why Mona brought Wilma in to me, because I was in bed. She was a fair bit embarrassed, you know, it was the first time that she'd had anything to do with any patient.'

When she was allowed some time off, Wilma became a regular visitor to Mona's family farm Bellbraes, her first experience of dairy farming. 'It was pretty rough in those days,' Tom Wilton recalled. 'You'd have to get up early, about half-past four or five. We only had about thirty-odd cows so we were milking them by hand. But that was a day's work by the time you milked them, hand separated, fed the pigs, did all those little things; fed the calves, took the cream up to the depot where it would be picked up by a horse and cart from the factory.'

Nursing was Wilma's first experience of living away from home. It was compulsory to live in the nurses' quarters and, as a trainee, to obey everyone who had seniority. This turned out to be just about everybody else in the building, apart from the patients. Pecking order in hospitals was firmly established from top to bottom and was not open to question. It was a bit like a convent with Matron in the starring role of Mother Superior. Here, however, the similarity ended because the behaviour of a student nurse could hardly be compared to that of a novice in a religious order.

Matron was in charge and Matron was *she who must be obeyed without question*. When Matron addressed you, you stood to attention with your hands clasped behind your back. The only permitted reply to Matron's questions was either 'Yes, Matron', 'No, Matron' or 'I'm sorry, Matron', depending on the circumstances. 'And you didn't dare talk to Matron unless you had your sleeves rolled down and your cuffs on,' Sheilah said. In the busiest part of the day this would pose a problem, should Matron happen along unexpectedly. Matrons tended, though, to do their rounds at regular hours and much preparation would go into making sure that nurses, patients and wards were spick and span, ready to meet the boss's eagle eye.

Whenever a group of young women is confined and expected to follow a strict regime, it is natural for them to challenge this expectation. By the time Wilma arrived, Mona and Sheilah had already discovered a hiding place for contraband. Mona and Wilma did not work together often, Mona being a little ahead of Wilma in her training, but they did share night duty so Wilma was exposed to Mona's clandestine activities. Nurses were traditionally badly fed or at least traditionally hungry even when they were not badly fed. 'When Mona and I were the juniors we had to cook for the six night staff,' Sheila recalled. 'The kitchen had a dark room with slate shelves. They used to put the vegetables in there when they got them in fresh. Mona and I discovered that there was a passageway leading into the nurses' dining room.' In the dining room a large board covered a fireplace where the fire was never lit. 'We'd go into the cool room and nick whatever vegetables we could eat for the whole week, then we'd shove them in this fireplace, so when the others were having mashed swede and pumpkin, we'd still be eating peas and beans.'

Money was an ongoing problem. 'We used to go to Tommy Rob, who was the hospital secretary, and borrow a couple of bob [20 cents] to go to the pictures,' Sheilah remembered. 'Then he took it out of our pay at the end of the week. We got 12/6 [$1.25] a week for the first year, 15/- [$1.50] for the second and 17/6 [$1.75] for the third.' Mona solved her financial embarrassment by going to the local store and charging everything to her father's account. He seemed to accept these bills in good humour: 'Funny,' he would say, scratching his head, 'I don't remember buying myself two pairs of scanties?'

In contrast to her memories of Mona, Sheilah recollected that Wilma was 'always talking about this brother of hers. He lived by the "absolutes": absolute honesty, absolute truth. She admired him, saying what a wonderful brother he was. I don't know much about her family because she didn't talk to me about the rest of them.' The brother under discussion was Jack, who was to live his life by a strict code of ethics. That Sheilah did not recall Wilma talking about the rest of her family is not surprising. Wilma was never a gossip, nor did she talk for the sake of talking. When she said something it was because she had something to say. Sheilah recalled, 'I couldn't imagine Wilma stepping out of line, she was very respectful and responsible. She was very popular. Everybody liked her. Some of the girls were "narks" but not Wilma.' Although Wilma's dignity and responsibility are qualities that most people recall, she also had a sharp but subtle sense of humour. Whereas someone like Mona might do something ridiculous or risky, Wilma could assess a situation with detachment and sum it up with a throwaway line and a half smile.

Mona finished training and went off to gain additional qualifications at the hospital at Daylesford. Meanwhile Wilma 'stuck it out for the three years', as she put it, and completed her third year in 1937. Then, in January 1938, she moved to the Jessie McPherson Private Hospital in Melbourne. This institution had been founded seven years previously in a church hall in central Melbourne when a group of female doctors banded together to supply services to the women of Melbourne. (In some cases, women were then still undergoing major surgery at home.) The State Premier, Sir William McPherson, donated £25,000 to the building fund and the hospital was subsequently named in memory of his mother.

As soon as Wilma joined the staff she went on duty in the operating theatre, where she worked for the next two-and-a-half years. It was during this time that Wilma first met Vivian Bullwinkel,[5] who was also a staff nurse at the Jessie McPherson. Their relationship had a subdued beginning. Both women were reserved by nature and at that time it seemed unlikely that the two would ever be close.

Midway through 1940, Wilma transferred to the Royal Women's Hospital in Melbourne where she found she enjoyed midwifery, although she still preferred theatre.

At some point during her time in Melbourne, Wilma met a young man by the name of Alan Livingstone Young, who was seven years her senior. Alan had bought himself some scrubby acres in Gippsland, on the eastern side of Melbourne in the area known as Cardinia, a village that consisted of little else other than a small garage and an equally tiny general store. His aim was to turn the property into a dairy farm. Alan's parents were wealthy enough to assist him but Alan had a recalcitrant streak and refused to ask for help. Instead, he worked alone to clear his property and was eventually milking a few cows and keeping pigs. He continued to develop his dairy business until the outbreak of war in September 1939, at the same time involving himself with the linked communities of Officer and Cardinia and attending social functions.

It is likely that Wilma and Alan met at East Brighton where Wilma sometimes spent days off with friends of her parents, a family called Higgins, who lived next door to the Young family. Wilma always described the beginning of their association as just a 'casual acquaintance'. Well-educated, handsome and articulate, there is no doubt that Alan was considered to be one of the area's most eligible bachelors.

WAR

By early 1940 World War II was gathering momentum and Lance Oram made the decision to enlist. Like many young men of the time he was already a member of the local militia, and in April he joined the 7th Division Cavalry Regiment, which later became the 9th Division Cavalry Regiment. After months of training, he and a mate named Nevil Campbell sailed out of Sydney. They were bound for the Middle East, first to Palestine and then to Syria, working most of that time on Bren gun carriers. After a short stint with this regiment, both Lance and Nev attained the non-commissioned rank of Corporal.

Alan Young, meanwhile, granted a lease to a tenant on his Cardinia farm and, on 9 August 1940, along with his younger brother John,[6] joined the 2/3rd Light Anti-Aircraft Regiment and started training as a gunner. After the intensive four-month training period he and John were shipped to Palestine where they fought alongside a mate from Cardinia, Ces Donelly, who had enlisted at the same time as Alan. The regiment eventually transferred to Crete where fighting became intense. On the night of 28 May 1941, Alan found himself involved in the evacuation of Heraklion. The destroyers *Havoc, Hereward, Hotspur, Imperial* and *Jackal* were standing by to evacuate 4000 men that night.

Alan and his brother were aboard the *Hereward* when the convoy put to sea. At about 6.30am on 29 May, the *Hereward* suffered a direct hit. The convoy's Commander-in-Chief, Rear Admiral Rawlings, who was in charge of the British Eastern Mediterranean Fleet, gave the order to abandon ship. Alan helped a mate, 'Basher', who was a poor swimmer. Although he could not see his brother, Alan was not overly concerned about him because he knew that John was a much better athlete and swimmer than he. Alan held Basher afloat and they swam for their lives, towards the distant surf along the shores of Greece. After six hours in the sea, Alan and his fellow survivors, including a badly wounded Ces Donelly, landed and were captured by the Italians. At this point Alan began to fear that his brother was not among the survivors. They were taken to the island of Rhodes where Alan finally learned that John had perished.

Tom Wilton did his best to get into the army, too. 'I was in the 4th Light Horse Regiment, camped away at Hamilton. War was starting in earnest and I wanted to join up, so I came home and said to my Dad, "The Light Horse is folding up, I want to join the AIF," and he told me, "But you can't go, Mona has just joined." So she beat me to it.'

Wilma, meanwhile, was inclined to regard the war with an air of detachment—until one day in May 1940 when an event occurred that spurred her into action. 'I was on night duty in the middle of this midwifery course,' she said. 'I woke up in the afternoon about four o'clock—and you feel pretty low when you wake up after night duty—and the first thing I heard was that France had fallen. Immediately I knew: I've got to go to the war. That's a terrible thing to happen.'

Since she could not decide which service she should join, the air force or the army, Wilma took the medical examination for both, passed both and filled in both application forms, even though she would not be turning the minimum age of twenty-five until the following August. Uppermost in her mind, however, was the knowledge that she had acquired a skill and that this would be much in demand.

By sheer chance, Wilma was standing beside a post box near the Women's Hospital in Melbourne with one application in each hand, trying to decide which to post, when along came her old friend from Warrnambool, Mona Wilton. Mona asked what she was doing and, on being told Wilma's dilemma, she promptly replied, 'I've joined the army, so you'd better join up with the army too.' So, Wilma posted the army application. This, like taking up nursing, was another whim that was to change the course of Wilma's life.

The army application was accepted on 3 July 1941. Wilma became eligible for an overseas posting with the Australian Army Nursing Service (AANS) six weeks later on 17 August, her birthday. 'I think everybody was rushing off to join up,' she recalled. 'It was a bit glamorous, an overseas trip. You go to the war and you never in your wildest dreams expected to die. After all there's been a hundred years of nursing and there's only been ninety-five deaths, and so many of those died with us [in World War II]. The percentage of nurses who've died isn't great. The chance of us being killed was so remote, then, as not to be even thought of.'

Although they were part of the army, nurses were non-combatants who held no formal military rank, unlike male orderlies and members of the Voluntary Aid Detachments (VAD) who held non-commissioned rank. The nurses' status was honorary. This was to affect many of them later, in a horrifying way. Wilma underwent no specialised war service training other than a six-week period when she attended the Alfred Hospital part-time for instruction in brain surgery. There was no army training as such.

Wilma was one of the first nurses to be posted to Heidelberg Military Hospital, which was still under construction. Her colleague Jean Parry, later posted to the Middle East, recalled, 'She was there before I arrived. I was a VAD, not a [nursing] sister [like Wilma], but she was sweet. When we first arrived there was only a small staff. We all lived in. The sisters lived in a hut type of thing and so did we, at the back of the hospital. We didn't have uniforms. We went out in civvies and it wasn't till later that we were given a small allowance and got our uniforms. The allowance didn't cover much. I remember, then, working with Wilma and I came to know her quite well.'

'It was really very muddy and messy at Heidelberg,' Wilma said. While she was serving there she was informed that she was about to become a member of the Sea Transport Unit. 'I didn't know whether I could sail or whether I couldn't because I'd never been on the sea.

I came back from final leave and the principal matron called me in and said, "Would you prefer to change your Unit?"' Wilma immediately agreed to this, with obvious relief, and she transferred from the Sea Transport Unit to the 13th AGH (Australian General Hospital). 'I spent the weekend going through all the things that had to be done,' she said.

Jean Parry recalled that weekend: 'Oh, the excitement when Wilma found she was going overseas. I remember when her trunk arrived with her name on it. She talked about nothing else but going overseas and what she should take. It all came out of this allowance that we received, which was about £30, a ridiculous amount. But from that we had to buy our clothing. Underwear we bought out of our own pockets. We had to have a little brown suitcase, in case we needed to be evacuated. Again we bought that, and we put our army number[7] and initials on it. Wilma would have had one of those, and she would have had a kitbag and a hold-all.'

The women were also instructed to take a rug or an eiderdown, in case there were not enough blankets. Wilma remembered buying this rug, which was quite expensive. 'Of course,' she said, 'the family had to come and help because the money they [the army] gave us wasn't enough.'

On Wednesday 4 September, Wilma and her colleagues of the 13th AGH marched out; they were put into buses and taken to Lady Dugan's Dugout, a hostel near Armadale. (Lady Dugan, wife of the Governor of Victoria, was also President of the Victorian Division of the Australian Red Cross Society.)

When she arrived at the Dugout, to her delight Wilma found that— again by coincidence—she was a member of the same unit as Mona Wilton. The feeling was mutual. In a letter to Sheilah Jenkin on 4 September, Mona wrote, 'We are just here awaiting orders and you'll never guess who's coming to the same AGH—Oram! She was trans-ferred over at the last minute and gosh I'm pleased about it.'

Into this letter Wilma slipped a short note: 'Mona and I are together, which is absolutely marvellous, and unexpected. We are thrilled, and at the stage when we can't think very well.' Interestingly, at this time Wilma's handwriting was almost illegible, a careless scrawl indicative of a young woman with far too many exciting things on her mind to be bothered with letters. Later in life she wrote with a clear and careful hand.

The period from when the women were informed that they were to be posted to when the ship sailed was three days. 'We were pleased to be going to the war,' Wilma said, 'but when we found we were going to Singapore[8] we thought we weren't going to the war after all, because the war then was in the Middle East. Singapore was supposed to be impregnable, a fortress, and we really couldn't see that we were going to a dangerous situation.'

THE HALCYON DAYS

As members of the 13th AGH, the two friends sailed to Singapore aboard the *Wanganella*. Nobody was supposed to know that they were on their way but somehow Alf Oram found out. 'We boarded the *Wanganella* and to my amazement somebody came with the news that my father wanted to see me,' Wilma recalled. 'He'd managed to get down to the *Wanganella* to see me off. I'm not sure how he did it, or how he knew. He had some sort of uniform. Guards or something like that. I was quite calm, and not thinking of perhaps never seeing my family again, but I broke up when I saw my father.'

Together, Wilma and Mona watched the lights of Melbourne disappear and later, when at sea, the *Wanganella* passed by Bellbraes where Mona's family lived. The two friends went up on deck to wave goodbye to the distant lights on shore.

The voyage to Perth was rough. Mona and Wilma shared a cabin and both suffered seasickness. 'I was so sure that nothing would ever make me sick,' Mona wrote. 'Wilma is flat out on the bunk beside me, being seasick too. It helps such a lot to have a companion.' Mona's sense of humour could overcome any of life's problems and it kept Wilma laughing. Mona reported that, apart from an unfriendly ocean, they were comfortable: 'Nice soft water for showers and washing our clothes. Nice sunny decks with deck tennis, table tennis, quoits. We don't do any work, are guests of the ship's staff. The food is absolutely delicious and the service is extra plush. I'm looking forward to the day when I can sit up and go right through the menu.'

On dry land again at Fremantle they enjoyed thirty-six hours' leave, during which time they were driven all over Perth by a person Mona referred to as an 'old dear'. They were then met by some of the boys Mona had got to know at Darley, where she had first been posted, and were taken to dinner and a show before being escorted back to the ship. Clearly Wilma's new life in the company of Mona Wilton would not be dull.

On 15 September 1941 they disembarked in Singapore. Half of the 13th AGH was immediately sent to Malacca on the Malay Peninsula, to relieve members of the 2/10th AGH. Matron Drummond[9] took over the 13th AGH, after filling in as matron of the 2/4th CCS (Casualty Clearing Station) at Johore Bahru, and Sister Kinsella[10] transferred to the CCS.

Veronica Clancy[11] reported in her memoirs: 'I was surprised when I heard that Sisters Bullwinkel, Tate, Harris, Kerr, Rayner, Glover, Brewer, Cunton, Bridges and myself were to go to the 2/10th AGH. These instructions were anything but popular, as we of the 13th AGH had grown very attached to our unit and its members, and did not like the thought of splitting up.' While on stand-by for its own hospital, the 13th AGH was filling in as replacements—and replacements were regarded in the army as being one rung below members of established units. Their colleagues of the 2/10th AGH had been in Malaya since February 1941 and were well and truly established. This 'pecking order' was to gain more significance as events unfolded.

The other half, including Wilma and Mona, was sent to St Patrick's School at Katong to await orders. 'We were there for about a month settling in with our Chinese *amahs*,' Wilma said. (The nurses were supplied with servants to do their washing, ironing, make their beds and tidy their rooms.) 'They are such sweet little things—I'll bring one home to you—and we have house boys to wait on us at meals,' wrote Mona. 'At first we had our own troops and they were terrific, positively threw our food at us, but our Chinese boys wait on us hand and foot.'

'Our food is awful and we are perpetually hungry,' she continued. 'We have herring, awful meat—dead horse, we think—Chinese rice, and potatoes, potatoes and potatoes.' Occasionally Mona and Wilma would splurge on a hotel meal, but not too often because it cost too much.

Apart from army food, life was easy. 'It was just luxury seeing the sights of Singapore,' recalled Wilma. 'The heat was terrible but we soon acclimatised. We lectured the orderlies from 11am till 12 midday, then had a siesta and went to dinner at Raffles, Seaview Hotel or the Airport Hotel, having a wonderful time.'

Mona wrote blithely: 'Since arriving, we haven't done one bit of work. We have been sleeping, eating and growing fat while we wait for our permanent place of abode to be ready for us.' Mona's reference to a 'place of abode' was deliberately vague because censorship applied to any direct reference to location. She was able to report, though, that 'Wilma and I have a room to ourselves. It's good. We talk Victoria till all hours of the night, then start again early in the morning. We have leave from 10am to 12 midday every day and go along into the nearest city [Singapore] to see the sights and smell the smells.' The two stuck together. 'We shared the same room, our clothes, we looked after each other,' said Wilma. Mona remarked shortly after their arrival, '*We* means Wilma and me, as we go places together always and without any of the other girls, as we don't like them very much. They will be all right to work with but we don't want them trailing around with us when we are off duty.' Considering that few of the women of the 13th AGH had met before, that they were in a strange new situation and that they were undoubtedly homesick, this negative remark should not be taken too seriously. Those who had known each other beforehand, like Mona and Wilma, would instinctively have stuck together for mutual support.

The two women, who still regarded themselves as country 'girls', enjoyed going out with male officers, both British and Australian. They usually went in pairs, as was expected at the time, rather than run the risk of being labelled 'fast' or 'no better than she should be'. Apart from following the army custom of drinking the King's health in red wine, both Wilma and Mona drank only lemonade.

Mona delighted in poking fun at the colonial English and the British officers who dined at 9pm. 'The *naicest* places have ballrooms attached to their dining rooms, and orchestra and things. My friend Wilma and I can hop around now with the best. Our English friends took us to dinner one night. We commenced at 9pm and finished at 11pm. We didn't eat all the time, danced in the open ballroom. One moment, my *deah* fellow till I get my eye glass, *bai* Jove! But we still like the Aussies best.'

The night before the two were posted to Johore Bahru, Mona reported, 'Our Scotchmen turned up and took us driving. It was good and we made the most of our night. My Scotchman of course still wants to marry me, but I like my Harry of Darley.'

There followed a teasing reference to Wilma having fallen for one of the Indian taxi drivers, who drove them at their peril, 'We've missed death dozens of times by inches, dash past rickshaws, ox driven carts, around electric light poles on one wheel. Horror. And there doesn't seem to be any right side of the road to travel on. You just whiz along anywhere. Haven't been in a rickshaw because they are out of bounds. Bad luck.'

In mid-October Wilma and Mona were transferred to join the 2/4th CCS at Johore Bahru. 'When our nurses returned from Malacca,' Wilma recalled, 'the other half went up to Malacca, except eight of us who had to join the CCS.' The eight sisters were Iole Harper, Anna Baird, Blanche Hempsted, Eileen Short, Violet McInnay, Val Smith, Mona Wilton and Wilma. Mona wrote on 16 October, 'After six weeks of loafing around we are finding solid work a bit trying, but we'll manage,' she added.

When asked in 1999 what was the hardest aspect to adjust to during this period of service, Wilma replied, 'The hospital at Johore Bahru. It was ill-equipped and we never had enough supplies to do our jobs as well as we would have wished. I had never been out of Australia before and the experience was something of a culture shock—but we rose to the challenge by using our initiative and imagination to improvise.' They were stationed in a native psychiatric hospital, which spread over a wide area. Six miles of corridors ran between the various orderly rooms and twenty-two wards, only four of which were functional at first. The nurses used bicycles to get from one ward to another.

'Sister [JE] Simons[12] [Charge Sister], Sister [J] Kerr[13] and myself tried to set up an operating theatre,' recalled Wilma. 'It was just a room with a couple of beds in it and everything was worked with primuses. One of the stoves blew up, burned one of the men and he later died as a result. We had another very bad burns case. Another man from one of the units was walking past a tent, and just as he walked past someone threw out a lamp that had caught fire, and it caught this man and set him on fire. He didn't survive either.'

Mona wrote, 'I have sixty patients between myself and one orderly, Wilma about the same, so we don't have much spare time. But it's good to be working again and to feel as though we are really doing something to earn our 8/6 a day.'

The hospital, which was still partly occupied by Malayan psychiatric patients, was situated out in the jungle. When she was on night duty Mona was disturbed by the monkeys, which tended to stare at them through the unglazed windows. 'My orderly thinks I am a bit of a baby to be afraid of them. Perhaps I'll get used to that too, and creeping crawling insects of all kinds much worse than scorpions and centipedes. Something bit me on the bottom tonight. Hope I don't suffer any ill effects. Wouldn't it be awful if I couldn't sit down for a few weeks?' she wrote.

Their sleeping quarters, which Mona described as 'quite nice' and Wilma described as 'spartan', were a mile from the hospital and the nurses were transported by ambulance. 'The place isn't as elaborate as our last home [St Patrick's School in Singapore],' wrote Mona. 'No frangipani trees or gardenia bushes or wide balconies, but peace and quiet. We seem to be miles away from the noise and smells of Singapore. The only noises we have are the wind in the trees and the jungle birds singing to us. Wilma and I have a room between us and a little Chinese *amah* to look after our clothes, so we can't growl, can we? Our two nice Aussie officers—remember them?—are camped about a mile from here so find plenty of excuses to come up. They are nice bright boys and we enjoy their company lots. We don't feel so homesick when they are about and they tell us they like taking us places, so why not?'

Shifts were staggered. The nurses worked 7am–4pm, or 7am–1pm and 4pm–8pm. Night duty lasted from 8pm to 7am, which Mona asserted was 'a jolly long time. We can just manage to drag our weary bodies up the miles of corridors to the ambulance at 7am, then we go to bed and sweat all day.' Most of their nursing was of victims of malaria. 'One little mosquito you haven't heard about and I hope you never do. Hope he doesn't pick me as one of his victims. This disease is a most distressing, miserable sort of existence,' Mona wrote. 'We are opening more wards every day and will soon have all our own staff in action and will be the real 13th AGH as we left Australia.' In the same letter she remarked: 'We certainly have lots of fun, but we'd be silly if we didn't, wouldn't we? A day might soon come when we can't have any more fun for a while.'

Mona began learning to speak Malay, her tutors being some of her patients. 'Woe betide me if I don't learn and remember a few sentences every day,' she wrote. And both Wilma and Mona were going out with British officers. 'Mine a dashing tea plantation man and Wilma's a newspaper reporter,' wrote Mona. 'We are keeping them on our visiting list so that we can get some chests of tea free to bring home with us.' In a letter of 24 November, she joked, 'Our tea planter boy is still sweet to me. He goes to India next week unfortunately but will be back in a couple of months. Then our two Aussie Majors come to see us frequently. One of these days, my girl, one of these days all our loves will arrive at the gate at the same time and great will be the sorrow thereof.'

One day's leave late in October was spent exploring the palace of a Chinese millionaire. Wilma and Mona—chosen for the tour possibly because both were young and attractive, a good image for army nurses— were accompanied by an official photographer. 'The rooms were circular with the most gorgeous ceilings and very bright and decorated. The furniture and the carpets, I was just afraid Wilma would sink away or get stuck in them. We leaned up against one bright looking Buddha and took one another's photos. Wonder what the Buddha thought about it?'

In this same letter Mona mentioned that she had fallen for a Scotchman. 'He writes the most wizzerish love letters. Wilma enjoys reading them too.' Here there is an intervention in the letter in Wilma's writing: 'Oh yeah, Sheilah, she is not going to marry him because I won't let her. I am looking after her, never fear!' Then Mona resumes, 'She snitched this while I was out at the lav but I am getting used to her ways now.' The friendship was cemented; the two women were by now inseparable.

The Scot's name was McKinnon, not to be confused with another Scot called Jock Mathieson. Jock Mathieson was a member of the British counter-espionage team that was operating in Singapore. This team's job was to bring in and interrogate members of the local community who were suspected of collaboration with the enemy. Wilma and Mona went out a few times with Jock and his colleagues, or met them at social gatherings, and this casual acquaintance was to prove useful to Wilma only a few fateful weeks later. 'They were quite a bit older than we were,' she said. 'Mona and I had met them and had dinner with some of them, with Jock and I don't know who else. We'd only known them socially a little bit in Singapore. We really didn't know them all that well.'

On 6 December, Mona wrote, 'Unfortunately, for obvious reasons, our leave has been cut out, so that we miss the outings we were getting used to lots, but guess that war is war. We haven't come on a Cook's Tour. We manage to get a lot of fun out of life despite all the restrictions. As for worrying about the international situation, it just never enters our heads so please don't worry about us.' She reported that the only nuisance was having to cart their gas masks and steel helmets about with them and teased, 'Wilma wears hers in bed—in case! The trouble is the darn thing falls off when she goes to sleep, and rattles against the wall all night. Great excitement, we are getting a week's leave soon and going to the coolest place in Malaya. The two of us will be going together and are we excited!'

THE JAPANESE

Wilma knew nothing about the Japanese. She had never even seen a Japanese person. 'You had no conception of what you were letting yourself in for. And we got to Singapore and there was still no war on, and life was a bit of a ball. We didn't even have a hospital. We didn't know the Japanese war was going to happen. The Middle East war was going, the German war was going ...' There was a false impression that, even if the Japanese did enter the conflict, they would be easily held back.

On 7 December 1941 Japan bombed the United States naval base of Pearl Harbor in the Hawaiian Islands, thereby entering the war. Five days later, Wilma and her colleagues were in the thick of it.

'We are having grand fun here, getting used to air raids and sirens screaming at us,' Mona wrote to Sheilah Jenkin. 'It's when we have to get out of our beds at night and rush for safety that we get a bit savage. It's all so unnecessary. We'd just as soon stay in our beds and be damned to them all.'

A day or so beforehand they had witnessed their first air raid and thought it was artillery practice. 'We thought someone was having a game with sky rockets and it was all so beautiful, if a little loud and thunderous. We were all very interested and stood and gazed. Actually didn't mind being out of our beds at 3am. Imagine our surprise next morning when we discovered it was the real thing, no practice about it. Now we carry around with us enough kit to make a packhorse weary. Steel helmets, respirators, anti-gas capes and hats, and whatnot.

I'm thinking of sending to Bellbraes for old Tim the horse to carry my kit for me.'

Later in the same letter Mona urges Sheilah to reassure her family. 'There is nothing to be worried about at all. Impress that upon them, won't you.' Of Wilma she jokes, 'Wilma sends her love. By Jove, I have her well under control now that we aren't allowed out of camp. We go to bed at dark unless we are on duty and then only get up for air raids, blast them.'

Because information was restricted there could be no mention in the letters about the number of casualties they were treating. All she could say was, 'We are terribly busy. I am in a fracture ward for the duration, like it or not. As you can imagine, fractures are common-place these days. Our ward is about 1 mile from the entrance to the place so I am slimming, thanks to the exercise. Wilma is well and happy and sends her love. Don't worry about us, will you, we are as safe as we can be.'

Letters home were of necessity cheerful and lacking in hard infor-mation. To a modern reader they tend to give an impression of shallowness, but nothing about these women was shallow. They were determined to be cheerful under trying conditions, to reassure their friends and families, to keep their patients cheerful and optimistic, and they were themselves brave and realistic.

'New Year's Day Wilma and I both had the day off and had leave to go into the city we know so well and have not seen for six weeks. It was good,' Mona wrote. 'We spent all our money, had lunch with my Major, shopped again and then he drove us back to the camp. My first early night for ages and ages.'

The people of Malaya in general, and certainly Wilma and Mona, had no way of knowing how grave their situation was. By this time there was only one fighter squadron left in Malaya, with just seven airworthy aircraft—no match for an enemy that could put an average of 250 planes into the air for daily missions.

Things were not yet so bad, though, as to greatly affect the way of life. On Sunday 10 January 1942 Wilma wrote a rare note to Sheilah

Jenkin. 'We have just been to church parade and are relaxing until lunchtime. We have our siesta after that and then we will get up and go to church again this evening. Aren't we good little girls! I know Mona has written quite a lot about the tropics and believe me, Sheilah, I haven't changed a bit. No-one has proposed marriage to me as yet anyway. Mona and I were to have gone to a curry tiffin, whatever that means, today but it's all off.'

By 17 January Mona was able to report, 'We work like the very devil these days, sleep when we are off duty. One's fracture ward is getting along nicely and is most interesting. It's a cheerful sort of a place too. We pride ourselves that it is the most interesting and the nicest ward in the whole place. And we have 20 wards now, 110 patients to each.'

Wilma was working in the operating theatre, only a few paces from the fracture ward, so the friends were able to see a lot of each other, both day and night.

'Wilma and I have a day off today,' wrote Mona, 'and are going into the nearest little township in a few minutes. We will probably find all the shops closed and will be shoved down a slit trench while planes have a game overhead. But we enjoy the outings lots. We see rickshaws, natives in their colourful clothes, smell all the terrible smells we know off by heart, buy bunches of bananas, then it's time to come back and do camp again.'

The war was coming closer. Suddenly the 13th AGH's sister unit, the 2/10th AGH, was forced to evacuate from Malacca. Thelma Bell,[14] who was to become one of the *Wah Sui* nurses (see p. 50), reported that when Japanese forces advanced from the north much of Singapore's military, and those civilians who had fooled themselves into thinking this would never happen, were left vulnerable. On Christmas Day 1941, the nurses in Malacca got news that the Japanese were coming through Burma. It was claimed that hospitals had been attacked there and nurses raped. Patients had been murdered. Colonel Albert Coates,[15] commanding officer of the AIF 8th Division, which the 2/10th AGH had accompanied aboard the *Queen Mary*, expressed an opinion that the Malacca nurses would be 'trapped like flies' during a Japanese advance.[16] But to the higher authorities the hospital had seemed ideally placed just far enough away from Singapore—the expected front line—for the wounded to be moved up there for treatment. Evacuation from Malacca was therefore delayed until bombs and shells were actually falling.

During their retreat, the 2/10th AGH kept stopping to establish field hospitals and attend to increasing numbers of wounded, only to pack up again for a further move. Sleep was nearly impossible. 'At night the whole place shook,' Thelma reported. 'I was doing night duty and you couldn't sleep during the day for the bombing.' Eventually the 2/10th arrived at Johore Bahru and linked up with the 13th AGH. Although many members of the 13th had by now served as replacements with the 2/10th, this was the first time that the two units were functioning together.

Between 20 January and 30 January, recommendations were repeatedly made, unbeknown to the nurses, by Colonel AP Derham, Assistant Director of Medical Services, 8th Division, that the nurses should be evacuated to safety from Singapore. These recommendations were refused 'on the grounds that it would have, if carried out, a bad effect on the civilian morale of Singapore.'[17]

Derham's recommendation was repeated on 8 February. Finally, it was agreed to get as many of the nurses as possible away, together with as many wounded as possible, 'on the pretext that they were travelling on duty'.[18] In the event, only six nurses, all from the 2/10th AGH, were reluctantly evacuated, together with 350 badly injured patients, aboard the *Wah Sui*, which flew the Red Cross flag. What transpired for these six nurses is an unsettling story, and one that was hushed up for many years, although they eventually got back home.[19]

Wilma described the evacuation from Johore Bahru from her own point of view: 'The CCS was evacuated and after this we all moved to Singapore island. We [the 13th AGH] had to pack ourselves in a great hurry and move back to St Patrick's school to re-set our hospital. But of course everything has to be done in a hurry when you evacuate because you've got to work your hospital to the very last minute. Then you've got to pack it up and move.' Such was the haste that many precious personal belongings were left behind. 'Our personal things had secondary consideration,' Wilma stressed. Their patients were always their top priority. 'But I think I got most of my own personal things with me, thrown together and put on a truck, but most of those got left in Singapore anyway so it didn't really matter.'

Wilma's stoicism was beginning to emerge. 'Once the war started and our troops were in action, we had so many surgical casualties that the mind just can't take it in. We were operating round the clock in the theatre and we still had them lined up outside. We could not get through them fast enough. You have so many surgical casualties in a war.' As an operating theatre nurse, Wilma was now at the bloodiest core of activity. 'I think we had six tables going at once. There were only three trained nurses and a few orderlies.'

'Things got pretty tough,' she was to admit to a group of ex-nursing friends whom she addressed at Warrnambool in 1960. 'We went back down to Katong to this school [St Patrick's]. In twenty-four hours we had to uproot one hospital and get another one started in what was a school. Conditions were primitive in the extreme. Matron [Drummond] came one day and said that the Japs were just up the road and we'd all have to go. So we got ready, we picked up what we could carry. Then word came through that eight of us were to stay [at St Patrick's]. Mona and I were two of the eight who had to stay, so we got back to work again. Then word came through that half were to go and half were to stay. So Matron [Paschke][20] called us all together and said, "That half go and that half stay." Mona and I were in the half that stayed.'

Matron Paschke, head of the 2/10th AGH, assumed seniority and took this dictatorial decision because none of the women of either unit were willing to leave Singapore. In fact the nurses were openly protesting, agitating to remain at their posts and attend to the wounded. When asked in 1999 whom she most admired during this dreadful time, Wilma replied without hesitation, 'Matron Drummond, who fought without success for our right to remain in Singapore to nurse the wounded during the Japanese invasion.' There were discussions between the two matrons, but Matron Paschke had seniority and her decision was final. In any case she was following orders. The nurses were aware that, if they stayed, they faced the same fate as those wounded soldiers who had to be left behind, but they were prepared to accept this.

Mona's version of events, for the reassurance of her friends, was: 'We had great *fun* shifting. I'll never forget it and will always look back on the time as a nightmare, but we survived, so did our patients. Days off are a thing of the past. We are looking forward to getting home again so that we can spend a whole fortnight in bed and do nothing but talk. Wilma will be in bed with me. What stories we will have to tell you all. Wilma did all the washing—gowns, sheets, towels, masks and all, for the theatre was working twenty-four hours yesterday.' Again, the frivolous reportage only partly hid the descent into chaos that Singapore was becoming.

'We have the place full of patients and look for places to put some more,' Mona continued. 'Quite a few Warrnambool kids are in and I do a round every day to say hello to them. It's funny how they just find out that there is a Warrnambool nurse attached to the staff of the 13th AGH. Our officer friends all left us for a brief space but are back in the vicinity again and pop up to say hello to us occasionally, but always in the daytime as the curfew, whatever that is, won't let people wander about after dark.' Mona's ignorance of wartime procedure, such as a curfew, is both touching and indicative of the lack of preparation that these women had for battle.

When a bomb hit the hospital kitchen, Mona wrote, 'We didn't even jump when our kitchen was bombed out of existence. Fortunately the tin opener was not put out of action and that was all we were worried about.'

The 13th AGH kept the hospital going at Katong for as long as possible, then, on 11 February, orders were issued to move to St Andrews Cathedral and wait. They were taken there by ambulance. Half of the nurses then embarked aboard the *Empire Star.* There followed a perilous journey under fire and the ship was one of only two to get back to Australia after surviving the Japanese onslaught.[21] Having endured so much, it is an indictment that some of these returning nurses were presented with white feathers by some members of the public.

When Wilma was interviewed for the 1997 movie *Paradise Road* she revealed: 'We were conscious of the danger we were in. We knew. Some of our officers said they'd never let us fall into the hands of the Japanese; they'd rather shoot us. But my reaction to that was "You needn't bother shooting me, I'll take my chance on getting into the hands of the Japanese and getting out again, but I don't want to be shot." I was twenty-five and I wasn't ready to be shot.'

THE VYNER BROOKE

On 12 February, the remaining nurses in Singapore were ordered to board a small requisitioned steamer called the *Vyner Brooke*, a merchant vessel of the Sarawak Steamship Company, which had been sailing peacefully between Singapore and Kuching when she was commandeered. She had once been the private vessel of the Rajah of Sarawak. She was painted grey and equipped with a forward four-inch gun, depth charges and a Lewis gun aft.

The nurses were taken towards the wharves in the afternoon, but such was the chaos that the ambulances could not get through and the women had to walk much of the distance carrying their equipment. Elizabeth Simons[12] described the scene: 'We had a long trek through indescribable ruin, blazing buildings, acrid smoke and abandoned or wrecked cars.'[22]

Wilma summed up the situation tersely. 'We were quite horrified that it could have happened. We fully expected there'd be far more resistance to the Japanese. The Australians stood their ground well but unfortunately the Japanese just overran all the defences in record time ... There weren't enough guns, there were no aircraft. They [the authorities] weren't ready for it and they had no intention of being ready for it ... The defence of Singapore was a shambles, it's rather a disgrace to the higher command.'

Although warnings had been issued days ahead for civilians to get out of Singapore, so many had ignored them that civilian men, women and children were now struggling to board the few available ships. That so many people had not even evacuated their children to safety was a source of anger to many of the nurses, who resented the fact that, as a result, they were not permitted to rescue any of their patients.

Their small ship was packed with an estimated 300 people. 'Matron Paschke called us together and told us how grim the situation was and what to do if we were bombed. Those who could not swim were allotted lifeboats,' Wilma said. Neither she nor Mona could swim.

Sister Jean Ashton[23] of the 13th AGH wrote in her diary: 'We had a scratch meal out of tins sitting on deck. There are a few rugs, chairs and some stretchers. All the sisters are sleeping on deck and have life belts. Discover over 200 on board and only provisions for us sixty-five. Those were put on board from our mess kitchens.'

The nurses were soon efficiently organising things. 'The ship's crew were tired out,' Betty Jeffrey[24] recalled, 'and we were asked to go to the galley and prepare a meal. Some did this and produced a stew of army tinned meat and tinned vegetables. A chain gang of nurses was formed and the plates of food were passed up from the galley to everyone on board: civilian men, women, children, ship's crew and finally us. Army biscuits and cheese were the second course.'

The nurses agreed that there should be strict rationing so that everyone could at least have some food. 'Only two meals a day to be taken— with tea and biscuits at midday,' wrote Jean Ashton. 'We made out lists for lifeboat stations and instructions for all on board. As we sailed out of Singapore at 6pm large fires could be seen, burning oil tanks and ships. Huge black smoke clouds hung over city—such destruction is war.'

'Blanchie' Blanch[25] described what happened next. 'We started off that night. Very slowly. The next day the Captain[26] didn't want to go out into the open sea because the Japs would see us. We hid behind an island. I've flown over that area since, and there's no use hiding behind an island because you can see everything! Anyway that was Thursday 12th. Next day was Friday 13th and everybody said we'd better keep our fingers crossed. Well, we got through Friday 13th, then at night we went on a little bit further and hid behind another island. About a quarter past two in the afternoon we heard a plane coming over: Jap reconnaissance. The Captain told us we'd been spotted. He said, "There's nothing here on this little island, but there is an island about twelve miles away. We'll make for that." So we started off. Flat out, the poor little thing, and it wasn't long before six bombers came … The Captain was very good. He zigzagged. They came over and bombed us, and missed. It was a very small ship. They came back and it is said that they dropped twenty-seven bombs. And eventually one hit us right down the funnel. The boys down in the engine room were badly burned. And then we were given orders to abandon ship.'

Wilma and Mona had been sent below with other nurses when the ship was hit. 'Where I was, they blew the side out and some of the people were wounded. One man had all his stomach opened up. We couldn't save him,' recalled Wilma.

Wilma and Mona were both blown off their feet and received shrapnel wounds to the back of their legs. At first Wilma thought her legs had been blown off. A nearby nurse, Sister KM Neuss[27] of the 2/10th AGH, was severely wounded so Mona and Wilma helped to carry her up on deck. Then they helped her over the side and she was taken into a lifeboat by Pat Gunther, a friend in the 2/10th.

'There was no trouble, no worry,' said 'Blanchie' Blanch, 'because Matron [Paschke] had given us lifeboat drill. She was a marvellous woman and we just knew where to go and what to do. We only had two or three lifeboats. So those who could swim had to swim. Those who were wounded had to go in the lifeboats. The majority of the Australian sisters, sixty-five of us, could swim. Our main recreation in Singapore had been swimming, because it was so hot. Anyway we all knew what we had to do. I had a bag of dressings. Another sister had the hypodermic needles with morphia. Each of us had different things. We went about the ship attending to the wounded and there wasn't a sound. We knew where we were going and we didn't have to have orders yelled at us. I was one of the last getting off. We all took our shoes off except one Sister. I remember taking my shoes off and placing them neatly on the deck. I looked and there were two of my friends down in the sea. By this time the ship was listing the wrong way. I was getting way up in the air and they were calling out 'Jump, Blanchie, jump!' Well I jumped, and I thought I was never coming up again, I was so long under water. Anyway I joined up with those two girls ...'

Others involved have reported that there was in fact a great deal of panic, though not among the nurses, who followed their emergency drill to the letter and were the last to leave the sinking ship. However, it is logical, where there were so many women and children, that panic would be rife. The situation had by now deteriorated to every man for himself. At such times people are reduced to a basic instinct for survival. Some did things then that they will have regretted for the remainder of their lives; some will have blotted these deeds from memory. Veronica Clancy remembered some of the horror in her personal diary: 'Many of the people collapsed and died through shock and exposure and exhaustion. Their bodies carried by the tides floated with us—a grim reminder of the fate that seemed inevitable.'

'There were dead bodies floating around,' Pat Gunther said. 'When you jumped overboard, you were supposed to hold your life jacket down. But what happened when it hit the water, it broke the neck. In one sense, it was quick. And there was one girl, she was a very fat girl, her skirt had gone up revealing very big pink bloomers. I couldn't help it, I pulled the skirt down.'

One passenger who will figure largely in this story was a certain Dr Goldberg. Veronica Clancy's initial brush with her is on record: 'Dr Goldberg was safely aboard a raft (along with three sailors) and we nurses had to push the raft. When asked to get off the raft and make room for some of the exhausted nurses she said, "I am the mother of three children and my life is more important." This was just the last straw. I put my knee on the raft and supported myself with my left arm and just banged into her with my fist, determined I would get her off. My blows were not light ones and her back must have been bruised for weeks. Blanche Hempsted[28] came to my assistance, putting her arm around her neck and unceremoniously pulled her into the water. Our two girls then took turns at having a rest on the raft. The sailors were not any better. Words failed to make them budge and we hadn't the courage to tackle them as we had [Dr Goldberg].'

Probably the most reassuring story that emerged from the ship-wreck is that of Jenny Greer[29] and her four colleagues from the 2/10th AGH who, holding onto a length of wood, paddled off singing 'We're Off to See the Wizard'. Those five women fought for the whole of the next night to keep each other awake and alive and two of them almost did not make it. Betty Jeffrey, when interviewed for the movie *Paradise Road*, told flippant stories of bumping into dead sharks while she was swimming. She said nothing about dead bodies, but they were there in their dozens and they included the nurses' own colleagues, plus women and children.

Wilma and Mona, together with Jean Ashton, were ordered to jump too. This time it was Matron Drummond who called the order from a lifeboat. 'We went over the side amongst the ones that really couldn't swim,' Wilma recalled. 'We got into a lifeboat but that lifeboat was holed and grossly overcrowded, and we couldn't get it away from the ship, so that's when Mona and I got out of the lifeboat to try and dog paddle our way or to swim away as best we could from the ship.'

Jean Ashton wrote in her diary: 'Sisters Oram, Wilton and I went down into a boat full of civilians and tried to push off from the side of the ship … One of the sailors in the boat ordered us all to jump out and swim for it. As I thought I had no chance of swimming out far enough to be missed by the sinking ship, I swam along the side and kicked off from her end as hard as I could.'

'Mona couldn't swim at all,' continued Wilma. 'I couldn't swim very much, and we jumped out to try and get away from the ship but the ship tipped over on top of us. I said to Mona, "Oh, we're sunk this time!" It was only an expression that I used and I didn't realise the irony of it. I came up through the rails, put my hands above my head and caught the rails and came up through them, but when I came to the surface Mona was nowhere about and that was it. I never saw her again.'

Wilma assumed that Mona had been dragged under the ship, but there was more to it than that. 'As I came up,' Wilma said, 'I looked up to see the other side of the ship coming down, and all the things on it falling. As it came over, the rafts that weren't tied down on the upper deck and hadn't been thrown over, they came tumbling down. I could see them coming and I was hit on the head by several rafts one after another—they hit me bang on the head in the same place.' Wilma's scalp was cut to the bone and, from then on, a large lump and scar from the wound were visible beneath her hair.

Not until many years later, when a number of survivors made a pilgrimage back to Bangka Island, did Jean Ashton tell Mona's brother Tom Wilton that she saw what had happened to Mona. According to Jean, Mona was killed by one of the falling rafts and 'just floated away'. Wilma was at this time being repeatedly hit by the rafts and did not see this. Also, as Wilma did not relate this in any of her interviews, it is likely that Jean never told her about it, possibly feeling that Wilma had suffered enough from the loss. It will be learned that these women would develop an infallible ability to keep secrets.

Wilma managed to dog paddle and scramble onto one of the rafts that had hit her. Meanwhile she saw the ship roll right over, her keel upwards. Although Wilma had an acute head wound she was quite unaware of it. Alone now and in a daze, she saw a civilian woman paddling towards her on one of the other rafts. Everyone else had gone because somehow fifteen minutes had elapsed since Mona's disappearance. The woman asked politely, 'Do you mind if I get on your raft with you?' The black humour of this situation did not escape Wilma and remained with her. 'Fancy asking me in the middle of the blooming ocean. And I said, "I don't bloody well care what you do!" She got on the raft with me and said, "Quick, quick, paddle, paddle! It's going to blow up." And I thought, "Oh God, nothing else can happen, surely?" Anyway it didn't. People always talk about being sucked down but that's a myth. You're not sucked down at all because I wasn't. It just settled and went down. In the space of about fifteen minutes there was no ship.'

The woman who clambered onto Wilma's raft was Mrs Dorothy Gibson. Wilma always felt guilty about having sworn at Dot Gibson, and she did not want the incident reported in this book; but it is important to show the vulnerable side of Wilma, who was normally so unshakable. Considering what had just happened, it is no wonder that she lost her temper for that moment.

For the next sixteen hours, Dot Gibson and Wilma tried to paddle towards some land in the distance. They did not know it but they had set their course for Bangka Island.

During the night they saw the dark shapes of passing ships. This was to prove to be the Japanese fleet, which was in the process of invading the island. 'It's a wonder they didn't run us down, but they didn't,' said Wilma. 'We went up and hammered on the hulls, yelling for them to pick us up but nobody took any notice.'

At one stage the two survivors got close enough to shore to see light from a fire on the beach, but they could not get to it, the currents taking them further along the coast. 'In the morning when daylight came there were Japs everywhere. They were circling around us in motor boats. But they still wouldn't pick us up. They just thought we were a bit of a joke. And this lady who was with me, she got quite panicky and said, "They're Japanese, we can't land, let's go somewhere else!" I said, "There's nowhere else to go. If we can get to land we've just got to land." And we managed to get right to the shore ourselves.'

While Wilma and Dot Gibson were struggling ashore amid the invading Japanese some Dutch planes flew over. 'We thought they were going to drop bombs so we ran for shelter. They didn't drop anything as it happened, but the Japs were in the only shelter that there was—a small customs house. We ran into that.' When the planes had gone, Wilma and Dot made a move to go outside again. Immediately the Japanese prevented them. With much gesturing, yelling and jabbing with bayonets, Wilma and her shipwrecked companion were taken prisoner.

PART TWO:
INTERNMENT

CAPTIVES

Wilma and Dot had landed on the beach at Bangka Island on 15 February, not far from Mentok jetty—a wooden structure, about 500 metres in length, which jutted out from the shore. Along this jetty, under the supervision of guards, were natives unloading Japanese supplies. A few hours later their numbers would be swollen by male prisoners—Allied servicemen who would be used as slave labour. The Customs House, where Wilma and Dot had run for shelter, was a small building that stood opposite the landward end of the jetty.

These two women were the first prisoners to come ashore on this part of Bangka Island and the Japanese did not know what they were expected to do with them. Wilma was in a kind of daze, feeling nothing in particular apart from unbearable thirst. 'We picked their water bottles off their hips and had a drink out of them,' she said. 'They didn't take any notice.' Both women were covered in oil and filth from the ship-wreck and had lost their shoes. Wilma's hair was matted with oil and congealed blood from her head wound. She never mentioned, nor appeared to even notice, the shrapnel wounds down the back of her legs.

Dorothy Gibson, who was of mixed race, spoke fluent Malay. With that and by using gestures they were able to explain that they were the victims of a shipwreck caused by a Japanese bombing attack. The soldiers found this fact, in Wilma's words, 'hilariously funny'. It was the first example she would have of cultural differences between her and her alien 'hosts'. The apparent amusement of the soldiers was probably an expression of pleasure at learning that their air force had been successful in routing the enemy, rather than a reaction to the women's plight.

The Japanese offered no help. 'They wanted to know what had happened and so forth,' Wilma said. 'They turned us around, took our lifebelts, looked down the front of our dresses to see what sex we were. I don't think they'd ever seen white women before.'

More survivors came streaming into the Customs House: men, women and children. Other nurses came in, tragically few, and many of those were partly naked from having taken off their uniforms to make sails or bandages or whatever was needed.

'What a sight we must have looked,' wrote Jean Ashton. 'Wet clothes hanging and two girls without uniforms, one poor Malay boy badly burnt, arms and legs all blackened and a lot of skin missing. Another Malay boy (Billie) with only a shirt on. One civilian woman ill, had to be carried down the jetty. She had a miscarriage … Sr Oram and Mrs Gibson had arrived half an hour before us on the beach and were in the room when we arrived. Sr Oram had a nasty gash on her head, caused by a raft [sic] falling off the ship and crashing onto her in the water.' Jean and her group had already been given men's clothing by the Japanese, who distributed it out of a trunk. They also tore up some sheeting to put over the women. Their lack of uniform was to be a disadvantage to the nurses when they later attempted to argue that they were military personnel.

Wilma and the other captives were herded into the brick courtyard attached to the Customs House. Only those still wearing uniforms had medical supplies, which were soon exhausted when the nurses attended to the sick and injured. That they themselves were sick and injured, shocked and traumatised, was not a factor. Jenny Greer, whose gang of five had paddled 'Off to See the Wizard', used a pair of nail scissors to cut the matted hair from around Wilma's wound. As soon as this was done, Wilma went back on duty.

Eight shocked men staggered into the Customs House at the same time as Veronica Clancy and her companions. The men's lives had been saved by the arrival of Veronica's group. A Japanese soldier had lined them up, intending to shoot them, until the nurses emerged from the water and distracted his attention. 'When those people came in and joined us, they were a shaking mess,' Wilma said.

Not everyone was a shipwreck victim. Some ships had been captured by the Japanese navy and piloted to Mentok jetty where they disgorged their human cargo. These people were lucky, if anyone could be classified as 'lucky' under the circumstances, because they carried money and possessions. The nurses had nothing.

Nobody had anything to eat or drink until one English woman managed to scrounge a small glass of water, which was passed around so that everyone could take a sip. When food came to the Customs House, Wilma recalled that it was three grains of rice placed onto the prisoner's open hand. (In their captors' favour, it should be acknowledged that this was taken from the guards' own rations and the numbers needing to be fed were swelling minute by minute.) 'During the late afternoon a small heap of cooked rice was tipped out onto the floor and two tins of bully beef. We all had about a tablespoon of rice and a *little* meat,' Jean wrote.

Several buckets of water were rationed out in small cupfuls during the day. Billie, the Malay boy, collected several pieces of jewellery from the women, plus Jean Ashton's watch, and said he would bribe the Japanese for more food. As a result, around 7pm half a kerosene tin of hot milk, sugar and rum arrived. Dr Goldberg, whom Wilma knew already from the *Vyner Brooke*, approached the Japanese. 'She went up to the Japs and said, "I am ze German, I am ze German! I can go out!"' Wilma said, then added skeptically, 'I think she did go out, too. She had both a British and a German passport, that woman.'

People of many races gathered together. When she was interviewed for *Paradise Road* in 1997, Wilma explained the situation to a young interviewer who was vague about the history of the area. 'At that stage,' she said, 'there were British, Australians, people from Singapore who were called Eurasians—I don't think you refer to them as Eurasians any more, it's not politically correct—but they were people of mixed blood.

The English colonised Malaya and Singapore. They were the dominant power in that area, and the Dutch were the dominant power in the Dutch East Indies [now Indonesia]. The Dutch lived there, farmed there, did their banking, had their oil wells, their rubber estates and lived a life of luxury. The Dutch were in the Dutch East Indies and the English were in Malaya. That's how we came to have such a mix of people, and there were people of mixed blood because of inter-marrying between the cultures.' As a potted history, this explanation demonstrates Wilma's talent for fitting a large concept into a few direct words.

No provision had been made for hygiene. By the end of the day hundreds of people had arrived, all of whom were crammed into that courtyard with only one small toilet in a corner. The contents of this were overflowing onto the ground. 'One of our girls had got ashore with her shoes on, so we borrowed her shoes to go and paddle through to the toilet,' Wilma recalled, adding a phrase that she was to use often when describing this period of her life: 'It was a hopeless situation.'

Night fell and everyone settled down on the bricks, attempting to sleep. 'I was rather numb and I didn't anticipate living much longer,' Wilma said. 'I didn't think there was much use worrying. As for being frightened, well I wasn't. We had always been told that the Japs didn't take prisoners; that they would just shoot us. We expected to be shot. When that didn't happen we kept living from minute to minute. There wasn't much we could do about it.' Wilma's trance-like reaction was probably what has now been defined as 'psychological numbing' or 'emotional anaesthesia'—one of the recognised symptoms of post-traumatic stress. Most of the prisoners would suffer from this to some degree.[30]

With little sleep during previous weeks while she worked in the operating theatre, then having gone through the shipwreck and its aftermath, it is not surprising Wilma fell into a sound slumber when she lay on the bricks. She placed herself between a man and a young boy. Being first on the scene had given Wilma an advantage because she had found a white boiler suit which she put on. This nearly caused her a problem. During the night she woke suddenly from an almost comatose state to find a guard squatting beside her with rifle and bayonet, screaming at her in Japanese and shaking her by the shoulder. He indicated that she was to accompany him. She assumed that they were being taken one by one to be shot. 'The man who had gone to sleep beside me was gone, so I reached over to Sylvia Muir[31] and I said, "Hang on to me, Sylvia, there's a Jap here that wants to take me away and I'm not going!"' Finally Wilma yelled at the top of her lungs, 'Help!', which, in her own words, 'brought Japs from everywhere and a great old scuffle went on. The Jap officer and several other guards came racing in ... There was a lot of talking and finally they left us alone, didn't worry any more about me. In the morning I found out they were segregating the men from the women. I had on that boiler suit, and not much hair, and the Jap soldier had mistaken me for a man.'

The whole of the next day was spent in the courtyard. 'We spent the day there doing nothing at all, just sitting,' said Wilma. Jean Ashton reported that 'We tried to tidy ourselves up a bit. Many of the girls' hands were skinned from sliding down ropes to leave the sinking *Vyner Brooke*. Our chins were skinned too from the rubbing of life belts. We looked real wags!'

One of the Dutch doctors managed to get some ham and biscuits and distributed a small helping twice during that day. Then the women were pushed back into the Customs House itself when about a hundred male prisoners arrived and were marched into the courtyard. There were air force, navy and some civilian personnel. Jean Ashton described how these men handed some tinned 'eats' through the door to the women, plus some money. 'Did we make those eats disappear!' she exclaimed. The following evening on 16 February, at around 5pm, the prisoners were marched a short distance to a small cinema building. 'Found many more men, all ranks. Quite a number of officers, both navy and military. Must have been over 1000 in the hall,' Jean recorded.

'A bit of food appeared for us that night,' recalled Wilma. 'We got a bowl of rice, I don't know where it came from, and somebody had got hold of a tin of Carnation® Milk; so I had some rice with Carnation® Milk on it, which seemed like heaven.' With every new arrival the nurses hoped to sight more of their colleagues, but after their move to the cinema it was obvious that more than half of the original sixty-five *Vyner Brooke* nurses were missing.

A detail was sent outside the entrance under guard to dig a slit trench. Around this some sheeting was draped and this became the latrine. Wilma described how they were all let out to use the toilet and then shoved back into the cinema. 'Guards were put on the doors, which were barred,' she said. 'After that we weren't allowed out for any reason whatsoever. In the morning there was nothing to eat or drink. There was hardly room to lie down either. And we had so many wounded people, without any means of doing any dressings or looking after them.'

The doctors called for volunteers to help attend to the wounded. Several of the nurses went, Wilma among them. Sisters Blanche Hempsted and EM 'Shortie' Short,[32] both of the 13th AGH, were assigned to night duty. In the absence of Matron Drummond, who was still missing, Jean Ashton assumed her position as the senior nurse of the 13th AGH. She did not sleep that night. 'What a sight!' she wrote. 'One thousand people in all postures.' At some time during the night the Japanese placed a machine gun outside, pointing directly at the main door of the building.

The next morning at around 9am the prisoners were turned out of the cinema. They sat on the grass in the sun, doing nothing for more than an hour. Wilma was relieved to be out of those confined quarters, even though she did not know what was going to happen. Then the Japanese sprang into action and, shouting and prodding, lined everyone up in two long rows and marched them off without anything to eat or drink. Fears of imminent execution taunted the captives. 'We just meandered along in a stream,' Wilma said. 'We were barefoot and it was hot. We were without food or water in the heat, with the flies and insects.'

After a long walk, carrying whatever they had been able to scavenge, the nurses and other prisoners in their group were led to a Chinese school building into which they were herded. Typically, such was the unpredictable nature of their captors, this turned out to be a short respite. Wilma and the others rested for only about half-an-hour. 'Scenery very pretty, nice neat houses and gardens, everything very green,' recorded Jean Ashton. Then they plodded on again for about another thirty minutes and eventually arrived at a less attractive location: a large open shed that stood in the middle of an enclosed compound. This compound was bordered on either side by barracks buildings, which were divided into rooms.

They had been brought to the 'Coolie Lines'. In these primitive quarters the colonial Dutch had housed native labourers (known in contemporary parlance as 'coolies') who were recruited to work in nearby tin mines. Did the Japanese perhaps think there was justice in giving their European prisoners a taste of their own medicine? Probably not. The Coolie Lines were purpose built for housing large numbers of people. They were available, so they were used.

THE COOLIE LINES

On her arrival at the compound on 17 February, Wilma found hundreds more prisoners already waiting. The camp housed survivors from about seventy ships that had been sunk that week in Bangka Strait. Wilma estimated that about 600 people were present at that time.

The women and men were segregated and placed in opposite buildings, forty or so people to each room. Inside the rooms were two sloping slabs of concrete, each at an angle of about forty-five degrees, separated by a gangway. On these slabs they were expected to sleep. 'If one turned over, everybody had to turn over,' noted Betty Jeffrey. A shelf ran the length of the walls, and here they could place their possessions.

The Japanese guards housed themselves on either side of the compound's entrance. At the opposite end stood an open kitchen. 'At the end of the barracks there was what you call a *tong*, a little square tank,' Wilma recalled. 'You were supposed to bail water out of that to have a wash. There was an open gutter that we used for a toilet.' Everyone, including the Japanese, made use of the gutter and there was no privacy.

The nurses stuck together as a unit and shared a room with eight civilian women. The rooms were dirty and there was a lot of rubbish lying around. 'Some native mats and two old mattresses—but oh! the smell of those latrines adjoining!' wrote Jean.

In this room the nurses found some sailors' uniforms. Thinking the clothing had been abandoned they helped themselves to it. 'The girls' hands were all curled up.[33] They couldn't wash themselves, couldn't dress themselves, couldn't do anything,' Wilma stated. Her own hands were uninjured so she was able to help her companions into the clothes. 'But I had an awkward job trying to wash and dress all those girls,' she said. 'Trying to button them—because we hadn't lost weight straight away—into these sailors' pants was a work of art, and to get sailors' trousers on people like Veronica [Clancy], who was pretty big ...' Eventually, after all that hard work on Wilma's part, the sailors came back from a working party and demanded that their clothes be returned to them. A bargain was struck and not all of the clothing was returned.

Hopes rose when two of the missing Australian nurses walked shakily into the compound, 'their feet and legs badly swollen and sore, and both exhausted.'[34] They were Betty Jeffrey of the 2/10th AGH and Iole Harper of the 13th AGH. 'They were covered in bites, in a terrible state,' Wilma said. 'One of the doctors had some morphia and gave them each a bit. They lay down on the cement and slept for another three days.' These two, both strong swimmers, reported that they had been with Matron Paschke's raft for a long time, swimming beside it and trying to propel it to shore. They could also confirm that a large party, including many nurses, had made it to a beach that they themselves could not reach.

Among the men in the camp, Wilma located Jock Mathieson and his colleagues of the anti-espionage group. Wilma was to spend a lot of time with these men, talking quietly in the compound. 'They were apprehensive about any of the Japanese guards or officers who came into the area recognising them,' she said. 'They never gave any indication in camp that they could speak Japanese. They just kept to themselves.' They knew they were in danger because some of the people whom they had previously interrogated were now with the occupying army and might be among the guards. Recognition of Jock or his mates by a collaborator would have meant immediate execution, probably by beheading. Every day men disappeared to 'unknown destinations' and the anti-espionage group did not want to join them.

'There was a Japanese officer who used to ride a horse through us and flick us with his whip,' Wilma said. '[He] used to ride around with his rifle and men used to disappear out of that camp every day and not come back. We never knew what happened to them.' Those who knew the identity of Jock's group kept quiet about it, but nobody could be trusted. Too many desperate people were locked together. The practice of total secrecy on certain issues was to become a normal and necessary way of life.

Realising that execution was not necessarily imminent, the prisoners started to organise themselves. Three women doctors were among the English-speaking female prisoners, including the opportunistic Dr Goldberg. Several doctors were among the males. There was also a group of British nurses. 'Margot Turner,[35] a British army nurse, came in,' Wilma recalled. 'She'd been in the water several days and came in very sunburnt.' The British and Australian nurses cleared a dormitory for use as the hospital. The male doctors had commandeered three rooms in the men's barracks for this and Wilma was one of the first to volunteer for duty. 'Wilma Oram was walking about the place doing her job of nursing with an awful looking scalp wound on top of her head—she must have the skull of an ox!' commented Betty Jeffrey.

A medical and surgical clinic of sorts was soon established. 'Only about half of the AANS were in a fit state to do any nursing because of skinned hands,' Wilma said. 'Quite a number of hospital orderlies helped.' The nurses were each on duty for only two hours per day but were exhausted by even these short shifts because of the starvation rations. 'Of course, we had no facilities for looking after [our patients],' Wilma said. 'We had no bedpans, we had no linen, and we had trouble with dysentery, sunburn, malaria. We just did what we could.' Inevitably, some deaths occurred.

Wilma kept imagining that she would not be in this situation for long. 'The general opinion was that we'd be there for three months. The quality of the rice was so shocking that I thought I wouldn't be able to eat it, and somebody said: "Well you'll have to because you'll be here for three months." I said: "I won't survive, I can't stand this for three months." But, anyway, it wasn't long before we started eating this shocking rice.' (The rice was tainted by grubs, dirt and rat droppings.)

'We'd get a bit of rice in the morning and a drink. I don't know whether it was tea or coffee, we never knew. The rice was always very badly burnt. There was no flavour in it. The taps dripped, they didn't run properly, they just dripped. The children in camp by this time were very distressed, not given enough to eat or drink. They cried a lot.'

Still Wilma and the other nurses scanned the new arrivals, praying that among them would be more members of their units. Only thirty-one nurses were accounted for. Surely more had survived? Where were the matrons? Matron Drummond had been in the only relatively seaworthy lifeboat with other nurses, including the casualty Kate Neuss whom Wilma and Mona had rescued. Blanchie was able to confirm that her group had drifted close enough to the beach to see that Matron Drummond and her people were safely ashore, having lit a fire as a beacon. Jenny Greer, Joyce 'Tweddie' Tweddell,[36] Beryl 'Woodie' Woodbridge[37] and Flo Trotter[38] (the 'Wizard of Oz' lot) had also seen them. Their colleagues *were* alive. Had they perhaps been transported to another prison camp?

By 22 February, eight days after the sinking of the *Vyner Brooke*, all the women felt weak, languid and hungry. 'Can hardly eat rice—but must,' Jean Ashton wrote. 'Several girls sick.' Wilma recalled ruefully: 'While we were in the Coolie Lines I remember one of our girls saying she was afraid she might get constipated, because she was used to taking things for constipation, but she needn't have worried, because it wasn't long before our bowels were running with dysentery.'

On 28 February, Jean Ashton recorded: 'Over 2000 now in compound, 40–50 in each room. Very crowded, many crying children, washing spread on grass and hanging on verandahs all day. We are counted by guards in groups several times a day. All names taken. Sentries parade hourly at night. Mosquitos fierce.'

That same morning Colonel Wynn, a New Zealander from the anti-espionage squad, gave Wilma a pair of his own raw silk pyjamas. He also gave her a terry-cloth coat, acknowledging that her need was great. Wilma accepted the pyjamas and was looking forward to wearing them for the first time that night.

The pyjamas, however, were destined for another use because, late in the afternoon of this same day, clutching a water bottle to her side and accompanied by a badly wounded British soldier named Kingsley,[39] Vivian Bullwinkel walked into camp.

Vivian's welcome arrival made a total of thirty-two nurses accounted for out of the original sixty-five. Maybe there were still more to come? But when Vivian pulled the water bottle aside to reveal a sticky, stiff mass of pus and blood, it was obvious that she had suffered a bullet wound. Quietly, Vivian informed her colleagues that she had something important to tell them. Wilma and the others of the 13th AGH listened silently in the barracks, huddled together, while Vivian, in her soft matter-of-fact way, told them what had happened to Matron Drummond's nurses; the group who lit that beckoning camp-fire beacon that so many of the others had struggled to reach.

The Japanese separated the nurses from their male patients. They took half the men behind a bluff, then came back and took the other half away. She said that the ship's officer tried to explain to their captors that the nurses were army personnel and were giving themselves up as prisoners of war, 'but they just ignored him and took the two ship's officers away,' said Vivian. 'After the second party, they came back and cleaned their rifles and bayonets in front of us. Then [they] lined us up and signed to us to march into the sea. Then they started machine gunning from behind.' Vivian stated that Matron Drummond, Sister FR Casson[40] and Sister RJ Wright[41] were killed before they reached the water's edge. 'The rest of us got quite a distance out to sea, nearly up to our waists, before any of the bullets hit us.' Only superficially wounded, Vivian hid among the bodies of her colleagues and eventually drifted to shore. She crept up the beach into the jungle, where she encountered the wounded soldier Kingsley. They remained together in the jungle for two weeks before deciding to give themselves up and risk the consequences.

Twenty-one nurses were massacred. It should have been twenty-two, but, as fate will so often take a hand, there was one survivor to give an account of it. Of Vivian's wound, and the reason she survived, Pat

Gunther reported, 'There's a gap between the hip and the ribs and that's where it went through. Thanks goodness, because it missed anything of vital importance. Even if one of the intestines had been penetrated and had leaked, she probably wouldn't have survived. It would have turned to peritonitis.'

Once Vivian had finished telling the nurses what had happened on Radji Beach on 16 February, they swore a vow of secrecy. In later years Wilma said, 'We knew what had happened but we never, ever spoke of it again. Never spoke of it once; that was the end. We just spoke of it when Viv came in, found out who had been shot and it gave us some idea then about what had happened to the others. We could only assume that some of them had drowned if they hadn't been shot. And we left it as it was.'

There were twenty-one massacred. 'The others were what we called "lost at sea",' Pat Gunther recalled, 'because we didn't know whether they reached the shore and were murdered or what happened to them. And the ones that were floating in the water, when I got in, we turned them over to see who they were anyway. Sort of an automatic thing, we were probably looking for some trace of life. Yes we would have accounted [for them], but we had to say "lost at sea" because they had relatives back here.'

Wilma had known Vivian only vaguely during her stint as a staff nurse at the Jessie McPherson Hospital. Since joining the 13th AGH Wilma's social life had been wholly tied to Mona Wilton and, by Mona's own admission, the two had not mixed much with the others. Now, on learning all the various aspects of her colleague's horrific experience, Wilma's heart went out to Vivian Bullwinkel and she determined to look after her.

Everyone agreed that, because of the nature of her wound, Vivian could not be nursed in the hospital in case questions were asked. The wound itself must remain a secret, they decided. Wilma gave Vivian the blue silk pyjamas 'because they did cover up the wound on her back and her ribs. She was very grateful for those. And never did I get to wear those blue silk pyjamas; Viv wore them until they fell to bits.'

Wilma also tried to wash Vivian's dress. '[There was] a lot of blood on the uniform, which I washed out with the little bit of water that we had, but that uniform is still very stained. I couldn't get the bloodstain out.'[42]

Wilma made space for Vivian on the concrete slab next to her and started to nurse her back to health. This was tricky, Wilma explained, because, 'all night long while we were trying to sleep, which of course we couldn't do very well, the Japanese patrolled up and down through the barracks with their rifles and bayonets.'

Vivian's wounds healed quickly and there was no lasting infection, possibly because they were thoroughly scoured by sea water while she crouched among the bodies of her comrades. 'I used to wash those [wounds] every morning and just keep them clean,' Wilma recalled. 'The bullet didn't apparently hit anything terribly vital and the wound didn't really worry her. She's fortunate that she's that bit taller than the average girl and they were shooting [at the chest]—she was hit just a bit lower than it was on the others. Although she was badly shocked, of course, she didn't really look bad.'

In her interview with the ABC in 1983, Wilma was pressed for information on whether Vivian suffered nightmares resulting from the massacre. 'That must have been quite an amazing responsibility,' the interviewer, Margaret Evans, observed regarding the vow of secrecy, 'and also for Vivian in particular; a difficult thing not to talk about when perhaps she had a fever, and nightmares during her fever?'

Interestingly, Wilma's reply was immediate and she stated firmly, almost snapping at the reporter: 'I don't think there was any difficulty! We all knew the seriousness of the situation and we all accepted that! It had been spoken about and there wasn't any need to speak about it again. Vivian never called out at any stage in her sleep.' Wilma was in a position to know the answer because, for most of the next three-and-a-half years, she and Vivian slept next to each other. In the late 1990s, however, a student contacted Wilma to check a school project she was preparing on the subject of Vivian Bullwinkel. As Vivian had by then suffered a stroke, Wilma would answer questions on her behalf. When asked by the student 'Do you experience things such as nightmares and flashbacks as a result of occurrences in the war?', Wilma replied, for Vivian, 'The answer is "yes". Experiences so horrific will always return.'

Throughout their lives it was difficult to get any of the POW nurses to talk about the massacre. Once the pact of silence had been agreed, that silence became virtually unbreakable. In the minds of her colleagues Vivian remained the only one who had the authority to discuss the subject, and so it remained. 'Some things are best taken to the grave,' commented Wilma.

On the day after Vivian's arrival, 1 March 1942, Wilma, Vivian and the others were assembled in the afternoon and informed that they were to be shifted to Sumatra. They were promised better food and quarters. Some of the men were to move without delay and the women were to be ready to go at 5am the following day. The nurses decided to carefully preserve their remaining AANS uniforms so that they could wear them on their day of liberation. They were confident that release would come soon, because defeat of the Japanese should be swift at the hands of the Allies.

BUKIT BESAR

On 2 March, after a sparse meal of rice, the prisoners were lined up at dawn and marched to the wharf, a half-hour walk. Each person had been issued with a small amount of rice wrapped in a banana leaf to sustain her on the journey which, though Wilma did not know it, was to take them 20 miles (32 kilometres) across Bangka Strait then 50 miles (80 kilometres) up the Musi River. 'Some of the civilian women, who had a lot of their luggage with them, found it was too much to carry. Although we'd all been in the compound together, us without any clothes and these people with clothes, they'd never offered us any,' she observed.

Before they left, one Australian woman came to the nurses, asking: 'Does anybody want a pair of shoes? I can't fit them in.' 'Del' Delforce,[43] an outspoken nurse, told the woman exactly where she could put her shoes. 'But one of the girls carried the case for a British woman, who said: "You can have this dress if you carry the case for me,"' Wilma recalled, 'and she did carry it. And when we got to the next camp, believe it or not, the woman came and asked for her dress back.'

Wilma could not understand how this kind of thing could happen when everyone was equally desperate but, although she was never willing to confirm it, selfishness was manifest in the camps. 'One woman had a case full of evening dresses. Well, she kept patching them up and she was well dressed the whole time, but she never gave anybody anything,' she said. Wilma would, and did, give away belongings that she could ill afford to part with.

When they got to the end of Mentok jetty the captives were left waiting for quite a while before being loaded into a motorboat, which took them in relays to a battered old freighter moored about a mile off-shore along with three other ships. Into it they crammed about 200 of the women and children, including the Australian nurses. The ship weighed anchor during a beautiful sunrise and they left the island of Bangka behind. A machine gun on the upper deck was uncovered and fired over the passengers' heads. The gun was left uncovered and loaded throughout the trip.

'Conditions weren't all that wonderful,' Wilma observed. 'Toilet facilities? Well, going to the toilet in the public view, that didn't worry us any more. But this ship had two planks jutting out over the sea, from the edge of the ship. You had to climb the rail and balance on these two planks to go to the toilet. If you're on a ship for a day and a night you've got no option but to go.' A large number of the prisoners were suffering from dysentery and there were other illnesses too, so conditions were squalid.

After about three hours crossing the Bangka Strait the ship entered the Musi River. Several native villages were passed on the way upstream with fishing boats drawn up at the water's edge. The town of Palembang was reached late in the afternoon after seven hours chugging up the river. Wilma and the other prisoners disembarked and were left sitting on the wharf for another two hours, after which they were lined up by the Japanese for the inspection, known as *tenko*. Their captors then took photographs.

After the second ship discharged its cargo of servicemen, who were immediately marched away, the European women were loaded into lorries and paraded around the streets of Palembang 'for the benefit of the natives who jeered and cheered at the sight of so many captive white women,' Wilma said. 'We had to stand on the back of these trucks without any sides on them.' During this move the nurses put on their uniforms in the hope that some sympathiser might identify them and report where they were.

They arrived at their destination at nightfall. It was another Chinese school building, consisting of a series of big square rooms. Around 200 prisoners were already there when Wilma and the other nurses arrived. They were met by British and Dutch servicemen, among them Air Commodore Modin (RAF Senior Training Corps, Mechanics) and Group Captain Rice.[44] 'Air Commodore Modin and some of his men had gone over a few days before we had from our camp, and they had some soup ready for us,' recalled Wilma. 'We thought this soup was wonderful … The only problem was that the soup went in one end and out the other. The Japanese guards were trigger happy, and you had to ask if you could run off to the spot where we had to go. You were in such a hurry that you didn't always ask and they'd fire a shot after you.' It amused the guards to fire over the heads of the sick women, with no intention of hitting them.

Vivian Bullwinkel sought out Air Commodore Modin and in secret told him about the massacre at Radji Beach, meticulously listing the names of the nurses who had been shot. This was as a safeguard in case she did not make it through captivity and, in any case, it was rumoured that some of the men had access to radios that might relay the information to Australia. Rumours of impending relief or release were rife during the whole term of captivity but, unfortunately, few had substance.

Meanwhile, hungry for news, Wilma had a conversation with Group Captain Rice who told her about the evacuation of Singapore. 'They had sent out messages to the [destroyers] *Prince of Wales* and the *Repulse* not to come in to Singapore harbour because the allies could give them no air cover. But in spite of orders, they still came in.'

The women were packed about forty to a room to sleep. After the meal the women lay on the floor. 'They left the light on all night,' said Wilma. 'The guards patrolled in and out and told us to lie down and go to sleep. We were sitting up swatting mosquitoes. Of course we didn't get any sleep; the children were all crying. A terrible night.'

The next day Wilma found herself in line for another long hike. Everyone had been told that they were to move into houses, but few believed it. 'The Japs were in cars and we were walking,' Wilma said, adding that she and many of the others were still barefoot. 'If you ever saw photos of the long lines of refugees out of Poland … I'd seen them on a news reel before I went to the war and never anticipated that I'd join one of them myself. That's what we looked like. We were trundling along with our bedding and so forth, straggled out for miles. The Japs were taking photographs of us. It was very tragic for the women who had small children.'

Although, according to Wilma's memory, their captors gave them nothing to eat before they left, Jean Ashton recorded that they were able to barter a few bananas—enough for the 'girls' of the 13th AGH to have a whole one each. The usual delays followed before they moved away on what their guards assured them was no more than a ten minute walk. Three quarters of an hour later they arrived at Bukit Besar (which means 'big hill') to a street of empty houses and were halted. It seemed that the Japanese had told the truth this time and the prisoners were being moved into houses, which looked quite pleasant. They were double fronted and built in the Dutch style, standing separately with steps leading up to the front doors.

The exhausted prisoners were left standing while a Mrs Blake, who could speak Japanese, had a long harangue with the guards about who should be housed where. Jean recalled, 'We happened to be halted opposite a small native shop, so we purchased a few eggs from the owner on the roadside who came out to stare at us. I also obtained a pineapple from a hawker on a bicycle before we set off to our allotted house, Number 26.' Jean had already sold her watch and no doubt others had done likewise, so there was a little money between them making it possible to barter with the locals. The women from the 2/4th CCS joined with the 13th AGH to occupy Number 26 while the 2/10th AGH occupied Number 24 next door. Jean Ashton was head of Number 26 and Nesta James head of Number 24, but it was Sister Nesta James—pint-sized, but possessed of the forceful nature of many tiny women—with whom outsiders tended to consult whenever matters arose concerning the nurses.

Even after the experiences they had already shared, the nurses still saw themselves as separate and agreed to remain with their own units. Army habits die hard. Other people regarded the Australian nurses as one team, so it is remarkable that they did not view themselves that way. There was a need, on the part of some, to preserve their identity. Perhaps this was left over from the old hospital-to-hospital rivalry that existed in the days before nurses worked, as they do now, under contract in a variety of locations and with no particular allegiance to one institution.

Wilma was careful to point out how their training and discipline helped these women to survive. 'We were a tight knit group who were used to living in close proximity. We were used to observing seniority and rank. [Conversely] the civilian ladies were used to being individuals in their own right. I dare say they probably found it more difficult to live in the very cramped conditions. Some of them had children, which made it even more difficult. I think maybe we settled down rather more quickly and accepted that we were prisoners.'

Wilma and her colleagues slept on the cold tiled floor. Fifteen or so were squeezed into each bungalow that would normally house no more than four. The toilet could not cope with so many, but it was a proper toilet connected to a primitive septic tank system, which broke down under the strain after a couple of days. However, with conditions so improved, spirits rose and Wilma began to hope that life as a POW might not continue as badly as it had begun. Part of the reason for the improvement in conditions was that the colonial Dutch population had not yet been interned. It was mainly through them that welcome extra food supplies were arriving. Japanese victuals consisted of the usual filthy rice and rotten vegetables.

Elizabeth Simons later recalled Wilma's powers of survival with admiration and typical self-deprecation: 'Wilma could and would do *everything*,' she said. 'Some others did nothing in particular. I, on the other hand, could never quite make up my mind *what* to do!' In fact, Simons kept herself very busy, along with Mavis Hannah,[45] making hats out of grass and selling them.

One of the first things Wilma did, when she had a moment, was to make for herself a set of 'trompers'—wooden-soled shoes hewn out of rough timber and held on the feet by either a strap of leather or layers of canvas. Nails were hard to find. Instead, barbs were cut from barbed wire to form staples. These were knocked into the wood with whatever could be found to do the job.

At Bukit Besar Wilma and some of the others did the rounds of the camp, functioning in a capacity similar to a district nurse. Patients in need of more intensive nursing were sent to the Dutch Charitas Sisters who were still running their hospital, as best they could, in Palembang. Although a purpose-built hospital existed there, this had been requisitioned by the invaders for use as an administrative centre, so the Sisters had relocated to a nearby, much older, construction.

Whenever a sick nurse was sufficiently recovered, the Charitas Sisters would rope her into working in the hospital until the ambulance came to take her back to the camp. The Charitas Sisters turned a blind eye to black marketing and enabled clandestine meetings between husbands and wives. Despite the obvious dangers, notes were relayed between those prisoners who could not get to the hospital, and the ambulance transported a certain amount of contraband food and medicines. In condoning such activities these Dutch Sisters placed themselves in jeopardy.

For the time being, life at Bukit Besar was a bit kinder to Wilma and her colleagues of the 13th AGH. Jean Ashton wrote in her diary: 'We have a nice large house. Clean, electric light, bathroom, but no stove. Several large pieces of furniture but all the small stuff is gone. Sr [Mavis] Hannah went up to the store and bought some goods on 'tick'—bill 5 guilders and 27 cents—leaving 10 Singapore dollars as security. We hadn't been long in the place when some Dutch people arrived with bananas, bread and butter.' Later the 'girls' from the 2/10th AGH came in with cushions, a few chairs and a table because their house was fully furnished and complete with an electric stove. 'We made a fire place on the verandah and decided to eat,' Jean Ashton wrote. 'Found some Bovril, spices and curry in a cupboard. Word came to go and collect some rations at Number 7 (Mrs Blake's). We received some rice and dried fish. Commenced our evening meal with Bovril, beef tongue (tinned), bread and butter, cakes and tea with milk.'

'Of course we overate, which made us sick,' Wilma remembered. 'One of the [native] servants, Siti, who had worked for the Dutch families, didn't live far away. She came over, a marvellous woman. She brought us some beautiful sweetened tea.'

Siti had reason to be grateful to Wilma and she repaid her with kindness. 'The first few weeks we were there, Gladys Hughes[46] and myself used to walk out of camp and go and see that Indonesian [sic] lady and her mother or mother-in-law,' said Wilma. 'They lived in this native house not far from where we were. We went to see her every morning and she always had some beautiful sweet tea ready for us.'

The mother-in-law was suffering from a severe tropical ulcer on one of her legs. 'We would dress it and look after it for her,' Wilma recalled. 'We told Siti what medicines to get, if her husband could find them in Palembang, and we'd use those on it. She'd cook in a *kwali* (or wok) small pufftaloons [sic]. She'd deep-fry them in oil with flour and onion. They were beautiful. She would sit over this brazier, fanning it, with a few coals and a bit of smoke and no chimney in the little hut that she lived in. Then she used to make up a bed: white sheet, mosquito nets and so forth. We never had a sleep in it but she wanted us to because we didn't get much sleep where we were, with the mosquitoes and in the conditions we were living under. We'd only be there perhaps half-an-hour or an hour in the morning, then we'd think we'd better get back to camp before anybody missed us. She'd always come with us because she said the Malays followed us; she said the Malays were very bad people and it was dangerous. Siti was really a wonderful friend.'

Only about two weeks passed before trouble loomed. The Japanese Commanding Officer, Captain Miachi, habitually came in to sit and talk in Wilma's bungalow. 'He could speak English,' she said. 'He'd been in Malaya before the war and knew a lot of the people in camp.' After two weeks of this unwelcome socialising the reason for Miachi's interest in the Australian nurses became clear. 'We'd apparently attracted the Japs and, when they came, Iole and I used to rush out into the back and hide in the jungle,' said Wilma.

Both groups of nurses were informed that they must move two doors further down, into the buildings which had until now been occupied by those benevolent Dutch families. The Nipponese intended to make use of the nurses' dwellings to set up what they dubbed an 'Officers' Club'. Far from visiting because of a desire to polish his English tongue, Miachi's desire proved to spring from the opposite end of his torso, as Nesta James confirmed. 'They prepared several houses near the club. I suppose you would call them pleasure houses. They told us we had to attend the club and made it pretty obvious that they expected us to become prostitutes.' The pleasure houses were nicknamed 'Lavender Street' (after Singapore's red light district) by the Australian nurses in their doggedly humorous way, but the situation was not funny.

Wilma was scared of this sudden twist in events. Until now their captors had not molested the nurses to any significant degree and they had nearly allowed themselves to become complaisant. Their fears were confirmed when three members of the 2/10th were summoned to visit Miachi. These were Nesta James, Winnie May Davis[47] and 'Blanchie' Blanch. 'They asked for us by name, to go and "discuss our living",' reported Blanchie. 'I went in and here was this Japanese sitting at a table, who could speak perfect English, and an officer lounging in an easy chair next to him with his sword well bared. He told me to sit down at this table. He gave me a piece of paper and told me that they wanted me to sign it. I read it and got as far as: "The Japanese want you to work for the Japanese." I refused to sign, "No!" And he spelt it out: "N-O or K-N-O-W?" I said, "I K-N-O-W—and the answer is N-O!" I yelled at him, and he yelled at me. We really argued about this. I still said I wouldn't sign. He said, "If you don't sign, you'll starve to death. We're going to starve all the Sisters." And I yelled back: "As far as I'm concerned I'm not signing it. I'll die first." He said, "How will you die?" And I yelled, "I'll lie down and die!" Which was stupid because I was so well at the time.' Here Blanchie paused to shrug regretfully at the memory before continuing: 'He got a bit sick of me and told me to go home. I didn't need to be told twice.'

For the other two nurses the experience was much the same. 'I felt dreadful,' Blanchie said, 'because I thought he was going to starve the whole lot of us, because of me.' This happened on Saturday 14 March, exactly one month after the sinking of the *Vyner Brooke*.

The three nurses went back to the two houses and a mass meeting was held to decide how they would cope. The following day the nurses were shifted into Number 20 (13th AGH and 2/4th CCS) and Number 22 (2/10th AGH) while their captors took over their former quarters. The new houses were much smaller and dirtier. Wilma's group still had no electric stove but there was a small brazier. The electric light worked and there was water on tap. Much sweeping and cleaning immediately took place.

On the Monday word came from the Japanese that the nurses must send six of their members to the official opening of the 'Club' on Wednesday, 18 March. On that same Monday Jean Ashton recorded in her diary that the 13th AGH only had enough rice flour left for five days. She concluded the entry with a single word: 'Hungry'. The nurses were being starved, orders having been issued to the rest of the camp not to supply them with food.

'The Japs were very puzzled that all these single women had been allowed out of Australia on their own without any men,' Wilma said. 'They had the wrong idea about why we were with the army and we couldn't convince them that we were nurses looking after the sick.' Officers among the male prisoners again attempted to convince the Japanese that the nurses were military personnel and should be treated as such. Some of the civilian men, however, believed that the nurses ought to cooperate because this might protect their own wives from being molested.

Two civilian male prisoners volunteered to act as waiters on the night. Their true reason for attending was to provide moral support to the nurses and to protect them if possible. The men were both British, a Mr Tunn and a Mr Stevenson, and the nurses always remained grateful to them.

The Japanese refusal to accept the presence of women in military service was couched in the fundamentals of Japanese culture. Women in Japan were subservient; there was a certain amount of respect between husband and wife, but from the husband's point of view his wife was his physical, intellectual and social inferior and must *earn* the honour of any respect bestowed upon her by her lord and master. Even in the 1940s such sentiments were unacceptable to British women, and especially so to the Australian military nurses.

To the Japanese mind, women in a prison camp were not only inferior because they were women but also because they were prisoners. This compounded the disgrace because, under the traditional law of *bushido*, a Japanese would (or should) commit suicide rather than be captured. That these prisoners were still walking around was an affront.

The Japanese officers who were put in charge of prisoners of war failed to practise just about every one of the eight principles of *bushido*: *jin* (to develop a sympathetic understanding of people); *gi* (to preserve the correct ethics); *chu* (to show loyalty to one's master); *ko* (to respect and to care for one's parents); *rei* (to show respect for others); *chi* (to enhance wisdom by broadening one's knowledge); *shin* (to always be truthful); *tei* (to care for the aged and those of humble station).[48] It was considered a disgrace to be put in charge of such non-persons as prisoners. The officers smarted under this disgrace and took it out on anyone below them on the social scale. Likewise, ordinary soldiers who were put to the duty of guarding internees resented their own low station and would vent their wrath on their charges, sometimes by physical violence, often by verbal abuse and always by humiliation.

Wilma was worried when the nurses decided that there was safety in numbers and that, therefore, not six of them but every last one would turn up on the night. Having agreed that all should go, there were nevertheless four who did not attend. These were Shirley Gardam,[49] Iole Harper, 'Mickey' Syer[50] and Wilma. 'One of the girls had a broken toe, so she wasn't going,' explained Wilma. '[Then] Mavis Hannah came and said would Iole and I please *not* come to the Club with everybody. So I said: "Yes, that's okay Mavis, I won't go if it's going to cause trouble ..." I suppose because we were young, and I hadn't had my chin scraped, and I hadn't been knocked about. I had the head wound but that hadn't altered my face.'

The rest of the girls duly went to the 'Club' after making themselves look as horrible as they could. 'They looked dreadful, and twenty-eight of them turned up and the Japs only wanted four or six! It rather shattered the whole purpose of the exercise,' said Wilma. 'There was food there so the girls got stuck into the food. There was no holding back on *that*. If they had pockets they filled them with whatever they could grab, sugar and all sorts of things. The Japanese kept saying would they like to drink, *sake* or whatever it was they had. Betty Jeffrey said: "No, we only drink milk, we never drink anything else." So then they said if the girls were cooperative they could go into town and buy cosmetics, clothes, have everything they wanted. The girls said: "We don't want cosmetics, we don't use them. We're quite happy the way we are." Meanwhile they grabbed toilet paper and whatever they could lay [their] hands on.'

'Finally one of the officers, Miachi, said that four of them had to stay behind and the rest could go home,' said Wilma. So Blanche Hempsted, Eileen Short and Val Smith,[51] all three Queensland girls, said they'd stay, and the fourth one was Mavis [Hannah]. They were all able to look after themselves; all on the ball, those four. One of the Japs took Mavis for a walk around the block and at one stage he went to kiss her, so she pushed him over. He went sprawling on the ground and the sword went one way and he went the other, and Mavis took off and ran home thinking that her last moments had come. She never heard any more about it. I suppose he was ashamed that he'd been pushed over by a woman. The other three coped with whoever was with them. Nothing happened. Eventually they all came back home with nothing having happened.' Elizabeth Simons observed, 'Even so, I might add, people do not believe we escaped scot-free, even now.'[52]

In the end, a Mrs Chan intervened on behalf of the four nurses. She promised the Japanese that some of the Eurasian women would be willing to go to the Club instead. 'Matron Drummond had been good to her aboard the *Vyner Brooke* and this woman took us under her eye and held the attention of the Japs, meantime telling the girls to leave and get back to their houses,' recalled Vivian Bullwinkel.

Through the years various members of the media quizzed the surviving POW nurses on the 'true' version of the Officers' Club incident. They found it hard to believe that the women escaped. Constant pestering for additional information eventually led the nurses to close ranks and refuse to discuss it. There is no reason to doubt that the incident took place much as it is reported above. If the nurses wanted to suppress it, the event could have been hidden under another veil of silence. It might easily have been erased from history. Wilma and Iole Harper were actually terrified at the time, and it was only in retrospect that amusing anecdotes came to dominate, as Elizabeth Simons put it, 'this horrible experience'.

For as long as the infamous Club lasted some of the camp's women were quite willing to go along with it. 'They went to the Club and we became the cleaners,' Wilma said, revealing an interesting detail that has not emerged anywhere else.[53] Mrs Chan became one of the Club's hostesses and the nurses at Number 20 subsequently earned a little money by babysitting for her.

'The Club functioned for about a fortnight,' Wilma said. 'But word was got through to the Japanese governor about what was happening in our camp and he was pretty furious and cleaned the whole lot up. Then we were left alone.' As a result of the incident, and thanks to Miachi, rations to the entire camp were cut and the nurses were not supplied with anything at all for several more days. As everyone else had been ordered not to supply them either, this resulted in total starvation of the Australian nurses.

On Wednesday, 1 April the guards burst into their houses at 9am with fixed bayonets, yelling, '*Inchi, inchi!*' which Wilma knew was Nippon's gentle hint that it was time for them to get going. Some women, who were ill or recovering from night duty, were still resting on their grass-stuffed rice sacks but soon everyone was up and packing as many supplies as she could carry. 'Some of the things we'd acquired we had to get out in such a hurry that we just had to leave them behind,' Wilma said.

She left the house to find everyone from the camp assembled in an open area. They had been joined by many Dutch, who were now also being rounded up for internment, plus a number of people of mixed race—anyone in whose veins ran a drop of Dutch blood. 'The guards went through our luggage to see if we had knives but I think we managed to hide one. We sat out there in the boiling sun, and after some considerable time they took the men one way and the women and children in another direction.'

The men were marched in groups of up to twenty under guard to an undisclosed destination. Wilma and the other women walked about a mile to a much shabbier part of town where they were halted in a street lined with small houses. As if the area were not depressing enough, the Japanese had added an extra homely touch: a surrounding fence of barbed wire. 'These houses were locked,' Wilma recalled, 'but they broke down the door and said that we were to go in there to rest a while. So we went in, thinking we were to rest before we went on somewhere else.' She was destined to 'rest' in that place for fifteen months. Because the street was called Irene, the women named this camp by its Dutch translation—Irenelaan.

IRENELAAN

There were ten three-roomed cottages in the street, originally built to accommodate three or four people. Into each of these were squeezed thirty women and children. The Dutch, British and Australians were mixed together at this stage. 'You went in the front door and walked straight into a room which you'd refer to in normal times as a living room,' Wilma said. 'There were two bedrooms off that. Then out the back was a native type of bathroom and a kitchen. And another very small room. There really wasn't much space. We had enough to lie down but the whole floor was taken up at night.'

The bathroom contained a *tong* with a tap, plus a floor level toilet connected to a septic tank. Sanitation consisted of open drains that flowed past the windows and these ran into open drains along the street. Within days the septic tanks were overflowing into these, their contents oozing down the road. A guardhouse was erected at one end of the street and Wilma was disturbed to find that their commanding officer was the ubiquitous Captain Miachi.

The nurses occupied houses next door to each other, Numbers 7 and 9, again segregating themselves according to their unit. The next door house, Number 5, was full of Dutch people. Into Number 7, with Wilma and the rest of the 13th AGH, moved an Irish family by the name of Close, consisting of a mother and her four children: two boys and two girls. Mrs Close, who was the wife of a British soldier who had been stationed in Malaya, was described by Wilma as: 'Short and fat; she hadn't lost weight yet. She'd been shipwrecked [not on the *Vyner Brooke*] so she didn't have much, and she'd had her teeth out when the ship was bombed and forgot to put them in, so she spent the three-and-a-half years without a tooth in her head.' Whenever she spoke about Mrs Close, Wilma was unusually vehement, describing her housemate as: 'An awful woman, she was terrible. She and her four children commandeered one whole room—the best room in the house! She insisted on them having that to themselves.'

Wilma had reason to shudder at the memory of the notorious Mrs Close, as Betty Jeffrey recalled. 'To start with, fifteen Sisters lived in the living room and dressed in the tiny dingy room at the back of the house while the Closes lived in one large bedroom and managed to keep it filthy, stinking and noisy all day long.' The Closes were to be a problem for the 13th AGH and one that would not immediately be solved. Other civilians moved in too—among them a Mrs McKecklie and a Miss Murray. Both allied themselves with the Closes.

During the first day at Irenelaan, a Chinese family gave the nurses of the 13th AGH some bread and butter but this outside help stopped when Miachi issued orders that no trading was to be permitted through the fence. To emphasise the potency of his edict he strung a Chinese trader up beside the guardhouse, in full view of the women and children. A few days later a Malay man was flogged and tied to a post near the guardhouse, not far from the nurses' quarters, where he remained for two days without food or water. His crime? Selling eggs outside the fence.

As soon as the camp was established at Irenelaan, Dr Jean McDowell, a Scot for whom all the nurses had respect, called for volunteers to do night duty. Wilma was the first to volunteer. She attended to isolation cases that were being treated in one of the garages. 'Vivian and I both did night duty, looking after a couple of the women who had bad dysentery, and you could only use tins and then try and bury the excreta. We kept every utensil we could salvage. If we passed a rubbish tip we'd salvage things from there. You had to keep everything.'

The Charitas hospital was still functioning at Palembang, and Wilma's disapproval of Dr Goldberg again surfaced when she spoke of it. 'That woman had arranged for herself to go out of camp and live at the [Charitas] hospital,' she said. 'Dr Goldberg lived in her own room and worked there; she got a lot of perks for herself.' Wilma and some of the other nurses voiced a deep suspicion that the doctor, if she was a doctor at all, was not a doctor of medicine. They were cautious not to antagonise her, suspecting her of being a collaborator. Goldberg was forever trying to find out what had happened to Vivian Bullwinkel during those two weeks before she gave herself up.

A few days after the move from Bukit Besar a group of internees arrived from the camp at Mentok, many ill and all emaciated. These extra people had to be accommodated in the already overcrowded houses and garages. In Number 7, the Closes still had that one bedroom to themselves. 'There was the little room off the kitchen which we could use, so a couple of us slept in that,' Wilma recalled. 'Then there was the other bedroom and two of our girls plus four civilian women took that over. The rest of us had to fit the best way we could into what would normally be the living room. In the camp there were Dutch, English, Scottish, Irish, French, Indonesians, Eurasians, Germans, Swiss, Chinese, Australians; there was a girl from Borneo. Americans, Canadian, Malay ... I think that's about all the nationalities.' Wilma reeled them off fifty years later as if it were yesterday.

With Miachi's rule against outside trading, the only rations were those delivered by the Japanese. 'We [the nurses in Number 7] were all taking turns at trying to cook and wash our rice. We had to pick it over grain by grain, it was so filthy. We found a coffee grinder and Blanche Hempsted spent time grinding up some of the rice so that in the morning we could make a sort of sloppy mess and call it porridge. The rest of the time we spent cleaning it, or trying to cook it, or to cook our vegetables which were few and far between and in very bad condition when we got them.' The camp name for the porridge was *boeboe*.

'Our rations came in a truck,' said Wilma. 'The Japs just threw the food off onto the bitumen road in heaps. If they brought any meat they put their foot on it and carved it up with their bayonets and threw it at us as though we were dogs.' While this was happening the children and dogs were running all over it too. 'The food, they would often let it rot outside the fence. We'd eat it just the same. I've eaten rotten meat, you don't die of it.'

There was strict rationing for each house. 'A woman called Anne Livingstone—who was a missionary, and who was a brilliant mathematician—she used to work out how much ration had been brought in. She'd do a whole lot of figures and then put the food in heaps for each house. I think there were fourteen separate groups of people because some of them were living in garages. The missionaries were all in a garage. Then the captain from each house would go down and collect that bundle of rations for that particular house and then divide it up as equally as she could. Jean Ashton was our captain. She would put aside what she considered was enough for the nurses, then divide the rest into two separate lots for the two civilian groups.'

Wilma recalled that everybody cooked separately at Number 7. The 13th AGH cooked as a unit but the civilians cooked for themselves. 'Mrs Close was never happy with what she got. She always said that we got more so Jean overcompensated and gave them more than their share to try and keep the peace.' The Chinese cemetery was just behind the nurses' houses and the Chinese would traditionally leave food for their dead on the graves. 'We'd slip out and collect a bit of food from there,' Wilma revealed.

Starvation was taking its toll on the nurses in various ways, not all of them inconvenient. Wilma found menstruation under the circumstances to be a nuisance. 'We found pieces of rag, and so forth, that we used to wash out as best we could. It was a bit of a problem right at the beginning, but then a lot of the girls' periods stopped altogether, and eventually everybody stopped.' Although the cessation of menstruation might have been a relief, it was a clear indicator that the women were suffering from malnutrition.

One day late in April some duck eggs were included in the ration. 'First taste of egg for over a month,' Jean Ashton recorded jubilantly. It was Wilma's turn to discover something more about her physical deterioration: 'Duck egg, one between fifteen people. We'd scramble it or do something so we could each get a little bit,' she said. 'Even that little fifteenth of a duck egg ... I was eating my bit and I was getting the most ghastly pains and didn't realise what was the cause. Then I suddenly woke up that I couldn't even tolerate a fifteenth of a duck egg, so that meant I had to give up my share. I got Dr Smith[54] to come one day and have a look. It turned out that I had developed a very enlarged liver. To this day I couldn't touch duck eggs—I can still remember those pains.'

Small gardens were established by some prisoners; they tried to grow food by planting seeds from their rations. The tropical climate was conducive to the quick growth of almost anything, providing something could be found to plant. As everything edible was being eaten, including seeds, this was not easy. One staple diet was *kangkong*, a spinach-like weed that grew along the drains. Wilma was not one of the gardeners, but she gathered and ate *kangkong* whenever she could.

A daily routine soon developed at Irenelaan: the women had to get up early in the morning and be counted, then again at night. This was known as *tenko*. 'We were guarded with fixed bayonets the whole time,' Wilma recalled. 'They'd do a lot of their bayonet practice just near us, and they'd make terrific noises.'

The rations came following morning *tenko,* after which the nurses did their hygiene patrol. The sisters took turns to perform this trying duty as it was not easy to persuade people to clean their houses or clear their garbage to a safer area. Garbage was not being collected and no-one was allowed to deposit it outside the barbed wire enclosure so there was no alternative but to bury the rotten mess inside the compound. Someone would always salvage anything useable, so garbage was kept to a minimum, but there was no collection at all for six months.

Because the septic tanks were not being emptied, a sanitary squad was formed. Payment was offered by the Dutch to whoever was willing to take on this repulsive job. For the time being, Wilma did not volunteer. She took the view that she would do the camp work and not labour for money because of the energy that it consumed. 'It didn't appear to me that the food you could buy would make up for that,' she stated practically, 'so I'd try and live on the rations and do the camp work that I had to do.' Eventually the Japanese were persuaded to bring in a tanker to pump out some of the sewage, but this did not happen often enough for the sanitary squad to disband.

The women burned makeshift lamps fuelled with red palm oil, but finding wood for a fire was another matter. 'We'd burn all sorts of things,' Wilma said. 'I took down parts of the hut we were living in and the Japs got mad.' Next door, the 2/10th practically demolished everything but the four outside walls: 'All the doors, everything was burnt because we had no wood.'

A wood chopping detail was formed. The Japanese brought in green rubber trees from the jungle. These had to be hewn with blunt axes that were supplied to the women, who sharpened them using stone or concrete. A couple of serious injuries resulted from the heads flying off those axes and one of the nurses chopped off part of a finger. 'We'd try and burn that green rubber wood to cook our rice,' recalled Wilma. 'After a bit, the Men's Camp got permission to chop wood and send it into the women's camp. Loads of wood came then, and among the wood there'd be notes. Husbands would bury a note in a piece of wood. We did quite a bit of smuggling through this wood coming in.'

After her first few weeks at Irenelaan, Wilma received a pleasant surprise—a gift from the men's camp. 'It was a mosquito net, a brand new mosquito net sent to me by Jock Mathieson.' She described Mathieson as 'a kind and considerate man, a good and thoughtful person.' Life in the men's camp was no better than it was for the women, but the male prisoners still saw it as their traditional role to try to do what they could for the 'girls'. Along with the mosquito net came an equally precious gift from Jock: a tin of bully beef, which was carefully stored by Wilma for a special occasion.

The mosquitoes were driving everyone mad and malaria was rife. 'I slept under that net in luxury and it was just heaven,' said Wilma. 'I could see Jean Ashton slapping at mosquitoes, and sitting up, and I thought: "two can sleep under this." There were two wooden beds [without mattresses] about the same height in the room. I had one and Jean had the other. And after a couple of nights I suggested to Jean that we should push these two beds together, so that she and I could both sleep under the net. People were trying to rig up all sorts of odd contraptions to keep the mosquitoes off, so we did that.'

Vivian Bullwinkel was sleeping in the same room on top of a cupboard (some odd bits of furniture had been scrounged in the intervening weeks). 'It dawned on me that Viv was being eaten by mosquitoes, too. She was getting up with great splotches over her. There were some outside blinds hanging at the windows, and they had a black lining. One blind was pretty rotten, so we borrowed a needle and cotton (from the Dutch, I think) and took the lining out of that. We took the top out of the net, sewed the black lining into the top and sewed the top into the side. This made the net bigger. These two wooden beds were both for only one person, but the three of us slept under that mosquito net.'

And so, through ups and downs, except when they were separated by hospitalisation, the three nurses slept under that net during the rest of their internment, for the greater part of three-and-a-half years. 'There was just room for us,' said Wilma, adding with a twinkle, 'but I slept in the middle because if you slept on the edge you were likely to get bitten.' After pausing, she added mischievously: 'Well, it was my net! I needn't have invited anybody under it.' Mosquitoes were not the only wildlife to contend with; one night when Wilma got out of bed she nearly stepped on a snake.

There was a short period of respite from Mrs Close during May when the Irishwoman and her daughter Joan fell ill with dysentery and had to be taken to the Charitas hospital. The Japanese guards sprayed her room with carbolic. 'It is full of rubbish,' Jean Ashton noted in her diary, adding that the other Close children were being cooked for in the house by Mrs McKecklie. Both Closes returned a couple of weeks later to resume hostilities.

To cook inside the house was uncomfortable for everyone, so Jean built an oven on the verandah outside and this was where the

13th AGH nurses did their cooking. There were arguments when the smoke wafted through the window of the Close domain, as it often did, because there was no glass in this native-style bungalow.

Wilma and Vivian continued to nurse critically ill patients in the garage. 'We were barefoot and we were frightened of snakes, scorpions and all sorts of things.' From somewhere they salvaged an old pair of shoes, sharing these in order to inch their way, alone, into the jungle at night. 'These people had dysentery and we had to dig holes and we had a tin for the patients to use and we'd bury the ordure.' As a result, by the end of May both Wilma and Vivian were victims of tinea. 'I suppose we picked it up out of the shoes and our feet being always damp in the jungle,' said Wilma. They continued to do night duty but eventually both had to be hospitalised in Palembang.

'They did have some medicines in the hospital,' said Wilma. 'Our tinea got much worse. Viv had it on her hands as well as her feet. She had to keep them dry; had to be washed every day. I used to do that, wash her and dress her.' Their method of getting to hospital was surprising. 'Captain Miachi came one day and we must have looked pretty awful because he said, "Get into the car and I'll take you to hospital."' This was the same Miachi who had strung up a Chinese trader only a few weeks before, the same man who was the driving force behind the Officers' Club. The nurses continued to find it impossible to read the Japanese mind, and this was a two-way enigma. Whatever his motives, Miachi now came to the rescue of Wilma and Vivian.

Veronica Clancy recalled that before being sent to the Charitas hospital, 'Women were forced to strip while they [the guards] ran their hands over our persons and suspiciously examined any bulges.' Nesta James reported: 'I saw a woman who was punched. She was Mrs Rottier. She has since died. It was really a very terrifying place to go [the hospital], because guards were everywhere. They were extremely nasty. They included Sikhs who had turned to the Japanese.'

'You only had access to and from the hospital once a week,' recalled Betty Jeffrey. 'The ambulance would take you there and back. It was a small room with thirty to forty women in it. Absolutely no ventilation.

No windows, no air vents. There were two doors, which were shut. The only chance we had of contact with our Australian men was through this hospital. There were guards around, especially around the civilian men and women. The only place where there was no guard was the lavatory. When you saw an Australian making for the lavatory you would follow him and say, "What's the news?" They had radios and we didn't, and often you would see an Australian walk over to the lavatory and he would look towards us. We would follow and exchange notes.'

'My tinea got better fairly quickly,' said Wilma, 'but Viv's didn't recover to the same extent. Of course in the hospital you had a little bit to eat, more than in the camp. I can remember seeing Viv: we'd eaten our rice (we had a plate at that stage in the hospital) and right around the edge there were these white grubs that she'd picked out. She hadn't wanted to eat them. But it wasn't long before she was eating grubs and all.'

Because she recovered faster than Vivian did, Wilma was returned to camp leaving Vivian at Palembang. 'We didn't like ever leaving Viv anywhere on her own but there was no option. We were always trying to be protective of Viv in case the Japs found out she had survived the massacre.' Vivian came 'home' about a week later.

Wilma experienced an even more bizarre exit from the Charitas hospital than her admission to it had been. 'I came home with a woman from the camp,' she said. 'She was Eurasian, and was in camp with her niece and her niece's baby. Aunt Lottie, we called her. Aunt Lottie and I came home with Miachi in his staff car, which was very good. Miachi *knew* we had brought stuff from the hospital but he just turned his back and let us fill up the boot of his car.' Again there was this singular benevolence on the part of the camp's commandant.

'Normally they used to drive the people right into the camp area if they came by ambulance,' she continued, 'which meant that somebody could run around and get the stuff out of the car while the guard was looking the other way. But Miachi brought us home and he stopped at the guardhouse, which was quite a way out of the camp. Aunt Lottie got into a panic and said, "What are we going to do?" And I said, "Oh, don't worry."' Wilma got out of the car and ran around to Miachi, demanding, 'What about our *barang* [luggage]?' He just muttered something and went into the guardhouse,' she said. 'Sure enough, he sent a couple of guards out and they picked up all the stuff out of his boot, shouldered it and carried it into the camp for us. I've never been so taken aback in all my life!' This was the only connection with the rampant black market trade to which Wilma ever admitted.

Miachi seemed to take pleasure in being unpredictable. He had lived in Malaya and knew the ways of the British; he spoke English, combed his hair in the European style and wore a small pencil moustache. 'He was a funny [odd] man really,' Wilma said. 'But, anyway, there were no repercussions.'

The contraband would have consisted mainly of food and notes that the men were sending to their wives, as well as money. This route would have been the same one taken by Wilma's bully beef and the mosquito net, and it had its perils. The perpetrator could be punished by slapping, punching, kicking, being left standing in the sun with their arms stretched out, or perhaps standing for hours with the forehead and toes pressed against a wall, and many other simple but effective modes of torture. Wilma and Aunt Lottie were lucky that day.

Vivian's tinea continued for the duration of the Irenelaan sojourn and beyond. Veronica Clancy recalled: 'A fortune teller in the camp told her that she would not be able to walk into the ship that was to take us home, on account of her feet. Vivian's feet became a barometer, deciding the day of freedom, and when they looked a bit worse we were almost pleased—surely the ship must be near now? With mixed feelings we watched them get better.'

The women created their own amusements. 'A Mrs Anderson taught us to play contract bridge here,' Wilma recalled. 'We played it a lot until the Japs got mad one day and came and scattered all our cards, and accused us of playing for money which we didn't have.' Mrs Anderson was an Englishwoman. 'She was probably a planter's wife. Most of the English women seemed to have been planters' wives.'

The nurses made their own packs of cards, using old photographs that they found on a rubbish heap, or squares of cut-out cardboard.

The workmanship was fine and detailed because time was plentiful. 'We'd make knitting needles out of fencing wire and then sharpen them on the cement by rubbing. I knitted quite a few socks for people who had cotton material.' Some of the garments and other items that Wilma made are in the collection of the Australian War Memorial. These include a felt pincushion decorated with feathers; a cotton beret crocheted on a fencing wire hook; a red-and-white checked dress, hand-made from material issued in one of the camps; and a red vest knitted out of cotton. This is very faded behind from the sun beating down on Wilma's back while she worked.

'In our house, we started up community singing on a Saturday night,' said Wilma. 'There was a piano in the house next door [the Dutch house]. They didn't want it, so we said we would take it. We manhandled this piano over the top of the fence and up these nine steps. It was a job. We put it into our house and somebody slept on top of it for a bit. Then we started up community singing.' It began in a small way, but soon became a regular weekly event for as many as could cram themselves inside. 'As well as that we did little skits, we'd impersonate one of the guards,' Wilma added.

'Wilma Oram and Sylvia Muir as 'The Light of Love' of the Japanese guards were screamingly funny. Many characters were portrayed. The acting was excellent,' recalled Veronica Clancy.

'We found some khaki clothing,' said Wilma. 'One of our girls would dress up as a guard and this was incorporated into some of our skits. But the trouble was that we had to be super careful because the Japanese guards were just as interested in skits and singing as we were, and they used to come to watch. We lived in terror all the time of that, but it was our entertainment. The piano was wonderful.'

When Wilma was asked how she reacted to the constant lack of privacy during internment, her answer is indicative of the serene person that she was (that is when she was not portraying 'The Light of Love' at a Saturday night singalong). 'Privacy is in your own mind, isn't it?' she said. 'The fact that you have to go to the toilet and wash and so forth, does it really matter? Everybody has to do that. I don't

think it's very important. You keep your brain ticking over and thinking. That's where your privacy comes, in your own particular way of
looking at life. Nobody can alter or intrude on that if you don't want
them to; not even the guards. The fact that the guards were always
around, it didn't disturb me. The guards were *there,* they were a fact of
life, and if they were going to shoot us, you had to accept that as well.'

When asked if there were any moments when she feared that she
was about to be shot, Wilma replied, 'There were several times when
I thought that it was going to be the end. If they're going to shoot you,
you have to accept it. You don't want to give anybody the satisfaction
of showing that you're frightened. That would be a letdown for yourself.'[55] On another occasion she said: 'You didn't think necessarily
every day that you were going to die today. You just kept thinking,
every day, maybe things would get better. Hope keeps you alive.'

Although she was brought up in a household where religion
played a major role, Wilma was not overtly religious at this time. In
2001 she said that she never remembered praying at any time during
internment. On being asked the reason for this, her reply was interesting. 'The thing was that we would pray to God that we were
helped (and I don't know how He was going to help us) but the Japs,
some of them were Christians, too, and the Germans are
Christians—we were all falling on top of this 'figure' that we call
God. And we were all saying "help us to beat the other." I didn't see
any real future in it [i.e. prayer].'

Stoicism became one of the keys to Wilma's survival, but this was
combined with a single-minded determination to get through the
experience. Nor was this true stoicism because, on a close reading of
her sentiments as expressed above, it can be seen that she had clearly
sorted out her priorities. She knew what was important to her and
what was not. She discarded emotions that would waste energy on
something that she could not change. She got on with what had to be
done and she did it as well as she could. She got satisfaction from helping others and from getting her allotted job done, no matter how
irksome it might seem. She wasted no time on even considering

anything to be irksome. She cherished her internal privacy; she kept her head down and her spirits up.

During internment, Wilma perfected another tactic for survival: she could disappear. That is not to say that she physically disappeared from view but, when she felt threatened, or if she found herself in a situation or setting where she did not wish to be, she would disappear metaphorically. Like a delicate sea anemone when it is touched, suddenly she would no longer be there. She was still present in body but her self had withdrawn. It was not a cringing or a hiding from anything; it was a case of mentally removing herself from the moment. This ability was intriguing to watch, and it remained with her throughout life and protected her. It probably saved her life in the camps.

NEWS

Following the fall of Singapore, the Oram family was anxious when they heard nothing of Wilma, but hopes were raised when six unsigned cables were received, one after the other, at home in Murtoa during April 1942. One of the cables, they thought, seemed exactly like Wilma and they pinned their hopes on it. It was therefore not until later when they received official notification that Wilma was listed as 'missing' that they became really concerned. They still could not believe it and sent all the cables to HQ to have them traced, hoping against hope that at least one would prove to be from Wilma. When word came back that all had been sent by Lance a gloom settled over the house. Jane Oram sank gradually into a depression, although she was careful to hide this from her other children. 'Mother was never demonstrative, that was how she was, but she certainly felt it,' recalled Jack Oram.

On 14 July 1942, Wilma's sister Phyllis was the first to take up a pen and write to her lost sister. This was a letter crammed with family news and Phyllis was determinedly cheerful throughout, her aim being to brighten her sister's life, wherever she might be. Wilma was not to receive this, or any other letter, until late in 1945. This letter, plus more that would follow, was received by the Japanese but for some perverse reason it remained undelivered.

The family itself concentrated, as so many others did, on 'doing their bit' for the war. Lance's future wife Kayla[56] was doing first aid exams with the aim of becoming a member of the VAD. Alf Oram was a security officer in Ballarat and sister Pat was now a trainee nurse and hating it as much as Wilma had. 'Every letter she offers to come home, and every letter Mum tells her firmly to stay where she is,' Phyllis wrote to Wilma. She closed this first communication by saying, 'I hope Mona is still with you, and that she is well.'

Lance was seeing plenty of action and was soon to be posted to El Alamein. Alan Young was a prisoner of the Italians and working with fellow captives, including his mate Ces Donelly, on a large farm growing wheat in the Piedmonte area in north-west Italy. Most of the prisoners' concentration went into thinking up possible methods of escape; but although Italy was having a hard time in the war, being pushed back on all fronts, the Swiss border was more than 100 miles (160 kilometres) away and the prospect of a break-out seemed remote. Still, such plans took a man's mind off his plight and gave him some sort of hope. On 9 August Phyllis Oram was again writing to her sister. There was a sad coincidence, too, because the family received the last parcel that Wilma had sent to them from Malaya, prior to evacuation. 'Everything was very nice and gratefully received,' Phyllis wrote brightly; but those at home shed tears that the parcel had arrived safely but that Wilma had not. On the back of this letter was a note from Jack that included the words, 'Soon we hope to have definite news of you, but in any case you are always in our prayers. Also Mona. Cheerio. Love from Jack and Phyl [Jack's wife].'

At Irenelaan, children around the camp were running wild, so some of the missionaries who were also teachers started a school. For the adults there were French lessons, talks and lectures and, under the guidance of the missionary Margaret Dryburgh, a choral society was established.[57] Despite the squalor, the majority made an attempt to preserve a semblance of civilisation.

Around this period a civilian woman joined the 13th AGH in their house. This was Mrs Valda Godley. She was unhappy in her previous quarters and, having become friendly with Vivian Bullwinkel, Viv suggested that Mrs Godley should transfer into the already overcrowded Number 7. 'Valda's husband was British army,' Wilma recalled. 'Her husband's father had been the governor of Gibraltar.[58] Valda was not a very big woman, and a perfect lady, a lovely person. She didn't really fit in with the other English people so she joined us. She slept where we slept. She used to get up very early in the morning to try and have a wash on her own. She hadn't been shipwrecked, so she had her clothes. She still tried to shave the hair off her body, but she tried to do it when there was nobody about. None of us had razors, but she did. It was hard for Valda to fit into camp life, she wasn't used to anything like that, but she was a very nice lady.' To a person like Valda Godley, the lack of privacy was an ongoing nightmare, which, when added to the other humiliations, took its toll on her health.

British, Dutch and Australians shared nursing duties. When it was their turn, Wilma and the others would visit the sick twice a day, do any dressings and sponge the patients. While this reads as a fairly normal routine for a district nurse, it should be remembered that the nurses themselves were ill, starving and, through no fault of their own, dirty. The 'dressings' were scraps of rag gathered from anywhere and washed in tainted water; the 'sponge' was another piece of rag, squeezed out and then re-used to sponge another patient.

During June there were eighteen people in the Palembang Charitas hospital and about eleven people confined to 'bed' in the camp. Depending on their condition they would be either at the makeshift isolation unit in the garage, awaiting the irregular services of the ambulance, or in their various overpopulated houses. Dr Jean McDowell and the other camp doctors, together with the nurses, carried on their duties regardless. Among those ill enough to be in the Palembang hospital during June were Vivian Bullwinkel and Valda Godley. Vivian returned on 22 June with smuggled goods and some scraps of eagerly awaited news. By the end of July Vivian was again in hospital, the tinea on her feet so severe that she could not walk, despite Wilma's care. During August a camp shop was opened in Irenelaan by a Chinese tradesman known as Gho Leng. His goods were marginally better and of a greater variety than Nippon's offerings. An Indian trader was also given permission to operate and his stock included pieces of material and other useful household items.[59] Instead of being dumped onto the ground this extra food would arrive with Gho Leng in his ox-drawn cart. The price was generally more than the nurses could afford but prisoner volunteers had formed a camp branch of the Red Cross and funds were being raised, within the camp, to help the needy. Among the needy were most of the Australian nurses. 'Only two or three of the nurses have any money,' observed Jean Ashton in her diary. Ignoring their own needs, the 'girls' made and raffled items and goods in aid of the camp's Red Cross.

During this same month the Japanese were replaced by Javanese guards, known as *hei hoes* but often nicknamed 'haw haws' by the internees. Although this led to a slight softening of discipline, and relief from the yelling, face slapping and jabbing with bayonets, it also led to increased problems with the indigenous population outside the wire. They would sneak in at night to steal whatever they could from the internees, and they did not differentiate between prisoners who had and those who had not. Wilma's 'home' at Number 7 was repeatedly broken into and pilfered of badly needed clothing and rice. These nocturnal visitors were barefooted and as silent as a snake. There was no lighting, so it was not too difficult to 'freeze' in the total darkness if someone stirred in their sleep, then go on again to carry out the theft. How anyone could have slept is a mystery because, with the departure of the last of the Japanese guards, the *hei hoes* would spend the night walking around camp and flashing torches in the windows, not seeing, or choosing not to see, the indigenous intruders.

Wilma's first birthday in captivity, 17 August 1942, was marred by the fact that Viv was again admitted to hospital that day, but Jean Ashton recorded in her diary that a party was given for Wilma and that it was attended by several visitors in addition to her friends in the 13th AGH.

On 1 September Miachi arrived in camp and called for volunteers. He claimed that American and Dutch prisoners outside had asked to be nursed by Europeans. Initially, about twenty-three of the English, Dutch and Australian nurses showed interest. Then they held a mass meeting and Wilma and the others came to the conclusion that there was 'something fishy' about the proposition. Suspicion increased when a request was refused that Dr McDowell should be allowed to inspect the hospital before the nurses gave Miachi an answer. The Australians decided not to volunteer for any more Japanese 'schemes' and it was to turn out that their suspicions were correct (see p. 129). Meanwhile, a group of English nurses, including Margot Turner, volunteered for Miachi's proposal. There was supposed to be pay attached to this job and the British nurses, having also been ship-wrecked, needed it as much as the Australians did.

During September there was much speculation in the camp. One of the Australian Officers sent a clandestine list from the men's camp through to Sister 'Ray' Raymont,[60] informing her that he believed that the men would soon be moving, that he had heard that the nurses were to be sent home and that this list was to go to HQ when the nurses arrived in Australia. This turned out to be another false rumour, which raised hopes only to dash them when the truth emerged. Meanwhile, some parcels arrived from the men's camp and these were real enough. They contained tinned meat and butter for the AANS. There were cigarettes too and five tins of coffee. The following day all the nurses walked down to the barbed wire fence to yell 'thank you' to the men when a working party passed by in the distance.

During October three of the houses were abruptly emptied of occupants for no obvious reason, leaving even less accommodation for more than 350 people. Every other house had to fit more into it and the consequences were to be severe for the 13th AGH. This was not a good month for Wilma and the other nurses in Number 7 because a disagreement arose between them and the 2/10th AGH. On behalf of the 13th AGH, of whom she was House Captain, Jean Ashton put in an application for a loan of $1000 from the camp's Red Cross, to be repaid after the war. Due to a misunderstanding this money went to the 2/10th AGH which, it should be stressed, imme-diately offered to share it with the 13th AGH. However, passions ran high, at least for a while.

Also during this month the Japanese announced with great dramatic emphasis that there was no rice left in Australia. 'Hooray,' wrote Jean Ashton. 'We have had rice at every meal for eight months!' Nippon also issued an edict that the women were to wear more modest clothing. Because those who had been shipwrecked were, for the most part, dressed in threadbare sun tops and shorts made from various scraps of material, patches by now being sewn to patches, they were mystified as to where this more substantial clothing was expected to come from.

The camp choral society gave its first concert, using Number 7's piano, and was an instant success. As a final touch to this surreal month, a garbage truck arrived to clear away the accumulated rubbish. To cap off her worst month in captivity so far, Wilma was shocked when Elizabeth Simons was admitted to hospital and diagnosed with a case of dengue fever. Illnesses were becoming graver and more frequent.

'Dear Willie,' Phyllis wrote to Wilma while the above was unfolding in Irenelaan. 'This is another letter in the hope that some mail is reaching you. It carries everybody's wishes that you and Mona are still together and hopes that things are not as bad with you as we think. Mum has improved in health. She is almost her old self. She had the doctor and he said that Mum was living under a strain of suspense.'

This letter contained many good wishes from people that Wilma knew, including Mrs Higgins of Brighton, the woman who lived next door to Alan Young's mother.

Phyllis was determined to bring comfort and support to her missing sister. She concluded: 'I have been writing once a month but I see you [sic] can write more regularly now, so I will write oftener. I trust this finds you and Mona in the best of health and spirits. Love from all of us. Good luck for the future. Phyl.'

In November, hidden in a banana from the men's camp, came news that the men were again attempting to get the Australian nurses recognised as a military unit '... so that we can receive some of our pay, the military men have notified us of their efforts to help in this way. They get their pay and so are allowed to buy extras. We have been told we are not to receive any pay,' wrote Jean Ashton. So the Japanese continued with their stubborn refusal to officially recognise the women as military. On the other hand there was no serious effort on the part of the allies to help any Australian POW nurses. While the Americans managed to negotiate for themselves an exchange of prisoners with the Japanese,[61] no such efforts were made on behalf of the Australian women.

Meanwhile, an election in the camp kept everyone busy campaigning and canvassing and, after the votes were counted, Dr Jean McDowell was re-elected the British Commandant by the necessary two-thirds majority.

One of the first jobs Dr McDowell had to do in her new term of office was to face Mrs Close. Despite the addition of several people to Number 7, the Closes had continued to occupy a whole room to themselves. So the commandant and her deputy presented themselves and ordered Mrs Close to remove to the small rear room so that yet another family—a Dutch woman with five children—could be accommodated. There was an argument, the Closes being supported by their cronies Mrs McKecklie and Miss Murray, and, to quote Jean Ashton: 'All girls' nerves upset by this attack.' But Wilma was to suffer much more grief from the Closes.

Christmas came and went, Wilma's first Christmas in captivity, and the burden was lightened by the men who sent over onions, potatoes and fat, together with coffee, tea, limes, soap and pineapples. 'Also a 6lb tin of butter,' Ashton recorded, 'and a tin of beef. Talk about Christmas, quite the real thing!'

As a thankyou, the nurses assembled by the barbed wire and, when the men passed in the distance on their work detail, they sang to them a Christmas carol. The men paused to listen and, a few days later, stopped to sing an English and a Dutch carol to the women. Wilma always remembered this as a very moving experience and yet more proof that, no matter what savagery their captors inflicted on them, civilisation would prevail for the vast majority in the camps.

Civilisation seemed to have been lost, or at least mislaid, by the Close family. The Dutch lodgers did not materialise and soon Mrs

Close agitated to reoccupy her former room. On New Year's Eve she forced her way into the nurses' area and attempted to throw their belongings out. When Wilma tried to reason with her, the woman attacked Wilma, grabbed her by the hair and hit her, scratching her face and drawing blood. At the same time one of the daughters lunged with a knife, calling the nurses, including Wilma, 'officers' playthings' and screaming that they had 'run out on their patients' in Singapore.[62]

This incident was distasteful and distressing to Wilma and was never fully described by her. Forever diplomatic, the nearest she would come to relating the story was to admit in understatement that 'we almost came to verbal blows'. She was a woman of peace and logic. There is little doubt that she approached Mrs Close quietly. Such an approach must have been like a red rag to this bullish Irishwoman.[63] Wilma did once admit: 'Mrs Close was the bane of our existence. Eventually it got so bad that she was running down and bringing the guard up because she said we were doing things to her that she didn't approve of. And she'd bring the guard up, and we had great trouble and were frightened of what might happen.'

After the fracas ended, most of the 'girls' from the 2/10th AGH came in and the 13th served them supper while the nurses saw the New Year in together—an indication that, regardless of any recent friction between them, reason prevailed between the two groups of nurses.

In contrast to her own Christmas, a note to Wilma from Jack told her what his family did that Christmas. 'We decided to go for a short run in the car and camp for a few days. By careful saving we were able to get enough petrol to go to the seaside down at Inverlock. The weather was perfect all the time we were there, so we had a wonderful time. The only trouble was that I foolishly went to sleep while lying in the sun the second day we were there and was well burnt. I have been peeling ever since.' Jack closed with a reminder to his sister to maintain her faith.

Life in Number 7 went from bad to worse. During January Mrs Close and Miss Murray attacked 'Ray' Raymont. Dr McDowell was called in to hear both sides of the argument. 'Yellings, hittings, kickings, were the order of the day for quite a while. Then, after three or four weeks of this disgraceful behaviour on the part of the wild Irish element in that house, the Close family swapped rooms with the other mad Irishwoman and settled in the front room.'[62] During this period, Iole Harper found that she was unable to cope with any more of the Closes' barbarism and shifted next door to live with the 2/10th AGH. Betty Jeffrey reported the episode with humour: 'Iole came over some weeks ago to live here before she went completely crackers (she is only half crackers now).'

The nurses of the 13th AGH might have been moved to greater action against their tormentors at this stage, had it not happened that both units were approached by the Japanese command for proof of everyone's identity. The Japanese officer announced that he had heard from Australia, and he passed on the message: 'Keep smiling, love to all.'

'We are quite overcome,' wrote Jean Ashton. 'He says he will send all our names over to Australia. Takes full list of AANS and next of kin.' This renewed hope of imminent release, or of exchange, strengthened Wilma and the rest to cope with the ceaseless turmoil in their house. A list of the nurses' names may have been sent by the Japanese, for some names, including Wilma's, eventually found their way to Australia.

On 2 February 1943, matters worsened for Wilma and the remaining nurses in Number 7. Jean Ashton was trying to cook some jam in the oven on the verandah when Miss Murray and Mrs McKecklie came rushing out and attempted to knock the pot off the fire because smoke was blowing in through their window. When Elizabeth Simons came to Jean's rescue, the banshee brigade ripped off both nurses' sun tops. 'Miss Murray hits me with a tin over the left eye and blood flows,' Jean recorded. 'What a life! They rush down to get a Jap guard and Dr McDowell comes up and tells him to go about his business. It is Val's birthday [Val Smith]. What a day.'

The final showdown came five days later when, around 7am, Val Smith and 'Ray' Raymont were attacked in the bathroom by Mrs Close. 'We others are still in bed. We rush out to help. Miss Murray, from the back room, joins in the fray by standing behind Mrs Close and hitting Sr Gladys Hughes on the head with a piece of wood. Mrs Close goes down and reports us to the Japs at the guard room.'[34] Both camp commandants were summoned to accompany everyone to the guardhouse, where a Mrs Muller acted as interpreter. After investigations were completed, the Japanese offered to resolve the problem by locking Murray and McKecklie inside their room with their hands tied and depriving them of food for twenty-four hours. To this punishment the nurses would not agree, even though 'Mrs Close's story to Dr McDowell was all lies, as was Miss Murray's.'[34]

The 13th AGH nurses held a meeting and decided that there was nothing for it but to surrender the house. 'So the sisters have moved out,' Betty Jeffrey reported. 'Ten of them are here, the other 5 sleep elsewhere and mess here, and the whole thing is miles better and now old Ma Close has 32 good Australians to contend with if she dares cross the border.'[64]

The outcome of this whole distressing series of incidents was that, for the first time since internment, the two groups of nurses became one. On 16 February they held a short service of remembrance in the back room for their colleagues who had been killed one year ago on Bangka Island and those who were lost at sea.

March records from Irenelaan are sparse and depressing. Rations were in extremely short supply. On 7 March, five pumpkins arrived to be distributed among 357 people; on 9 March 'One whole day's ration for the entire camp is 49 bunches of *kangkong*, 44 cucumbers, 49 bundles of leaks. 356 people in camp. Work that out!'[34] By 14 March nearly every nurse was a victim of dysentery.

On 18 March, postcards were issued to the AANS women and permission given for them to write to Australia.

'Dear Mother and Father and the rest of my very dear family,' wrote Wilma. 'I am very glad that I can drop you a line—belatedly but that can't be helped. I can even wish Pa many happy returns of the day. I am very well and look exactly as I have always looked. My hair is growing nice and long, waving and curling like it used to when I was little.

We find shorts and sun tops plus trompers for our feet a very satisfactory form of dress, and have acquired a lovely sun tan. I hope and pray that you are all well, and please do not worry. Is Lance all right? Pat, you will know more than I do now.[65] We do a little nursing, but the very sick go to hospital. Will you let anyone who is interested know that I am all right, and could you send my love to Mr and Mrs Wilton. Mona is not here. May God bless you all and keep you safe, and I look forward to the day when we will be reunited. I can now play contract bridge, Phyl. We are very fond of rice, as you know. I miss my daily swim. Love from Wilma.'

Only one card was allowed, so it was important to know precisely what was the most important news to impart. Comments like 'I miss my daily swim' were a code which, as Wilma was a non-swimmer, indicated that hardly a word of the above was to be taken as written. 'This was one of the big troubles,' Wilma said, 'having no contact with home.'

When the card was eventually received by the Orams on 3 December 1943, they assumed correctly from the words 'Mona is not here' that, if Mona was not with Wilma, then she was probably dead. They saw to it that the Wiltons were gently told the sad news. Mona's mother had died only shortly before this news arrived, so her father suffered a double bereavement within those few weeks at the end of 1943.

Meanwhile, around the middle of March, even more internees were brought to the camp, among them a group of Dutch nuns from a convent at a place called Lahat on Southern Sumatra. The village of Lahat was to play a role in the eventual fate of the nurses but, for now, it was merely a name. Some of these new arrivals had nursing skills and some were teachers. The British and Dutch prisoners now separated into their own sectors and the Dutch elected Mother Laurentia to be their commandant. Separation was not exclusivism, but to facilitate organisation. It might also have been an attempt to retard the transmission of disease—typhoid had broken out.

As the nurses had already done, each civilian house now elected a House Captain. Among the civilians this post was to be rotated, so that no individual could assume absolute power. Because members of the

AANS plus the other nursing and religious units already followed an established order, no such rotation was necessary for them.

A clear structure emerged within the compound. In each of the Dutch and British sectors there was a Commandant and a Deputy Commandant. As has already been indicated, the British Commandant was the fair-minded Scot, Dr Jean McDowell. Her deputy was Mrs Gertrude Hinch, an American who was married to the English principal of an Anglo-Chinese Methodist School in Singapore. Her husband was being held in Changi. Below the Commandants were the House Captains and, from within the various houses, a Camp Committee was formed.

On 22 March 1943, Wilma received a surprise visit. She was elsewhere on duty at the time but Jean Ashton saw the native woman, Siti, with her husband, standing outside the wire. Placing themselves in danger of Japanese reprisals, they had brought eight small oranges as a gift for Wilma, the friend who had nursed their elderly relative, and they threw the fruit over the fence for her. That week the AANS house was able to make marmalade, among other things, by cooking the skins. Nothing went to waste.

Then, to add to all the other the challenges, there was again an acute water shortage: 'We are carrying water again. We go down to bath in Houses 12 and 14. The septic tanks are overflowing and running down the drains on the roadside,' wrote Jean Ashton.

Life was not all black and, whenever it was possible to create laughter out of very little, the women did so. Jean Ashton recorded flippantly at this time: 'Goodness me! We receive a ration of sugar, tea and soya bean sauce. The sugar works out at 1 small teaspoon per person, per day for a month.'

At home, there was still no news of Wilma (her letter of 18 March was yet to be received). Regardless of what had been written in the family's letters, Jane's depression deepened. When visiting Melbourne, she would go to St Paul's Cathedral and sit for hours in the quiet, praying or meditating. By now the family had all but given Wilma up for dead.

Then, abruptly, everything changed. Phyllis's letter described it: 'Dear Willie … Well at last we have had news of you! It came indirectly, from two sources, that your name was one of six nurses given over the air, that you were a Prisoner of War. We were all very pleased to hear that you are a Prisoner of War, bad as that is, but it is over a year since we had heard anything and we were beginning to wonder if you were still alive. The message stated that you were well and in 'good quarters' and we are praying that it is true.'

Jane was overjoyed and convinced that her prayers had been answered. 'Hearing news of you has put ten years on Mum's life,' Phyllis's letter continued. 'She has brightened up ever so much.'

'We couldn't believe! We couldn't believe! That word *incredible* doesn't really give you any idea,' said Kayla.

Although the Orams now knew that Wilma had survived and was interned, there was no further information and anything could have happened to her since. It is hard not to be touched by the determined optimism and bravery of those who were attempting to give support to those who had been caught up in the war, under conditions that none at home could imagine.

Lance was at home, enjoying twenty-one days' leave, when the news came through. By the end of his month's leave, he had made a life-changing decision. Armed with the knowledge that Wilma was alive, and that she was being held somewhere among the islands of the East Indies, he resolved to turn in his stripes. He applied to join the Infantry, and his mate Nevil Campbell did likewise, so that they could go and fight the Japanese. They underwent jungle training in Queensland, on the Atherton Tablelands.

At the same time, in Italy, Alan Young had become known around camp as 'the chief' because of his wide general knowledge. 'If some-body [in the camp] asked someone a question and they didn't know the answer they'd say, 'We'll go and ask the chief, he'll know,' recalled Ces Donelly's wife Midge. By this time Alan, Ces and the other internees were starved to the point where they could only crawl on hands and knees. To try to alleviate the situation, the men were

ordered to plant crops to supplement their poor diet. Such food as they
had was nearly devoid of nutrition because Italy was in disarray. Alan
immediately declared that he would plant radishes. 'Why radishes?'
everyone asked, imagining more palatable crops that might be chosen,
'Because,' he said, 'radishes only take three months to mature and
we're going to be out of here in three months.' He was the only prisoner in his camp to harvest a crop.

Wilma was in hospital when this was happening. She was suffering
the first of several physical problems that would plague her for the rest
of her life. Dorothy Gibson, who shared Wilma's raft after the ship-
wreck, was by profession a physical education teacher. Since landing,
Dot had traced her sister and mother and was living with them in one
of the other houses, but she assured the nurses that they ought to try
to keep fit and invited them to take part in one of her exercise classes.
Wilma willingly joined the class but, due probably to poor health, she
injured her back. 'My back simply collapsed, it gave up the ghost,' she
said. 'There were a lot of times when I had to either lie on my face or
stand up. I couldn't sit down. I eventually had to go to the hospital and
they put me under a shock cradle [a cradle over the bed with electric
light bulbs in it for heat]. My back never recovered.' She was discharged from hospital on 14 April without having had an X-ray but
there was some improvement.

While Wilma was away the Japanese transferred all the older male
children to the men's camp. This event Ashton described as 'a good
idea' because the boys were becoming troublesome and inclined to
run riot, with no male authority figure to control them.

At Irenelaan during June, the Japanese banned musical entertainment, including singing at church services. Jean Ashton remarked
sadly, 'It seems they don't like us to be joyful.' During this same
month, the Camp Committee sent out an appeal for extra rice to send
to the male prisoners. They had heard that food was getting scarcer in
the men's camp. Between them, the already starving female prisoners
amassed and sent two sacks full of rice. While this gesture was a way
of thanking the men for past kindness, Jean Ashton was fearful that

their captors might use it as an excuse to cut the women's rice ration still further.

A few days before Wilma's second birthday in captivity, an old nursing friend from Heidelberg days, Kath O'Toole,[66] sat down to write to her friend. 'My dear Wilma, it is very hard for me to write this letter, not knowing if I am writing to someone living or not. How I have missed you all this time and I am still missing you. And how I do hope you are well and as comfortable as possible under such circumstances. Do you know anything of Kit Kinsella?[67] How I worry about her too. I am still at the same place as when I said goodbye to you. It seems at least ten years ago … I only want you to know that I still think of you. If it is possible, dear, write to me. It would be just wonderful for me to know that you received my letter. I could then try and send some things to you through the Red Cross. Keep your chin up, dear, and keep hoping all will be well and someday we will meet and be able to talk of the things of the past, both good and bad. I have just recovered from a severe attack of 'flu and have lost a bit of weight but no doubt will pick up again. We have had a severe winter and now have frost and snow.'

On 17 August 1943, Wilma's birthday, the diary of Betty Jeffrey reports: 'Wilma had an afternoon tea party inviting the AANS. We had coffee and a tiny piece of loaf as birthday cake[68]—perhaps after four birthdays here we will be able to have real bread, cake etc. for our next birthday. We are terribly fed up with this woeful life.'

Wilma remarked, 'We knew that we were living on a knife edge; that we could be exterminated at any time. It was just at the whim of the Japs whether they kept us or not. We were starving and we were sick and we knew that if the Japs didn't kill us, disease probably would.'

Events in the outside world were changing. Barely two weeks after Wilma's birthday, the Italians surrendered and signed a peace treaty with the allies. The women at Irenelaan were kept ignorant of these developments but, for the men imprisoned in Italy, events moved swiftly. On 8 September there was a mass break-out of the camp at Piedmonte.[69] Among the escapees were Alan Young and Ces Donelly, but the two got separated. Alan found himself in a gang with four others who between them agreed that the best course would be to head south in the hope of meeting the allies. Soon they met other escapees who, having failed to cross the River Po because it was under such heavy German surveillance, decided to dig in where they were and wait for the arrival of the allied armies.

Alan was one of those who had learned to speak Italian. He and his group met a friendly local, who showed them a map and discussed the possibility of crossing into Switzerland via Monte Rosa, but they were warned that this course of action would prove too difficult. Disregarding the warning, the men walked north where they met and joined with more escapees. Here they discovered that a group of Italian alpine troops were forming a guerrilla unit and the escapees immediately volunteered to join this unit. Before long, the numbers of potential fighters rose to around 150 and, for a while, the prospect of offering real resistance to the Germans looked promising. With the help of guides, the would-be guerrillas moved into the foothills, dodging German patrols, but were eventually surrounded by armoured vehicles and again taken prisoner. Alan had been at large for a total of just twenty-six days.

Meanwhile, 13 September 1943 marked the return to the Irenelaan camp of Dr Goldberg from her job at the Charitas hospital with its accompanying perks. 'She brought quite a few medicines back with her, but she wasn't very generous with them,' was Wilma's sour comment on the doctor's reappearance. Goldberg accompanied the Charitas nuns and all their seriously ill patients, the Japanese having finally closed the Palembang hospital. 'The Dutch doctor [Dr Teklenberg] and the Indonesian doctor had their heads chopped off,' Wilma revealed. The Japanese had taken reprisals for the long-standing smuggling and note passing, which they had been aware of since the start but only now chose to recognise. The Charitas sisters took over one of the empty houses not far from the guardhouse. This they set up as their new hospital, stocking it as best they could with whatever they had been able to bring. This arrangement was short lived because, within the week, the entire camp was uprooted and transported yet again to an undisclosed destination.

For some time now the nurses had adopted a small dog—a fox terrier cross that they called 'Toby'. They fed him by reducing their own rations. 'We didn't have much rice but we shared it with the dog,' Wilma said. 'The Japanese didn't like dogs, they used to shoot them. The dogs were terrified of the Japanese. We were always hiding our little dog when there was a search.' The animal never made a sound, it seemed to sense the danger. 'A very intelligent little dog,' she asserted.

When their captors informed the women that they were to be moved yet again, the nurses decided to hide their pet and take it with them. 'We didn't know where we were going. But they put us onto trucks to take us, that time, with all the things we could carry. We'd accumulated quite a lot: old tins and little *kwalis* that we used to cook in.' And among their belongings, the nurses carried the dog. He shared their destiny for months, but eventually got sick and needed to be put down. 'Jean Ashton had the task of knocking it on the head,' Wilma said. 'We wouldn't ask the Japs to do it, so we had to knock it on the head ourselves.'

THE MEN'S CAMP

On 18 September 1943, Wilma found herself transported to what had formerly been the Men's Camp and it was by this title that the nurses referred to it from then on. The male prisoners had been shifted back to Mentok on Bangka Island. Believing that the camp was about to be used by the Japanese, they had vandalised it before they left.

It was amid this filth that the women now found themselves. There was nothing for it but to clean up and make repairs. This task was to occupy them for weeks and was never completed because of the shortage of materials plus the internees' progressive physical weakness.

'We lived in huts, wood and *atap*[70] buildings,' Wilma recalled. 'There was an open space in the middle. The British and the Australians were on one side of the quadrangle, the Dutch on the other. The guardhouse was at one side of it and what we called the hospital was on that side as well. On the other side of the square were the kitchens.'

'Each internee had a space just 6 feet by 2 feet [183 x 61cm] to call her own, on long communal bunks made of bamboo slats,' said Vivian. 'This space was all they had to eat on, to sleep on, to live on, and on which to store the few belongings they had scrounged. The climate was tropical. Oppressive heat causing a desert of dust in the dry season and, in the monsoon season, driving rain and leaking thatched roofs turned the whole compound into a sea of mud.'

'We had electricity,' Wilma continued. 'Sometimes it would go out. Sister Catherinia[71] used to fix the fuses—but when we had our tropical storms, the palm leaves that were our roof used to blow off. It was nothing to see Sister Catherinia up there with her nun's habit on still, sitting on top of the roof trying to mend it to stop the rain coming in. She was a remarkable woman.'

'Very crowded in our hut of 53 people,' wrote Jean Ashton. '27 inches[72] [68.5cm] on bamboo benches as sleeping and living space each side of aisle.' The 'aisle' was the dirt path up the centre which became slippery when it rained because of the holes in the roof. For most of the time these holes were tolerated because they afforded ventilation.

Wilma continued to share her mosquito net with Vivian and Jean. 'We had always had bed bugs and rats,' she admitted, 'but in that camp they got to plague proportions. The mosquito net in the mornings would be thick with bed bugs around the edges. We used to spend ages killing them and they smell awful when you squash them. There were rats but, having the mosquito net, we weren't so bothered by them. They would gnaw at your feet. If anyone had a duck egg … a rat can carry away a duck egg, just carry it! As well as the mosquitoes, and rats and bed bugs, we had ants crawling all over us.' At night the nurses had to take their food to bed with them in an attempt to protect it from those voracious rats. Veronica Clancy discovered a handy household tip: 'We found that sleeping on bananas ripened them.'

Of the sanitary arrangements, Veronica recorded: 'The lavatories in our previous hut were the European type but these were the worst form of Asiatic ones, a cement drain partitioned by a wall about 2 feet [61cm] off the ground [so] you could see the other occupant's anatomy and of course the reverse was also true. There was no water to flush the lavatories. No further imagination is necessary to describe this …'

Wilma described the bathing arrangements: 'For washing facilities we had a cement floor, and a bit of water in *tongs*. You'd bail the water out of that with half a coconut shell and pour it over yourself. The water … in wells in this camp. Just dirt wells, sunk into the ground, and you can imagine how muddy it was. We used that for cooking the rice.'

'The Japanese would walk to and from the women's barracks and hit us,' recalled Nesta James. 'They were to and fro all the time with their bayonets. They came into the lavatories, which had no doors; it was just a cement latrine and they made themselves objectionable to us in the lavatories, also in the place where we managed to bath [sic].'

Every shift of camp location was shortly followed by the addition of yet more prisoners. Four days after the move to the men's camp eleven more prisoners arrived, including several nurses who had served in the civilian hospital at Malacca and were known to the Australians who had served there in the military hospital which, in those halcyon days, was nicknamed 'The White Elephant'.

Around 25 September, Wilma witnessed the return of Margot Turner and the other British nurses who had volunteered to go out to nurse. Contrary to what the Japanese had originally claimed, not a single Dutch or American prisoner had been at the hospital, which turned out to be of the native variety. This did not deter the British nurses, who willingly cared for the indigenous people, but they were shortly accused by the Japanese of unspecified smuggling and spying 'crimes' and spent months under horrific conditions in a native prison, some in solitary confinement. When they eventually returned to camp, they had barely managed to cling to their sanity.[73] Very soon, they and the Australian and civilian nurses again joined forces to resume their district nursing duties. The Charitas Sisters had again set up their hospital, which was always full.

Veronica Clancy was to spend a lot of time in this hospital because of failing health. 'The hospital hut was just inside the entrance gates, at the top of the camp and of the same structure as the other huts; but the roof was lower, making it ever so much hotter,' she wrote. 'It was partitioned off into various rooms in this order: Firstly Dr Goldberg's room, then a cubicle for the sick and dying. Next was for nuns on night duty and, lastly, a utility room. The ward held approximately 30 patients. The bathroom and latrines were even more public than those at the camp. Seats had to be installed as the patients, in their weakened condition, were unable to support themselves over the drains.'

Later, when she caught typhoid, she wrote: 'My first thought was how wonderful to be in a bed again to feel linen, and turn and stretch my limbs without touching my neighbours. This on our 22 inches [*sic*] space at camp was accomplished in mid air.'

Veronica was no more fond of Dr Goldberg than was Wilma. On the days when rations were distributed at the hospital, Veronica observed: 'The wares consisted of brown and green beans, bananas, gula, duck eggs and chillies. Sometimes paw paws and dried meats. For hours before the goods arrived, Dr Goldberg would anxiously wait and be on the spot immediately to supervise the distribution to her own advantage. She was the cause of much strife among the ration officers.'

Dr Goldberg was officially the prisoners' doctor in the Charitas hospital, an arrangement that she had engineered for herself at Palembang. The other doctors served around camp with the district nursing service or helping within the hospital, as required. This so-called district nursing was a useful back-up for the Charitas hospital, which did not have the capacity to attend to the rising numbers of medical cases. The doctors themselves were often among the sick.

Dr Goldberg guarded her territory jealously. 'She worked very hard in the interests of the hospital patients but, like many other German women, she was provided with money through the Swiss Consul, and herself knew nothing of hardship during internment,' wrote Elizabeth Simons. 'Her temperament was as unreliable as Jap propaganda. At times she was rabidly anti-Aussie, and would even refuse to admit members of the AANS to hospital, but on another occasion it was she who raised the forty guilders to provide tinned milk for our typhoid patients.'[74]

Cooking facilities were as primitive as can be imagined. The British, including the Australian nurses, continued to cook in separate small groups. 'We all used to have our own little individual fires,' Wilma remembered. 'We used to perhaps cook [for] half a dozen people together, or even one person on their own. We called these groups *kongsis*.' Wilma's *kongsi* cooked in one corner of an open shed with seven other fireplaces around it.

The Dutch were better organised because they came into camp with so much in the way of goods and money. They hired other prisoners to cook for them, and their food was prepared on their communal fire. But the British remained typically individualistic, preserving their own little piece of personal space, and this did not work to their advantage because of the shortage of firewood. 'Val Smith got some mung beans,' Wilma recalled. 'She cooked some of these and we were all sitting around. We were looking forward to getting our share. Just as she got to us, she slipped and dropped the lot into the mud. Well, as hungry as we were, we couldn't rescue those beans. It was the most awful few moments. Val felt really terrible, and we were so hungry, but we just had to forget about it …

'The Japs had some chooks [chickens],' Wilma continued. 'Occasionally a chook made the mistake of coming into our camp. It was quickly dispatched but we never knew what to do with the feathers.'

In Italy, meanwhile, Alan Young and Ces Donelly were loaded onto cattle trucks to be railroaded to Germany. 'There were forty men to a railway truck, and the doors were locked, and we were let out once in the whole of the six days to go to the toilet. The rest of the time we had to use one end of the truck as a toilet.'[75] Alan and Ces ended up at 46 Stalag 344 in September 1943, where Alan found himself quarrying in deep snow for three months. He was later put to work constructing the foundation for a three-storey building. The local *Burgermeister* was a Nazi called Neubauer and he made the prisoners' lives a misery. Alan and his comrades were later moved to Lager 741 at Zwittau near the old Sudetenland border, from where they were drafted out to work parties until the end of the war.

On 2 November 1943, Jane Oram at last felt able to write a personal note to her daughter. It was not received by Wilma until May 1945. Jane wrote: 'Heard officially you are a prisoner. News welcome. Pray you are well treated. All well. Pa working at seaside, am joining him. Lance safe. Good health. Mother.'

Wilma's health was worsening. Even though her wholesome upbringing, her relative youth and her natural robustness equipped her better than many for this crushing life, she suffered from malaria and dysentery and all the symptoms of starvation. 'Jean Ashton, Viv and I were sleeping under that mosquito net when, one night, in the middle of the night, I got a sudden attack of dysentery,' she recalled. 'I got out and started to go as fast as I could down to the toilet, and it had been raining. Everything was slippery and wet and I just wasn't getting there in time …' Vivian followed close behind to help her, and it was just as well that she did because, halfway there, Wilma collapsed and soiled herself and the floor. Vivian immediately went to fetch a tin. 'She had to go out and bail water out of this well, in the rain and the mud, to clean me up—which she did willingly. You see, you did need a friend when these things happened, because they would just happen without any warning.'

When Wilma was asked in 1997 whether there was any angle or attitude that she would like to emphasise about her period in the camps, she replied: 'The sordidness of the camp hasn't been brought out. Perhaps also the dedication we had to each other, the helping of each other, what we did for each other when we were sick. We'd try to keep the others going … Individually we were very dedicated to our close friends—we did everything we could for them. That hasn't been stressed, neither has what you went through to help other people.'

The concept of mateship has long been recognised among men in Australia. It is revered as a traditional Australian male value. Yet those same men have been quick, in the past, to label the identical relation-ship between women as lesbianism. It is not; it is mateship. Mateship is non-sexual. It is that total commitment to another person in adver-sity, to the point where one would willingly lay down his or her life for the other. This quality exists among women, too, and probably the very highest example of female mateship is that of the POW nurses of World War II—those imprisoned on Sumatra and those who were transported to Japan.

At home in Murtoa, Wilma's lone letter had at long last been received and, with it, the sad news that 'Mona is not here'. On 3 December 1943, Phyllis was able to write: 'Dear Willie, we were all very pleased to receive your letter. Wired Lance, who is still safe. Pat in army now. Everyone well. Merry Christmas. Tons love.'

A short note to Wilma dated 16 December and also delayed, sent her Christmas greetings and reported: 'Lance wounded but improving. Everybody well and happy. Stick to Christ, Willie. Cheerio.'

Behind that short statement 'Lance wounded but improving' lay another story of mateship. 'Lance and Nevil were engaged in some very heavy action against the Japanese, during which Lance was severely wounded in the leg,' recounted Wilma at her brother's funeral. 'All of their other mates were killed. Nevil got Lance behind a tree and attended to the leg as best he could. He had to straighten the limb and then bandage it. There was a heavy storm and trees were brought down, blocking the track, which made it impossible for Nevil to take Lance back down to their lines. He went to procure help, but his request to the Lieutenant on duty was refused …'

'And poor old Lance was left there all night,' continued Nevil. 'The Japs came out after a bit and took all the boots off our dead chaps, and Lance's too, and they belted him up and he feigned death. They bashed him over the face with a water bottle. And it laid his cheek right back over his ear. He hung on all night. Where our section was, we couldn't hear him, but the other part of the battalion could hear him yelling out, "The Japs have gone!" He even used Arabic to try and get them to come and get him.[76] They didn't, of course, till first light.'

There was more to the story. Lance himself only spoke of it, years later, to his grandson who eventually told Lance's wife. 'When the Japs came back to make sure that Lance was dead, they twisted the leg and it finished up at the back of his neck. When he had nerve storms—when you lose a limb you have nerve storms—he still felt his leg at the back of his neck.' Kayla Oram's eyes filled with tears while she related this, and she added sadly: 'My husband had never told me that.' This phenomenon of keeping the worst of it from the folks at home was seen, at the time, as the right way for a man to behave. It was a code of behaviour that was to have prolonged consequences for war victims and for their families.

Lae, near where Lance was wounded,[77] was the focus of a major land, sea and air operation by Australian and American forces. Fighting lasted until 16 September 1943, when members of the encircled Japanese garrison were either killed, captured or escaped.

At around this same time at the Men's Camp, on Sumatra, the Japanese erected an open shed in the middle of the compound. While children played in and around it during the day, it also had many other uses, one of which was to shelter the now famous vocal orchestra[78] on the night of its first concert. Wilma was not one of the singers. 'I've got no possible hope of singing,' she laughed. 'I wasn't involved with the orchestra.' The rehearsals were so secret that Wilma was not aware at the time that they were taking place, even though her colleague, Betty Jeffrey, was one of the singers. 'As far as I know they practised behind the Dutch kitchen,' Wilma said.

Christmas approached, Wilma's second in captivity, and at home Lance was critically ill. He became one of the first patients in the world to be treated with penicillin. This was a case of kill or cure. He was so near death that they had nothing to lose by giving the drug a trial.

In Germany, Alan Young's Christmas was cold and stark but at least he was getting Red Cross parcels. From his mother he also had a Myers clothing parcel and so possessed enough clothes to be able to give some away to his fellow prisoners. Despite his deprivations, Alan made it his business to learn to speak German just as he had taken the trouble to learn Italian. By exercising his mind in various ways, he was able to get through.

Christmas in the Men's Camp brought little joy to the AANS. On Christmas Eve, Jock Mathieson smuggled a note to Wilma from Mentok on Bangka Island: 'Dear Wilma, Here I am again. It is Christmas Eve. Great preparations are being made for tomorrow's food. I believe we will be eating throughout the day. Three pigs have been slaughtered. They are being prepared just for the cooking pot. The local authorities have contributed a great deal towards tomorrow's food. There will be church services, carol singing. The weather has been shocking. We have had continual rain for days. I forgot to tell you before that I am doing a job of work with the hospital, so I am on the staff. It helps to put in the time. The lads are still in high spirits and they all wish you and the other lasses the compliments of the season. Well, Wilma, I wish you and all the lasses I know a Merry Christmas and a Bright New Year and I hope you will have plenty to eat on Christmas Day. What is your program for the festive day? I do hope that, for the next one, we will be out of here. Keep smiling and God bless you, with all the best for the coming year. Yours ever, Jock.

'Unfortunately I wasn't able to smuggle one back to him,' Wilma said sadly. Jock's attempt to boost her morale was timely, for the Australian nurses were low in spirits. 'Christmas dinner light on this year,' Jean Ashton wrote. Betty Jeffrey did a drawing of the entrance to the Men's Camp. On the other side of the wire stood three trees, the centre one of which was straggly and had less leaves than the others. Betty pointed to each in turn. 'Faith, Hope and Charity,' she recited, then added bitterly, 'Hope is dying.'

There could not have been a better moment for Nora Chambers to launch the vocal orchestra, on 27 December.[79] 'I remember distinctly the very first time I heard it,' Wilma said. 'It was wonderful. Nora Chambers just started it from dead silence then, all of a sudden, this beautiful melody drifted through the air ... It affected [the Japanese guards] too because they hadn't wanted us to congregate, they don't like groups of people, they think you're hatching something. They came yelling out as they do, in Japanese, with their fixed bayonets, but Nora started the singing off, and they stopped to listen, and there was never any trouble. They let us have those concerts.' Even at that first performance some of the members were too weak to stand. They brought with them various makeshift seats: upturned *kwalis* or kerosene tins. The vocal orchestra lasted for about a year, its members gradually dying of starvation and disease, until it could no longer continue.

Now that the family could be fairly confident that Wilma was still alive, they kept hopefully sending her notes. The correspondence was shorter, not by choice but by wartime regulation. On 12 January 1944, Jane wrote: 'Praying for your return during 1944. All well, except

Lance, who is improving after amputation of right leg.' On 20 January, Jack wrote: 'Mother with father at Portland. Lance in hospital. Right leg amputated. Off danger list now. Jack.' A little later, Jane again wrote: 'Dear Willie, Lance is improving, being fitted for leg. Everyone else is extra well. Your return should not be long now.'

Lance's daughter, Gianne Johnston, remembered her father's early prosthesis as 'so big and bulky that it had to be taken on and off and stored in the back shed. It always seemed to me he was putting on a harness, with a huge strap that buckled around his waist and another over his shoulder.' Regardless, one of the first tasks that Lance set for himself after his medical discharge was to learn to ride a fixed wheeled bicycle.

Food in the Men's Camp improved in February when permission was again granted for Gho Leng to bring in his daily wares. He regularly brought bananas, but also *gula*, a few eggs (33 cents each), dry opak biscuits and occasionally small onions, hard red beans and bean flour. Everything was at inflated prices which had to be paid for in advance. Although Wilma was allergic to duck eggs, hens' eggs did not affect her and she was proud that she was even able to stomach those that contained a partly formed embryo.

Together with Vivian and Betty Jeffrey, Wilma was elected to sort the bananas before they were distributed. '[We] used to go over to the guardhouse and collect the stems, which were pretty heavy,' she said. 'We'd carry them over to our side of the camp. Then we'd have to cut the bananas off, count them out and sell them to the people who had the money.' She then admitted to a subterfuge that was necessary to combat starvation: 'Viv and I had no money,' Wilma repeated. 'I think Jeff had a bit. She was able to buy for herself, but Viv and I had no money to buy bananas, so we stuffed in as many as we could while we were cutting them. The ones that were a bit overripe or rotten, we took those and put them with our rice and cooked them. There were ways and means of looking after yourself,' she added meaningfully. 'Betty Jeffrey was one of the workers on the shop committee for over a year and Vivian Bullwinkel and Wilma Oram did splendid work distributing the daily supply of bananas ...' recorded Veronica Clancy.

'We had to dig up the middle part of the camp and plant tapioca root for the Japs to eat,' Wilma recalled. Despite their physical weakness, they had to use heavy *chungkals* (hoes) and *parangs* (sickles) to do the job because the Japanese would not, or could not, supply the proper tools. 'We had to go for miles and cart water, nice clean water, and pour it on this *iti kaya* (tapioca), while we were drinking this dreadful muddy water out of the wells. We also had to cart it for baths for the Japanese officers. If you were caught switching the clean water for the dirty water, you were punished, so it just wasn't worth it.' The women had to cart this water in the hottest part of the day, standing in a queue to fill leaking buckets. 'One bucket was full,' said Wilma, 'and I was there, waiting to fill my bucket, when the guard known as Snake said, "Take that bucket!" I tried to say it wasn't my bucket, that it was some-body else's. He was very threatening, about to flatten me, so I picked up the bucket and ran. I wasn't going to argue with him.'

Violence was a part of life. Nesta James said: 'In the Palembang camp I frequently saw women punched and slapped. I have seen women with their teeth hanging out and faces blackened.'

During February, Wilma was forced to sign an oath. It is likely that all the women in the camp had to sign such a document. It was worded as follows: 'I sign my hand below in this internment place and swear in the name of God that I will not run away or plot ways and means to escape. If I break this oath, whatever punishment is meted out to me I will accept. W.E.F. Oram, 6 February 1943.'

March came and, at home, Lance was transferred to the Heidelberg Hospital where Wilma had first been posted. By the end of that month he was getting about on crutches and making good progress. 'Keep shining in your small corner,' Jack wrote to Wilma.

Wilma was shining as brightly as she could, under the circumstances, and unaware that she had received 'promotion this side of the ocean (so cheer up, my lads, bless 'em all!)'.[80] In Canberra an official document was drawn up that contained (in part) the following wording, signed by the Governor General of Australia: 'To Wilma Elizabeth Forster Oram. I do hereby appoint you to be an officer of the permanent Military

Forces of the Commonwealth from the twenty-third day of March 1943. You are therefore carefully and diligently to discharge your duty as such officer in the rank of Lieutenant. Given under my hand and the Seal of the Commonwealth this fifteenth day of April, One thousand nine hundred and forty-four.'[81] On 1 April 1944, the Japanese military again resumed responsibility for the camps and took over supervision of the *hei hoes*. Their Commandant was a tyrant called Captain Seiki. His deputy, Mizumoto, was nicknamed 'Ah Fat' or 'Fatty' by the nurses. 'Immediately we came under army control, things became very different and, almost overnight, the food became shorter,' reported Nesta James. 'Capt. Seiki was in charge. From the time we were under his supervision, until the end of the war, he paid very little attention to the camp and allowed his NCOs and guards to do just what they liked with the women.'

'The Japanese officer used to come and inspect us, and we'd all line up, then we'd have to bow low,' Wilma said. 'We were not allowed to look on the Japanese higher officers. Yes, you were stood out in the sun, and you could perhaps be made to stand straight and hold your arms out horizontally. Various things like that. And they would bash you as well, whenever they felt inclined.'

When the military moved back, part of the Australian nurses' dormitory was taken over by the *hei hoes*. 'We had a bit of a partition up between us but we used to peep through that. If they were being punished I've seen them have to stand there with a bucket over their head and their arms outstretched for eight hours at a time,' reported Wilma.

Wilma, along with Jean Ashton, Vivian and Valda Godley moved out and took up residence in Hut 8. The one good thing that came with April was the receipt, through the camp's Red Cross branch, of a payment of $40 for the Australian nurses.

Seiki was fond of the sound of his own voice. He was to call many assemblies. Everyone would then stand for hours while he made long speeches. These had to be translated, thereby lengthening the ordeal. On 22 April he called everyone together to announce that the Australian government had returned to Japan the ashes of Japanese submariners, who had lost their lives in Sydney Harbour when their midget craft were sunk. This, according to Seiki, was much appreciated by the Emperor. Wilma muttered an aside to those standing nearby, 'So long as they send our bones home with *us* wrapped around them.'

In May, Seiki issued orders that, from now on, all cooking was to be done communally. 'The Japs called for half-a-dozen strong women,' Wilma said. 'I went out and said I'd do whatever had to be done. They had these big *kwalis,* as big around as a table. We had to pick them up. They confiscated our little individual fires.' Wilma was ordered to gather bricks. 'We had no mortar. We had to build these bricks up high enough to sit these *kwalis* on and put a fire underneath them.' This was a belated precaution against the spread of fire. As the Dutch already cooked communally, it was the British and Australians who were affected. Gone was the opportunity to sit with friends and enjoy a short period of what passed for privacy. Instead it was a case of queueing for the ration in their sector.

When Wilma volunteered to become a member of the British cooking squad ('British' meaning also Australian), the squad was subdivided into vegetable washers and cutters, rice washers, water carriers, washers-up, etc. Rotten vegetables were sorted from those that were edible. Rice-washing involved the usual picking through it grain by grain.

Wilma's duty was to be a rice cook. 'They all jumped on me and said, "You can't cook rice, what do you know about cooking?" I said: "Nothing." But nobody else had volunteered so … It was a really big job cooking rice for 300 people, although we only had a cupful each. Anyway Louise Beeston, an Englishwoman, and myself were appointed for one squad and we defied all the critics by being as good rice cooks as any in the camp,' she said proudly.

Cooking the rice was a precise art. 'Our *kwalis* were probably 100 times [*sic*] bigger than the normal household wok. And we got up in the morning about 4am to cook what we called porridge.' Everyone was given a bowl of this *boeboe* (porridge) at about 7am. Then the squad cooked the rice for the midday and the evening meal. 'We tried to divide the rice into three meals and we had to measure it carefully with exactly the right amount of water for this huge amount of rice. We had a big fire under it, cooked it quickly. As soon as the water was absorbed, we would rake the fire out and cover the *kwali* with a big wooden lid. Norah Chambers made those lids, I think.' The rice would then be steamed until soft. 'You had to be very careful not to burn it, not to have it sticking to the bottom of the *kwali,* because every grain was valuable. It was measured out equally to each person. Each person got exactly the same amount for their midday and evening meal.' When divided among the 300 or so prisoners, the rice amounted to a small handful each.

On being asked what happened to any rice that was left over, Wilma replied: 'There was never any left over. It was dished out exactly, to the last grain. If it had caught on the bottom and there was some hard rice, it had to be scraped off. That was taken and given around to each hut. People were given a turn at being able to eat that hard rice.'

At about the time of the changeover to communal cooking, Dr Jean McDowell suffered a nervous breakdown. She had done an outstanding job as British Commandant for so long, and had continued her medical duties as well. Now the strain proved too much. Dr Smith came to see Wilma to ask if it would be acceptable for Jean McDowell to join the washing-up squad. The cheerful company of the other women on the squad was beneficial and Dr McDowell remained with them, washing out the *kwalis* and other utensils, such as they were, until her mind eventually recovered.

Mizumoto, or Ah Fat, was in charge of rations. He was forever hanging around the kitchen with his fixed bayonet and gun. 'We had to bow to him every time he came anywhere near,' said Wilma. 'He was always on about fire, but we just had to ignore that because we had to get the rice cooked. So we had to bow. Our shorts were in tatters, so by the time you hung onto your shorts and tried to keep all the bits together and bow at the same time, it was quite a work of art.'

'Fatty' derived pleasure from voyeurism and he was also one of the cruellest of the guards. He was later named as a war criminal. On being shown a photograph of him at a tribunal after the war, Nesta James stated: 'I identify [him] as Seargent Major Mizumoto. He was in charge of stores for the camp. He stood women internees and POWs out in the sun without head coverings for periods of an hour and more. Sisters Oram and Bullwinkel were subjected to this treatment for failing to see Seargent Major Mizumoto in August 1944.'

Vivian Bullwinkel described what happened: 'One day Sister Oram and myself were coming back from a gardening period and we did not notice Mizumoto there and did not bow; so we were called up and he spoke to us severely in Malay. Then he stood us in the sun for about an hour without our hats. After an hour he called us in and asked us why we had not bowed ... After we explained we had not seen him and that we were sorry, he let us go with a warning.'

Due to the salvaging of wood, the huts were in danger of falling down. Mrs MacKenzie, a Scot who was in charge of the vegetable cooking squad, was singled out one day by the Japanese. 'They took her out and stood her in the sun,' Wilma said. 'They gave her a terrible talking-to and then the guard stood back ready to slap her. She held her hand up and said, "*Nanti, nanti*—wait, wait!" Then she took her glasses off and her false teeth out, and stood and said, "I'm ready." He slapped her on one side, nearly knocking her over, then on the other.'

During June large squads of women were sent outside the wire to dig gardens to grow vegetables. '*Chungkals* weigh 7lb or more. Everyone very weak. Captain Seiki says unless we grow food we will have none by September. Sweet potatoes and *obikuya* planted,' wrote Jean Ashton. These gardens were located close to the Japanese, who helped themselves to the meagre crop.

On 7 June 1944 Valda Godley died. In the tropics dead bodies decompose quickly, and on this occasion the Japanese refused to take the body away. The women carried it out into the shed in the centre of the compound, known as the *pendarpo*. There was no coffin available and rats and feral dogs were everywhere. Vivian and Wilma sat up all night guarding the body of their friend, which was not due to be removed until the next morning.

'The following morning, before it was taken outside [the compound] to await removal Captain Seiki, Fatty and an interpreter made a spectacular entrance,' recorded Veronica Clancy. 'They demanded that everybody gather outside the *pendarpo*. Mounted on a box we were addressed in Japanese, the interpreter translating his oration into Malay. I was standing next to an Indonesian who spoke [English] fluently. She explained what this was about. With much repetition, the speech lasted about an hour.'

Valda Godley's body meanwhile lay there, by now having been transferred into a rough wooden box. 'In the middle of this speech a truck arrived to take away the remains of Mrs Godley,' Veronica wrote. 'It was a terrible moment. In the excitement of Capt. Seiki's address, the lid of the coffin had not been nailed down. This unpleasant procedure was hurriedly accomplished, with the hollow resounding blows re-echoing above the raucous voice of the Japanese tyrant.'

Viv and Wilma were permitted to go outside the wire to attend the funeral, such as it was. The grave was not dug until after the coffin arrived. The digging was effected by the *hei hoes* while the coffin rested on the ground and the mourners stood around. 'The guards would throw the shovels down and an air of frivolity prevailed at this sad interment,' Veronica wrote.

Valda left her personal effects to Wilma and Vivian. Wilma inherited a toothbrush and a long red evening gown, which Jean Ashton remodelled into a short day dress.[82] 'And this was my best dress,' said Wilma. 'I kept that very carefully, I would only wear it on special occasions like birthdays.'

On 1 August 1944 the Japanese Chief of Staff of the 11th Formosa Unit received the following orders: 'Under the present situation, if there were a mere explosion of fire, a shelter for the time being could be in nearby buildings, such as a school, a warehouse or the like. However, at such a time as the situation became urgent, and it be extremely important, the POWs will be concentrated and confined in their present location and under heavy guard, the preparation for the final disposition will be made. The methods of disposition are as follows: Whether they are destroyed individually or in groups, or however it is done, with mass bombing, poisonous smoke, poisons, drowning, decapitation, or what, dispose of them as the case dictates. In any case it is the aim not to allow the escape of a single one, to annihilate them all, and not to leave any trace.'[83]

It seems likely that the above was a general order issued by the Japanese High Command, though only one copy is known to exist, the rest having been deliberately destroyed in the Japanese retreat. Its timing coincides with the allied defeat of the Japanese in Burma. At the same time, in the Pacific, forces under Admiral Nimitz were making real inroads on Japanese strongholds while preparations were being made for General MacArthur's thrust into New Guinea.

Wilma, in a speech delivered at La Trobe University, Melbourne on 8 September 1998, stated: 'We did have some notion that things were going badly for the Japanese, as we had learned of their plans to shoot us all, in order to destroy the evidence of their brutality.' At what point the women learned this is uncertain, but it seems likely to have occurred around this time. There was an air raid over Palembang on 11 August and by 30 August nightly air raid alerts were the norm.

During August the wells in the compound went dry. The women were rationed to one bottle of drinking water each and one butter tin of water per day for washing. Sister Raymont had been ill in hospital for the past twelve weeks. 'Heart,' wrote Jean, adding, 'we are all weighed monthly.'

'Fatty lived in the house, just the other side of the fence,' Wilma recalled. 'We used to have to bring his bath water for him. He would sit in this hip bath and we used to peep through at him to see what was going on.' Obviously a fair amount of peeping went on one way and another, but in a camp full of 300 women, even the sight of a Japanese in a hip bath must have been better than nothing to look at.

On Wilma's third birthday in captivity there was a sudden welcome delivery of mail. Jean Ashton was among the recipients. 'I was having what we called a birthday party,' Wilma said, 'and letters arrived in the camp. Suddenly I wasn't having a birthday party, we were all having a party. Everyone was screaming out wondering: who's got a letter? Who's got a letter? But the trouble with letters [is that] only a few people received them. And the unfortunate thing was that you didn't always hear good news. Beryl Woodbridge heard her mother had died. Nesta James heard her father had died. One of the other girls heard that two of her brothers were prisoners in Germany. So it was wonderful to hear from home but it was very worrying to get that kind of news.'

Betty Jeffrey wrote: 'A little Jap interpreter told us three months ago that three hundred letters were here for us, but we wouldn't get them till they were ready to give them to us. Oh, how we all hope they are squashed and thoroughly broken! They are a cruel, untamed, uncivilised race.'[84] Afterwards, the AANS internees sewed their mail into book form and shared it with each other. Sometimes, for entertainment, extracts would be read aloud.

In honour of her birthday, Vivian made a small purse for Wilma which she treasured for many years. At Vivian's 'This Is Your Life' Wilma brought that purse into the studio and presented it to Vivian, saying, 'And, Viv, look it's still lasting and I've still got our money in it.' How the two of them earned that money will soon be revealed.

On 30 August the AANS were allowed to write home for a second time, but there was an unsettled air around camp and rumours of yet another change of location. Suddenly, on 2 September, everyone was lined up and given a tetanus booster injection, after which Captain Seiki confirmed that they were to shift camp. 'A wonderful camp,' Seiki assured them in a lengthy speech, which ended with the words: 'There's no light and no water.' Small hand luggage only was to be taken. Soon everyone was selling or bartering and the women were busy making haversacks so that they could carry the maximum.

In the middle of this there was another air raid. Every air raid alert was greeted with joy by the AANS, though not overtly. '[The Japanese] attitude changed immediately [after the first air raid]. All face slapping stopped and we were left by them alone, comparatively [sic],' noted Vivian Bullwinkel. Veronica Clancy was in hospital at the time, recovering from typhoid. The camp had suffered six deaths since the beginning of the year, though not as yet within the group of nurses.

Right: Wilma's father Alf Oram,
dressed for bowls.

Right: Wilma's mother Jane Oram,
dressed for church.

Right: A young Wilma in her nurses' uniform, while studying midwifery at the Royal Women's Hospital, around 1939.

Left: The official army portrait taken when Wilma first joined up in July 1941.

Right: Wilma with her brother Lance in 1941.

Below Left: Exploring Singapore with best friend Mona Wilton (left), 1941. Mona was later 'lost at sea' when the SS *Vyner Brooke* was bombed on 12 February 1942

Below Right: Wilma on the day of her release from the Japanese POW camps after three-and-a-half years of imprisonment, September 1945. Wilma is wearing her nurses' uniform—the women tried to preserve their uniforms, and kept the buttons shined for this very occasion.

Above: Some of the 'girls' at a ladies auxiliary function in Adelaide, 1946. The group includes Jean Ashton (second from left), Vivian Bullwinkel (second from right, sitting) and Wilma (third from right).

Left: Wilma and her husband Alan Young, 1947.

Food was now *boeboe* twice a day, produced by Wilma and the other rice cooks, because there was only a daily allowance of twenty-four Klim tins of rice for division between the three hundred British. 'Dry' cooked rice was available only for the evening meal together with tiny slivers of cooked fish or pork. If the Japanese had at least delivered international Red Cross parcels they could have prevented unnecessary suffering. Instead, evidence suggests that they intended to cause it.

During this same month there was, in fact, a delivery of Red Cross parcels. In a deliberate act of psychological torture, the desperate prisoners were forced to watch through the wire while the guards broke open the parcels and scattered the contents, which included badly needed medical supplies. The Japanese partly smoked cigarettes, then tossed them onto the ground and immediately lit up another. What little was left of the parcels was contaminated by the time it finally found its way into camp. 'We got out of that two squares of chocolate, twenty-five Chesterfield cigarettes, a tin of Spam,' recalled Wilma. These few items made up the total goods shared between the whole of the two nursing units. The greatest loss was the medical supplies and the cigarettes—a cigarette could be used as currency to buy goods on the black market.

Towards the middle of September anti-cholera injections were administered and the camp was accorded the services of a Japanese dentist. 'One woman went and had the wrong tooth pulled out. No anaesthetic. And you had to get up and bow to him afterwards!' Wilma smiled grimly. 'No good going to the dentist, it was just another form of torture. One of the girls used to get the rubber out of the rubber trees and push that into the holes in her teeth.'

At the beginning of October more mail was delivered, though again there was none for Wilma. Meanwhile her sister Phyllis had written once more, telling her of the marriage (on 9 September) of Lance Oram to his fiancée, Kayla, from before the war. Though Jean Ashton noted on 1 October that everyone had been packed and prepared to shift for a long time, matters would only progress at the rate dictated by the honourable Sons of the Emperor. Three days later, volunteers were called for to go ahead as a work party. 'We had to cook up our rice, then roll it into balls and deep fry it,' recalled Wilma in her professional capacity as a rice cook. 'They gave us a lot of red palm oil. While it [the rice] was still hot, we rolled it into balls and dipped it into the oil. You finish up with a little rice ball if you do that, and actually it's beautiful if you can do it that way. Then that was wrapped in a banana leaf and this was to be our ration. But we didn't all move together. One lot went over to this new beautiful camp by ship from Palembang to Mentok. Then the second lot went.' Wilma was with the first group.[85]

On 4 October Wilma's group of one hundred British and Dutch left the Palembang camp in lorries and was driven to the wharf. There they boarded a boat to cross the Musi River to reach what Jean Ashton referred to as the 'wharf railway station' where a train full of internees was already waiting. It was around 8pm and dark. The AANS had to carry and load the heavy rice sacks, a task which took them two hours or more. For food, Wilma and the other nurses each had only the single rice cake that Wilma had prepared.

'We were pushed and shoved towards a boat that lay at anchor,' recorded Veronica Clancy. 'As we moved away, another lorry carrying the rest of our party arrived. Walking unsteadily over a plank, we embarked on the ship. It was a small river boat—still clutching our supplies of food we mounted the steps leading to the higher deck where the people were already overcrowded but, with more cries from Nippon, they were herded still closer together. At last we all managed to get a spot to sit, but had hardly sat down when more cries from Nippon signified the other people were coming on. It just seemed impossible to get any more on board, but not to Nippon. With threats and yells we were pushed still closer together. At last all were on board. Two hundred women in that tiny ship. We couldn't even stretch our legs sitting on the dirty bare boards with our bones sticking into us. We could get no relief by leaning against anything as we were right in the centre with people all around us. There was no sanitation, so we used a bucket, which caused a lot of inconvenience. The person would have to stand up and this was not easy. If leaning on your companions you managed to get in a standing position, and then after using the bucket in the presence of the guards and the native crew, it was passed over the heads of the other passengers and emptied over the side into the river.'

'The smell was frightful by the time we got to Mentok,' recalled Wilma.

The edges of the ship near the rails were piled high with luggage, mainly belonging to the Japanese. There were bunches of bananas lying on top of the pile, but if the internees attempted to go near these they were threatened with rifles and bayonets and the usual strident shouting from their captors. The Japanese were also transporting a pet monkey which they fed with bananas throughout the trip, further emphasising their own sadistic nature. 'When we got there [to Bangka Island] the ship couldn't go into the wharf,' Wilma said. 'We had to get out into … like a barrel, it was [probably the hull of a Chinese junk]. Some said they'd stay on the ship and go in the morning. Some of us didn't want to stay on the ship. We knew that the people who had gone before us would have something for us to eat when we got there … Betty Jeffrey was with me in the barrel.' Their gnawing hunger out-weighed commonsense in this case, and what transpired next became one of the themes of recurring nightmares for Wilma and Betty Jeffrey throughout the remainder of their lives. 'We got on this terrible thing, and they shut the lid and there was no air and no light. The sea was rough and it was just rolling around. We were standing in what smelt like kerosene.'

'There was an escape ladder that came about halfway and then you had to jump the rest,' continued Betty. 'It was pitch black and then, in the middle of this, there was an air raid. They just kicked us out and let us bounce around the sea. We bumped into something after some time and found that we were back at the ship. We were all terribly ill and just couldn't stand … By the time we finally reached the wharf and they opened up the hatch we were just semi-conscious.'

Wilma admitted that this was one of the times when she truly believed she was about to die. 'A dreadful craft. I was sure, then, that I wouldn't survive. Anyway we did survive and we crawled out. It was the only time I ever hugged a Japanese, because he had to help us out of this onto the shore, and it was very rough and dangerous. The only way you could get from one place to the other was to put your arms around the Jap and let him lift you across. I didn't think I'd ever be pleased to see a Jap as I was when the lid came off and we saw a bit of fresh air and a chance to get ashore.'

'[They] treated us decently,' Betty said of the Japanese who met them at the end of the ordeal. 'They were soldiers manning the guns [on Mentok jetty] and they felt sorry for us. They lifted us out of the boat onto the pier and treated us very carefully. You could see they were really genuine. It was cold, dark and wet, and people just collapsed on the pier and couldn't stand up.' While even a lifetime could not heal the psychological wounds inflicted on Wilma and Betty, Jean Ashton, who waited to disembark from the original ship, fared a little better. 'We arrived at Mentok, Bangka Island, at 2pm,' she wrote. 'About 30 of us were taken ashore by barge, after which we sat on the wharf. We rescued our hand luggage, were bundled into lorries and arrived at the new camp, thankful to see cooked food already done by the men from the civilian camp, who had arrived earlier. We had a good feed and went to bed with full tummies.' The civilian men's camp was situated not far away, at the old Coolie Lines, and those prisoners had sent over as much food as they could spare for the women. 'Of course we all overate,' Wilma said.

Of the many terrible experiences that she endured during those years, Wilma identified that trip to Bangka Island as the worst. 'You see, when you get jammed into a craft like that, like a barrel with a lid on it, it's a bit of a hopeless situation and there's just no way out of it. It gives you a feeling that you don't want that to happen to you again. In 1997 an interviewer from the 'Today' program remarked: 'Wilma, it seems that, since the Japanese have apologised for their war atrocities, some people think that film makers and perhaps the media shouldn't dwell on those incidents. What do you think?'[86]

Wilma was suddenly adamant: 'Don't we want to know our history? Isn't that part of our past? Shouldn't it be portrayed? Shouldn't we know what happened during the war? Shouldn't it be obvious to everybody that the people that fought the war suffered? I think it's absurd to say we shouldn't talk about history.'

The outburst rocked the interviewer for a moment, then he asked tactfully: 'So you think that to remember and to study history is quite different to forgiving and forgetting?'

Wilma's reply was immediate: 'You have to do both. But you *must* study history, and that is part of history. The Japanese *did* these things, so why can't we talk about them? We *suffered* them. Why can't we tell people? Isn't it better for our young people to know what war entails instead of treating it like a fairy story?'

MENTOK

16 OCTOBER 1944

At first it seemed conditions might have improved, because the camp at Mentok was new and purpose-built. Unlike the previous Men's Camp, the new one was situated on a slight rise which should have afforded occasional breezes from the direction of the sea. Better still, it was built on a gravel surface so there should be no mud or clay bog when it rained. 'Everything was huge and brand-new and spotless,' Betty Jeffrey wrote. 'There was lots of room and bed space, each person had a new rush mat to sleep on.'[87]

'Here, instead of 24 inches we had about 36 inches each. Just wonderful, and it was clean,' Wilma confirmed. There were warning signs, though, for those who could read them, that this might not be an internee's Utopia. For instance, although nine large wells had been dug, and they were properly cemented, after the first twenty-four hours of use there was no water in any of them. Then there were the toilets. For the time being, these were also practically empty, but they were only large cement pits which had no outlet. Over them were thrown wooden slats, on which the user had to squat. Worse, they were situated next to the kitchens and on the other side of them stood the community bathrooms. This, plus the overcrowding which was to come, was a blueprint for disaster. A well-meaning girlfriend of one of the guards, a lass from Borneo, thought she was doing everyone a favour by persuading her protector to release a larger rice ration. This he did with the consequences that the ration ran out earlier. 'We had to make up for that and go on shorter rations than ever,' Wilma commented. Captain Seiki was again in charge, and would remain as their commanding officer until eventual liberation but, with less beatings, life was a bit easier. Also, Nesta James reported, 'We had a very much better guard in charge of [the] Japanese named Taratani. He did all he could for us.'

'But the food was very scarce,' Vivian said, 'particularly vegetables. During that time we lived on rice practically all the time, but occasionally we were given some fish. The position in respect to medical supplies was much worse … no medical supplies there at all. The food had been cut down considerably, to 150 grains of rice and very little vegetables. Quite often for weeks we were without any vegetables whatsoever.' With starvation worsening and everyone's weight dropping alarmingly, it seemed to Wilma that the time had come to break open the gift sent to her so long ago by Jock Mathieson. Lying with Vivian and Jean under the net, Wilma felt for the treasure hidden in her haversack. 'We were pretty hungry. And I said, "We'll eat this tin of bully beef, the three of us." So we did, and everybody could smell it. "Where's the bully beef?!" everyone yelled, but we scoffed it off, we didn't [share].' Though this needed no explanation, Wilma clarified that it was only a small tinful and, had she shared with everyone, nobody would have got more than a sliver. Because of the numbers involved, it was acceptable to share only with your own *kongsi*.

The toilet pits soon overflowed. 'They were lapping on your feet, and maggots and everything else …' said Wilma. 'Something had to be done about emptying those pits, so they said that everybody in the camp would have to put in 5 cents per week to pay somebody to empty them.' Until now Wilma had resisted taking paid work because of the extra drain on her energy, but her situation was now too drastic to avoid it any longer. 'I said to Viv, "We haven't got any money, so we can't pay out 5 cents a week, we'll have to go on the squad."'

At first Jean and Vivian insisted that they could never do such work. 'Viv then just went really mad. She said, "You're not going on that squad, it's a terrible job! You're working in the hospital, you've got camp chores to do!" She really went off the deep end about this.' After Vivian stopped protesting, Wilma made the point that if she ever got really sick, she was obliged to supply her own replacement. 'So that sent [Viv] madder than ever,' Wilma laughed, 'because, obviously, she would have to be the jolly replacement.' And Jean Ashton was no keener on the idea.

Wilma put her name down to work on the squad. 'We emptied the sewage into a kerosene tin with a stick between us on our shoulders. We'd do this about 5 o'clock in the morning. We'd fill [the kerosene tin] with half a coconut shell.'

The 5 cents per week came from everyone else in camp and it built up enough capital to pay this team of six or eight women their precious 5 cents per day. Following the war, Norah Chambers, who was in charge of the squad, told Wilma that she had been reluctant to put her on it because she was under the impression that Wilma had money— but this was not true and Wilma did not know how such a rumour got started. She did not volunteer for the fun of it. Not surprisingly, she soon fell ill. 'And Viv told me this in 1992: she said, "Jean and I lay there all night not getting any sleep at all. Just lying there. Not talking."' Wilma's two soul mates knew that one of them would have to act as her replacement, and they were not looking forward to it. It got to around 4am, when Wilma was supposed to get up to do the disgusting job, and Vivian got out of bed. Wilma said: 'She told me, "I got out of bed. You rolled over and went to sleep." So she did it for me.' Vivian also told Wilma that, when the time came that they needed a permanent replacement: 'I was quite angry when I wasn't appointed to that permanent vacancy!'

Eventually both Vivian and Jean served on the toilet squad and they remained on it, as well as fulfilling other duties, for the rest of their time in that camp. 'We'd do about ten trips, out into the jungle,' Wilma recalled, adding pensively, 'It was nice to get out of the camp for a bit. We used to just tip it on the ground, we didn't dig a pit or anything. We just managed to keep all these pits down just enough so that they were usable. It was a very necessary chore and we didn't mind.' By doing this work the trio was able to bring in money to buy those extras that, until now, had been out of their reach. (It was some of this money that Wilma placed in the purse that Vivian gave her for her birthday, and which she produced so many years later at Vivian's 'This Is Your Life'.)

'A couple of the nuns fell in one night,' Wilma revealed. 'Your mind boggles doesn't it—the nuns had on all those petticoats!' There were more incidents on the toilet squad, too. 'Viv was fairly tall and Iole [who was also on the squad] was a bit short ... the bucket slipped off Iole's shoulder and broke her collarbone. Norah Chambers and Audrey Owen[88] had their bucket swinging along, going out of the camp with their load, and the handle of the bucket broke in front of the guard-house and tipped it all out. They spent the rest of the day cleaning up the mess. The Japs were not amused.' These anecdotes, often repeated in postwar days, are typical of the black humour of the camps. A laugh helped the prisoners to get through their appalling days and there was always plenty of laughter and jokes on the toilet squad. Such an attitude helped to prevent its members from going insane.

The camp committee agreed that the toilet squad workers must be allowed a small amount of hot water so that they could have a 'proper' wash. Every day on Bangka Island, as soon as they finished on the squad, Wilma and her friends washed as thoroughly as they could then went straight to work at the hospital.

At home in Murtoa, Lance was negotiating a war service loan to enable him to buy the family house, Troon, which Alf was keen to sell. The house was now too big for him and Jane. Everyone decided that Lance and Kayla should share it with Phyllis and her husband Wally. There was plenty of room and Kayla was particularly fond of Phyllis. 'All well,' wrote Phyllis to Wilma on 12 October 1944, 'Pray you are the same.' On 23 October the final batch of female prisoners came over from Sumatra, among them the chronically sick and the nuns.

'The ones that were already there cooked rice [for the new arrivals],' Wilma said, 'but for some unknown reason they'd misbehaved. According to Captain Seiki, the prisoners had done something to annoy him en route and he would allow them to eat nothing when they arrived. We had this rice cooked so Vivian and myself stood guard over it all night to make sure it was still there in the morning for the people to have it. With 700 hungry women, you couldn't take the risk of leaving that rice unattended. We didn't even touch one grain of it, hungry as we were.' There was soon another, cleaner opportunity to earn money, this time from the Japanese, by sewing bags for the tin mines. In keeping with her policy of filling every moment of her day, Wilma made time to sew bags. 'We had to sew our name into them so that, if anything was wrong, they knew who to come back to, to punish. They were going to pay us for doing this job, so we did it and waited for payment, but it never appeared … but then they brought in some extra food, some durians and some duck eggs. And the ones who had done the sewing had the privilege of buying them.' Wilma and her colleagues took their share, then resold most of it. 'The durians, they're beautiful fruit but there's flesh around a seed,' Wilma explained. 'We sold all the flesh, which is what you usually eat, then we cooked the seeds and ate those. They were a bit like a potato really, but there were duck eggs and various other things came in. We had to sell those.' With the fetid smell of the camp, it is not surprising that Wilma made no comment about the famous odour of the durian. The internees probably did not even notice it.

In November, Jean Ashton's diary recorded: 'Fourteen British and Australian Sisters on the hospital staff as well as the Charitas Sisters, also the Tachong Karong Sisters. Over 90–100 patients in the hospital wards—dysentery, beriberi. Death rate increasing. Everyone losing weight, legs swelling, malaria and dengue fever. No medical supplies. Many of our AANS down with malaria every week or two.' At the end of this diary, Jean listed the names of the nurses who volunteered for hospital duty. It was voluntary work, there were no perks or advantages to being one of the nurses. They were AANS sisters Ashton, Oram, Bullwinkel, Harper, Jeffrey, Hughes, Muir, Smith, Blanch and Blake, plus British sisters McKenzie, McAllister, McCallum and Cooper.

'There were four doctors,' Vivian reported. 'Dr Goldberg, she seemed to have charge of the hospital and all supplies. She seemed to do anything that would bring her anything from the Japs. There was Dr McDowell [Scottish], Dr Thompson [Scottish] and Dr Smith [English].'

In addition to the illnesses already mentioned, another virulent disease appeared. This was called by the nurses 'Bangka fever' but was possibly cerebral malaria. Some nurses described it as a combination of meningitis and malaria, while others believed that the disease was a form of typhus. Under the circumstances a positive diagnosis was impossible, but the condition was lethal. 'We had about five different orders of nuns,' said Wilma, 'and in one order the whole five or six of them died quite suddenly.'

The normal strain of malaria was forever present, but it could abruptly develop into this fever. 'We had a mixture of Bangka Island fever and malaria and, at that time, 75 per cent of the people in the camp were lying down and simply could not move,' recalled Nesta James. 'There were about 700 in the camp at the peak.'

At the point of death there was a peculiar cry from the patient. It became known among the nurses as the 'Song of Death'. 'It's that cry that they make,' said Wilma, 'and they go pretty quickly after that.'

Wilma had more than one close brush with death. 'A lot of people were dying of it,' she said. 'I went just about unconscious—and Jean Ashton ran and got Dr Goldberg. She was the only one with quinine. She came over and gave me an injection of quinine, which nobody ever got. Normally you had to pay [her] for it but, anyway, she gave it to me, probably because I was on the hospital staff.' Here Wilma underestimated the appreciation of her fellow prisoners for her constant service. Since the beginning of internment she had always been one of the first to volunteer to nurse. Now even the unpredictable Dr Goldberg proved willing to help. 'That got me over the very worst of it, but I was still pretty sick.'

By now Dr McDowell had recovered from her breakdown. She knew Wilma well, because of her convalescence on Wilma's rice cooking squad at the Men's Camp. Now she, too, came to the rescue. 'She said to me, "Wilma, what's the matter?" I said, "I've got malaria." She said, "Well, don't say anything to anybody ..." She put her hand in her pocket and gave me some atebrin and I thought that was marvellous. Then Sister Rhynelda, who was in charge of the hospital, she came to me and said, "Sister Vilma, vot is the matter?" And I said, "It's this malaria, I just can't get over it." And she said, "Vell, don't say anyseeng …" and she lifted up her skirts and put her hand in her pocket and gave me some plasmaquin. So if there's a miracle, that was it! I never said a word to anybody, because you couldn't spread it around that the medicine was there. I never asked where they got it from.'

The combination of quinine, atebrin and plasmaquin saved Wilma, and for the rest of her life she never suffered another attack of malaria. The willingness of these three diverse people to help her speaks for itself about the high regard in which she was held.

Following her recovery, Wilma resumed night duty. 'For the Dutch nuns, it was not the thing to eat with people who were not nuns,' she said. 'If two of them were on, I'd have to wait and look after the hospital then have my [rations] by myself. But if I was on with Sister Wilhelmina, just the two of us, we would always eat together. But Sister Beninga and Sister Brighetta, they used to work there [and not eat with me].'

The AANS on duty shared living space with the nuns. 'We lived on one bed space and the nuns … were in the same hut as us. Opposite us. We were in pretty close contact with them,' recalled Wilma. Protocols continued to be observed, even under the cramped conditions. Sister Beninga, Sister Brighetta and Sister Rhynelda were in charge and the AANS sisters worked under their supervision. 'We did our best,' said Wilma, 'but we had a lot of deaths. [The patients] were dying all the time.' Some of the diseases would not normally be killers, but everyone's immune system was so depleted that the internees fell easy prey to almost anything that attacked their bodies. 'Apart from malaria, I had beriberi, dysentery, lice, worms,' said Wilma, 'so I don't know why I came through. You just manage to survive.' Even worm infestation was enough to kill many. 'People got so weak, you'd give them the worm medicine and they couldn't take it. The medicine would kill them anyhow—either that or the worms. We had a few died of cancer. A lot of deaths.'

Everyone started to carry their own coffin nails, mostly made out of untwisted and sharpened barbed wire. 'You were supposed to have six nails ready, in case you needed your coffin,' said Wilma.

'We buried our own dead,' said Veronica Clancy. 'The coffins … were stored in the back portion of the church with the rations. Volunteers were called to dig the graves. At first they used to go out every day and dig a number required but later they would dig about a dozen at once. The only instruments they had were *chungkals*, shovelling the dirt out with their hands. The funerals were usually in the afternoon. Four whistles from the guardhouse would denote that Nippon was ready. The pall bearers and the mourners for each deceased would gather at the hospital, carrying the coffin on three poles, three each side and one person supporting the foot and the head, they would slowly walk between Hut One and the Convalescent Ward. The coffins were covered with wreaths made of shrubs, and leaves or flowers if any were available. Many of the patients in the Convalescent Ward[89] would stand along the verandah while the cortège passed. Often the graves were not big enough and the coffins had to be taken out and the holes enlarged. Attending these funerals was a very grim experience, you stood while the graves were being enlarged, gazed at all the open graves, many half filled with water, and wondered who would fill them.'

Burials were even more stressful for those who were preparing the remains of their friends because, sometimes, the box was too small to fit the body. It meant having to force the corpse to fit. This made it necessary to mutilate the remains. Wilma was often a member of the burial detail but would never directly confirm this. When asked, she replied with a soft and enigmatic 'mmm'. The exact words of Audrey Owen in her interview for *Song of Survival* were: 'And we used to find it very hurtful when it was a friend whose body we had to make to fit the box.'

Back home, the Oram family at last received the brief card written by Wilma on 30 August 1944. This took less time to reach its destination than did the first that Wilma had written. With the allies relentlessly advancing, the Japanese perhaps found it prudent to be more flexible. Jane replied that they were happy to read that she was working and well. 'Praying that you are still in good health and spirits. Every one of us are well. Love, Mother.' But, like Wilma, who could only write 'working and well' to her family, Jane's note hid the ongoing psychological and physical struggle that Lance had in getting the better of his disability. 'He'd lost a lot of confidence,' his wife revealed, 'because he used to drive in the army, but he wouldn't drive the car when he first came home.'

'Christmas diet low this year,' wrote Jean Ashton. 'Nursing in hospital very hard. Patients lying up on *bali bali* with mattresses almost touching. Have to climb up on *bali bali* to attend to them. Sanitary conditions in camp simply appalling. 15 deaths a month. Open septic pits almost full.'

New Year was no better. One of the civilian internees, a Dutch woman called Antoinette Colijn, remembered: 'It was New Year's Eve and we had this terrible Bangka fever—shivering, cold, miserable. It was near twelve o'clock and, at the other end of my barracks, Sister Catherinia and other Sisters were singing the end of the year and the coming New Year. I was lying there, feeling horrible, and I thought "Oh, I wish I could sleep now, forever."'

'Ray' Raymont of the 2/4th CCS had been ill on and off for months. This followed punishment inflicted by the Japanese for some trivial offence, after which she was stood in the sun for several hours without a hat or water. At the end of this torment, the South Australian nurse collapsed with a heart attack. Since that day in the Men's Camp, she had been in and out of hospital, gently tended by the AANS.

On 7 February 1945, Dr Goldberg went to see her in the hospital and, in Wilma's presence, declared that there was nothing much wrong with Ray and that no medication was required. Wilma climbed up onto the *bali bali* to check on her patient's condition. For her and other nurses who were victims of beriberi, real effort was involved in getting onto this rough wooden platform where all the patients lay side by side in one long row. 'Beriberi is a terrible disease,' said Wilma. 'We had people in camp who looked like monsters. The tummies were swollen, and the legs got swollen with fluid. You had to lift your leg [with your hands]. You couldn't get up a small step, you had to lift it up.'

Wilma spoke to Ray, who was able to reply, although she was intermittently hallucinating. 'She had this terrible meningeal cry that people get but we thought it must be cerebral malaria.' It was 4pm when Wilma went off duty, expecting to be attending to her fellow nurse again the next day. During the night Ray's condition swiftly deteriorated and, by 6am, the AANS had lost the first of its members. Wilma never forgave Goldberg for not administering medication to Ray. She knew that relief was available and she blamed Goldberg for Raymont's death.

Somehow the nurses had never believed that they would lose one of their members. The tragedy brought them together and they decided to break out their nursing uniforms, or those parts that survived. These were put on and the nurses carried the coffin outside the wire to perform a military burial. The uniforms were tattered and stained, some were missing belts or buttons and those whose feet were not bare wore a pitiful assortment of footwear. It must have been a profoundly moving sight.

On 20 February, only twelve days later, Sister 'Rene' Singleton[90] died of beriberi. Twenty-one days later, on 13 March, one of the Queensland members of the 13th AGH, Sister Blanche Hempsted, died. On 4 April another member of the 2/4th CCS died: Sister Shirley Gardham, from Tasmania. Altogether, during the short time that the internees were on Bangka Island, there were more than one hundred deaths among the women and children. Sister Catherinia described it in her broken English: 'The mothers who died were the ones who took their own portion and gave it to their children. If she gave more to the children and ate herself less, she couldn't go on very long, and then she died. Then they came to us, and they were all clever little children. But they were all round little bellies, full of water.'[91]

Wilma told her Warrnambool friends in 1960: 'As the other girls died, we ourselves were getting a bit too weak, and we were sick, and we were not able to give them all the same military honours that we had given to our first girl that died.' She admitted, 'I was still not too good. Viv was looking after me and so was Jean. Then they told us we had to move camp again.'

This decision by the Japanese to shift the camp from Bangka Island is puzzling until it is looked at in the context of the progress of the war. It was the beginning of April 1945. For months, a concentrated assault by the allies had seen the gradual reoccupation of most of the Pacific Islands. On 1 April the Americans launched their offensive operation to capture the Japanese island of Okinawa. The plan was to establish a base from which the allies could directly attack the main Japanese islands. Between then and the end of April the Japanese would lose more than 100,000 men. A huge fleet from the British navy linked with the Americans in launching the decisive naval onslaught. The British fleet consisted of two hundred ships under the supreme command of Admiral Sir Bruce Fraser. With this coming together of the two major allies, the final phase of the war against Japan began.

None of this was known by the female internees. It might have given many the strength to survive if they had an inkling of what was going on outside, but they lived in an information vacuum. 'Camp life is just an existence now. No more concerts or charades or sing-songs,' wrote Betty Jeffrey.[92] The vocal orchestra had ceased to exist. Its founder, the missionary Margaret Dryburgh, was among the desperately ill.

Thanks to the loving care of Vivian Bullwinkel and Jean Ashton, Wilma was fighting her illnesses, but more members of the AANS were sick. 'Sister Sylvia Muir and Gladys Hughes have to give up nursing in hospital, both sick with recurring fever ?malaria,' wrote Jean Ashton.

Everyone was so debilitated that the prospect of another move was a summons to death. 'We didn't want to take the very sick ones with us,' Betty Jeffrey wrote. 'Our doctors begged the Japs to leave the ones who were going to die behind. But the Japs said no. There were five women who were unconscious, and they were definitely going to die.'

This move to Sumatra was not planned for the health of the internees. Both female and male civilian prisoners were being transported simultaneously from Bangka Island although the women did

not know that until much later. It is far more likely that this current
move, to a remote area of southern Sumatra, was part of an attempt to
conceal war crimes. Given the progress of the war and the Japanese
directive of 1 August 1944 it was also the prelude to a possible massacre.

BELALAU

Moving the internees from Bangka Island to yet another camp was again achieved in three separate trips, each as horrific as the last.

A few days after being told of the impending move, the AANS women were issued with about 5lbs (2.5kg) of uncooked rice plus their monthly ration of oil, sugar, tea and coffee. This they decided that they should carry on the journey, for safety. It would be a heavy load for them to shift, together with the rest of their pathetic belongings. Wilma was to move in the first group, along with Veronica Clancy and others. Their captors assured them that they would be able to spread their mattresses and sleep on the boat. Furthermore, the Japanese claimed, food and drink were to be provided after Palembang and for that reason the prisoners were to carry no more than twenty-four hours' supply. The rice was made into the usual little deep-fried cakes. In this form it was less likely to turn sour. Each woman took charge of her own small bottle of boiled water and, by 8am on the morning of 8 April, the first contingent was waiting at the end of the dormitory. Travelling with them would be six stretcher cases. The nurses were expected to carry these. 'At midday the motor transports arrived,' Veronica Clancy wrote, 'and we scrambled into them and, with our cries of goodbye from the people, we formed a convoy and departed.'

The convoy was soon rattling and bumping towards Mentok jetty. It stopped outside the Customs House where Wilma was first taken prisoner, and everyone started to unload the trucks while the Japanese looked on. Everything and everyone had to be marched the length of the long pier where, at its end, a tender waited to transport them to the ferry that was anchored offshore. In addition to lugging stretcher cases, and there were many of these by the time the entire group assembled, the members of the AANS had to carry the hospital equipment and supplies. 'We did the whole move,' Nesta James reported. 'Two sisters and I loaded all the sick. Most of them were sick. We loaded them onto a small tender on the pier and then on to the boat. They told us that we would be travelling under more comfortable conditions than the conditions under which we came over.'

Although Sister James did not travel with Wilma's contingent, conditions for each of the three groups were much the same, and their experiences almost identical. Far from being more comfortable, the vessel that would transport them turned out to be the same in which they had made the horrific voyage to Bangka.

Everyone formed a line in the blazing sun at the end of the jetty and made the traditional bow to their overlords. Now they were to stand while the Japanese performed their interminable *tenko*. In the first contingent, and in the midst of *tenko*, one of the stretcher patients died on Mentok jetty. A party of nurses and nuns from the hospital trudged back along its whole length, carrying the dead body on one of the makeshift stretchers so that it could be buried.

Veronica, meanwhile, was aboard the tender. 'We sat around and waited,' she wrote. 'Along the pier could be seen other members of the party straggling along … It was stifling hot. Looking back we could see the nuns and our sisters carrying the sick down the steps in their arms, it was impossible to use the stretchers because the stairway was too steep and the boat [the tender] too small.'

'So many sick,' Blanchie recalled. 'And the pier where we had to board the little boat, it was so long, and we had to carry these sick people. *We* had to carry them—the Japs never helped us at all.'

'I wasn't properly better,' said Wilma. 'And I got on this ship and went back to Palembang.' Everyone was crammed aboard the ferry and another terrible journey began. 'The ship was horribly overcrowded and the toilet was over the edge as usual,' Wilma said.

'There were stretcher cases on the deck without shelter and altogether there were about 400 people sick aboard,' recalled Vivian. 'There was no shelter, nor room, nor sanitary arrangements … no cover, hardly room to sit down, and no room to lie down.' There were seventeen stretcher cases aboard apart from the walking sick.

Wilma saw a small brazier standing amid the piled cargo. She climbed across the stretchers and sat on it, shuddering at the thought that she would have to spend the next day or so perched that way—but it was better than sitting on the filthy deck. 'It rained,' Wilma recalled. 'Somebody put down a basket of limes, so we pinched those as fast as we could.'

On the deck in the open air, Wilma was luckier than those who were herded below. 'Aboard the coaster those who could walk were forced down through a small hatch into a hold lined with sacks of verminous rice. It was black, airless, stinking and as hot as a furnace.'[93] After her last such experience there was no way, walking or not, that anyone was going to force Wilma to go down there.

Betty Jeffrey came with the second group, four days later, but conditions were no different. At first she was put into the hold but she and Pat Blake[94] used the excuse that they should go up on deck because both were suffering from dysentery and they did not want to risk passing it on to others.

With this second contingent were Iole Harper and Nesta James. Nesta James reported: 'During the whole of that trip there was no protection. The patients and ourselves [who] were on the deck—it got so hot we could hardly touch them—they were burning. The remainder of the sick and other people we carried were put down in a hold and remained there the whole time. There was no sanitation whatsoever on this boat and quite 75 per cent of the people suffered from dysentery and diarrhoea.' The nuns had brought along a couple of bed pans, and Iole Harper took her life in her hands by hanging from the side of the ship, with Pat Blake holding her hand, while she washed the bed pans in the sea.

Wilma had not been sitting on her brazier for long when she witnessed the death of a nearby stretcher patient. Because of the condition of the dead woman's mattress, the nuns lifted both the body and the mattress and dropped it overboard. Wilma immediately leapt forward to grab an inflated air cushion that had been underneath. She put this on top of the brazier and spent the rest of the trip seated on it. These days it was a case of first come, first served. The rule was the same for everybody.

To Wilma's former easygoing personality, as revealed in the relationship that existed between her and Mona Wilton, unwelcome life experiences had added new layers. Her desire to help others remained, as did her soft and caring personality, but the foundations upon which her character was built had toughened. Beneath the outward softness lay a firm resolve. 'You realise that you're in a situation where it's essential that you get on with each other. And you do. You don't try and impose your personality onto other people. You make absolutely certain that you get on with people. It's a conscious decision. You respect everybody's right to do their own particular thing.' To her conventional Anglican upbringing under Jane Oram's benevolent but strict supervision, Wilma added Alf Oram's more practical philosophy of 'God helps those who help themselves'. The country lass had grown up.

Wilma's memories of the journey from Bangka Island became haunted by the sight of the body of the woman who floated on her mattress, caught in the wake of the ferry, which refused to let her sink into her watery grave. As a result, bodies of the additional people who died were kept aboard, with the intention of burying ashore. 'We lost about twelve women through death on that ship,' said Vivian. 'Cause of death: exposure to the sun. They were all sick women, and being exposed on the deck and without medical supplies or water, and the tropical sun was just too much for them. They died from sunstroke, because of their emaciated condition. We buried one at sea and the others were buried when we got back to Palembang.'

'Yes,' Wilma smiled tensely, 'It wasn't much of a boat journey, that one.'

On arrival at Palembang, the boat had to stand to in the Musi River to await the tide. Unloading then took as long as the loading. Prisoners still had no food or water other than what they had carried aboard. As each group disembarked, it was lined up for *tenko,* first bowing to the guards. While this was going on, the nurses and nuns carried the stretcher cases into some shade near the railway station. When the Japanese could not reconcile their numbers, they ordered the stretcher cases to be returned to the jetty while the count was repeated. Then someone tactfully pointed out that the reason the figures did not tally was because there had been so many deaths. The bodies had been removed, presumably for burial, although nobody knew for certain what happened to them Eventually the prisoners were marched to the railway station, where those who were not ill were crammed into coal-encrusted carriages, while the sick were packed into goods wagons, which were enclosed apart from a small slit high up in the sides. Wilma travelled with the sick, to help look after them.

On the railway station, another stretcher case died. She was Mrs Anderson who had taught Wilma to play contract bridge. 'A very charming lady, very understanding,' said Wilma. 'She said she would survive two years. And that was about all she did manage.' The women did not perform this burial. The Japanese disposed of the body.

Of the second group to come over, Nesta James reported: 'We were stationary in the Musi River when darkness came. We stayed there all that night without any protection and were bitten severely by mosquitoes. We had no warm clothes and it became very cold in the early hours. We started off again next morning … one patient died before we arrived at Palembang. Just as we arrived at Palembang another patient died. We were completely exhausted by this time but had to remove all the patients from the ship and put them onto a train. Two other people died in the trucks. We stayed on that train all that night. [The corpses] were taken off the train that night … I do not know where they were buried. Presumably it was somewhere in Palembang.'

Wilma's train trip took all day, so this meant that the first group had so far travelled for two full days since it left the Bangka Island camp. On the train seven more women died. Their bodies were placed together and Wilma sat and watched over them, trying to keep off flies. She remained on duty over the bodies for several hours in the heat.

Conditions inside the wagon were unimaginable. Faecal waste had to be ejected through a small sliding hatch high in the walls of the wagons. 'One girl went mad,' recalled Betty Jeffrey.

'We had to keep the shutters closed,' said Wilma. 'We were not allowed to peer out and see what the country was like we were going through.' At some stage during the second group's journey the dead bodies were slung under the train.

The journey from Mentok to the railway station at Loebok Linggau, a remote town in central southern Sumatra, took three days. After everyone was taken off, they again lined up for *tenko* before being loaded at dawn onto open trucks for a breakneck drive of several kilometres, over rough jungle tracks, to an even more remote location. Again, because of deaths, the numbers did not agree with the Japanese tally and *tenko* was repeated again and again. The prisoners had still received no food or water.

On 12 April 1945, the internees arrived at what was formerly the largest rubber plantation in southern Sumatra, a place called Belalau. The property had been trashed when its owners left and it was overgrown and neglected.

They were taken to the edge of a gully. Here the scenery was picturesque. A steep track wound down one side, from a cluster of newly built bamboo huts, to where a small stream flowed. On the banks of this grew ferns and other vegetation. Up the gentler slope, which formed the other side of the gully, grew rubber trees. Among these, lush jungle vegetation encroached. At the bottom, several long bamboo huts formed part of what had been the former 'coolie' quarters. These would serve as the communal kitchen, as the hospital and as its nursing quarters.

Crossing the stream was a small bridge that linked the two separate sectors, the upper and the lower camp. Slightly down from the lower camp, toilets extended across the stream. The prisoners could squat over these so that the excreta were carried away. Upstream from the toilets a section of the stream could be used for washing. This seemed a much better arrangement than conditions that they had recently endured. What they did not know was that, further upstream, stood the civilian men's camp and, still further upstream of that, the Japanese guards were encamped. Effluent from both of these areas flowed down the creek through the women's camp.

On 12 April, the second contingent left for the trip to Loebok Linggau via Palembang and again took three days to arrive. 'Although we had scarcely nothing to eat, apart from a little rice on the journey, and in spite of the fact that food was waiting, Captain Seiki refused to allow us any food that night, and we did not get any until next morning,' reported Nesta James. Seiki remained true to form and for no obvious reason.

The third and last contingent left Mentok on 15 April.

A routine was established without delay. Wilma moved into the hospital area with Iole Harper, Betty Jeffrey, Val Smith, 'Blanchie' Blanch, Flo Trotter, Nesta James, Chris Oxley,[95] Vivian Bullwinkel and Jean Ashton. These nurses were in what would become known as Hut 13. As always, Vivian and Jean shared the mosquito net with Wilma. Wilma was still suffering from beriberi and none of the others was well. Betty Jeffrey recalled: 'Most people were living on the upper part, and you slid down the cliff and across the little bridge [Wilma described it more bluntly as a plank] to where we had the hospital and the kitchen. And, because the hospital was there, we were living alongside and the Dutch nursing nuns were alongside us.'

In the unseen world outside, momentous events were occurring. On 7 May 1945 the Germans surrendered. Ces Donelly recalled that the prisoners, including Alan Young and himself, discussed trying to reach the American forces at Pilsen, but to achieve this would involve a 500-mile journey. Instead, on 9 May, the group of former prisoners met the Russians at Gahlene on the Czech border and promptly found themselves at the centre of a battle between the Russians and three German SS battalions that refused to surrender. These German forces were also attempting to reach the Americans at Pilsen, but with a different aim. They craved a final battle.

Ces and Alan reached Prague at the time of the Russian victory and its accompanying celebrations. It seems quite possible, though it can not be confirmed, that it was somewhere on these travels that Alan saw the sight later described by his son David. 'One of the events that affected Dad was seeing young German boys, only thirteen or into their early twenties, strung up on lamp posts.' Such atrocities are recorded as having been committed, at the time, by the victors against the Germans.

Five days later, Alan's group reached the Americans, who took them to Regensburg on 14 May. They were then air lifted to Rheims and from there to England, where Alan was hospitalised. He was badly undernourished. After his release from hospital he stayed for a time with his English cousins Wilfrid and Marion Masheter.

Conditions at Belalau were bearable until the rains came, after which Nesta James reported: 'The accommodation was even worse than the camp at Palembang [the Men's Camp] as regards the *atap* huts, because they all leaked. Frequently one could not get any sleep because there was nowhere to go to get out of the wet. We were ankle deep in mud.'

'There was more crowding than the previous camps, frightfully muddy and filthy,' said Vivian. Blanchie remembered: 'We had lice and parasites, and we had to have our hair cut. We'd line up for *tenko* every day. When we were waiting for the Japs, the one next to you would inspect your head, but you couldn't pick anything out. We had nothing to put on them [the lice], so we would have our hair cut right off short. Flo [Trotter] and Jeff were the hair cutters.'

Nesta James took charge of distributing rations. 'We were told we were being taken to this camp from Mentok because it was situated in the Dempo Mountains, where vegetables grow profusely,' she reported, then added, 'We did not see the profuse vegetables ... The food did not improve. We had some meat, but not much.' Fruit grew in what had formerly been the plantation's gardens, but Captain Seiki's guards forbade the women to eat it. 'There was quite a lot of face slapping in that camp,' said Sister James, 'The whole camp would be punished for individual alleged offences. For instance, rations would be taken away from us.' No clothing was supplied, and no medical supplies until after peace was declared.

Some of the nurses who were not working in the hospital moved to other huts. One hut was known as the 'melting pot' because so many different races shared it. 'Some degree of discord in the daylight hours was evidently a cultural necessity, understood by all, but at the root there was tremendous loyalty and generosity.'[96] In this hut they had no qualms about eating monkey, snake, skunk, rat. One of the British women fried grasshoppers in palm oil. She declared that they tasted like shrimp. There is no record of any of the Australian nurses eating rats, though they ate most of the other unique meats on offer. Some of these supplies were shot by the guards and then presented as the usual gourmet fare, flung onto the ground and hacked apart with a sword. 'We have had wild boar, venison, monkey, bear, yak. The guards shot them nearby in forests. Skunk has been caught by some and eaten. Rats have been eaten by one or two families,' reported Jean Ashton.

The nurses were nothing if not enterprising. Blanchie commented: 'We had all sorts of bugs, rats and things [in Hut 13]. One day they gave us corn for our ration. I had some corn in a little basket tied up on the rafter for my next day's meal. I looked up, when I woke, and here's a rat in it. So I grabbed him and went off to sell him to the Eurasians. I said, "He's lovely and fat and a good healthy rat!" and he popped out of the bag and I lost my $2.50—they were going to pay me $2.50 for a rat.'

Vivian Bullwinkel attested that the Belalau camp had very poor vegetation. 'Actually on the shore there was a banana plantation, and ferns and grass which the natives told us we could eat. We used to cook them.'

Blanchie related another alarming food story: 'In this little creek were some shellfish like periwinkles. Val [Smith] and I said we'd go and get some and boil them up. And we ate a few. But then along comes the doctor [Goldberg] and she had seen us getting these things, and said if we got sick after eating them, she would not treat us. We didn't do it again. You see, the toilets were over this creek above us, and you can imagine what was in there. But we were so hungry we'd eat anything.'

Captain Seiki let his guards do whatever they liked to the women. 'Ishimara, the rations officer, was very objectionable ...' Nesta James reported, and Vivian Bullwinkel confirmed this in her 1946 testimony: 'Shigemura [sic][97] had most to do with us. He was quite objectionable. He hit people with a stick he carried around with him. I saw him beat a woman one day and there was a lot of face slapping.'

The hospital was full to overflowing. During May 1945 there were fifty-four patients in the hospital itself and many more being treated in their own huts by the still functioning and vital district nursing service. 'Some [patients] on cement slabs in one hut and others on *bali bali* bench. Dirt floor,' Jean wrote.

Malaria was as big a problem as ever and there was nothing with which to fight it. 'We were given some quinine bark which we discovered was much worse than having fever because it gave us violent diarrhoea in addition to having malaria,' recalled Nesta James.

As for the toilet facilities in the hospital, Wilma remembered: 'We had tins for [the patients] to use because they couldn't get to the river. We had an old fashioned wash tub at the door which we would empty it all into. When it was full, two of us carted the tub down to the river and emptied it. The jolly thing used to leak so there was sewage all over the place. But we'd walk down to this river with it of a night, then we'd come face to face with the wild pigs or any other thing that happened to be in the jungle. I don't know which used to get more frightened, the pigs or us.'

Wilma found herself rostered on night duty with Sister Wilhelmina. 'We'd go along to the hospital arm in arm, singing,' she said. 'The nuns had the hut next to us. They were running the hospital, we were just helping them. Sister Wilhelmina would want to heat up the rice at night. She had a brazier there. And of course it was supposed to be a blackout. She'd light this brazier, put the rice on it, stir it up, and the guard would be going mad. And there'd be this terrific conversation between Sister Wilhelmina and the guard, shouting at each other in fluent Malay which I couldn't really understand. He was trying to put the brazier out while she was trying to heat the rice. He was going on about the blackout. It didn't take long to heat up a little bit of rice, so as soon as the rice was heated she'd put the brazier out. But every night it happened.'

And being firm friends with a Charitas Sister was no protection against theft, especially as that Sister was also starving. 'If anybody called out while we were trying to eat our rice, and wanted anything, Sister Wilhelmina used to tell me to go. I did, and I'd come back and there wouldn't be a grain of rice left. She'd have scoffed the lot,' said Wilma, then added, 'She and I got on very well together.'

Wilma recalled the time when Mavis Hannah was a patient. 'Mavis had trouble with her heart and every now and then she'd call out, "Wilma, Wilma! My heart's stopped!" You'd dash up—there was nothing much you could do about it—and feel her pulse, and sure enough she'd have very little pulse. I used to dash off through the jungle—the doctors lived in a little hut up through the jungle—and get Dr Goldberg. Of course, in the jungle at night you're not too sure what you're going to tread on. A lot of snakes about. By the time you got back to Mavis her heart would've reasserted itself and she'd be all right again. So you never knew whether to run for the doctor or just to wait. Anyhow Mavis survived all of that.' Wilma's use of the verbs 'dash' and 'run' should be tempered by the knowledge that she had beriberi.

The sight of Wilma and Sister Wilhelmina arriving arm in arm and singing must have been a morale booster for those in the hospital huts, even given Wilma's tone deafness. The smaller of the two huts housed the worst cases and it was not long before Vivian Bullwinkel was included with these, having herself only recently been nursing the desperately ill Wilma, who was still recovering. 'Somebody had some aquaflavine and we gave her that,' said Wilma. 'We did everything we possibly could to get her right … Nobody knew what to do or what to give her. Anyway this Goldberg, she said to me, "If you can get hold of some Epsom Salts we'll give her chenopodium." That's for worms, but you've got to follow it with Epsom salts. I didn't know where I was going to get Epsom salts. The only money I had was what I had earned from emptying toilets [on Bangka Island] and that wasn't very much. Anyway, I found that Chris Oxley had some Epsom salts.' Wilma asked if she could have some of Chris's Epsom salts for Vivian. 'She very kindly let me have them, and we gave Viv the worm treatment, and from then on she started to improve. I followed it with the Epsom salts, and then I watched and watched for worms, but I never found any.'

Thanks to Wilma, Vivian eventually recovered but she was ill for many weeks and came close to death. 'She wasn't eating,' Wilma continued. 'I'd take things over to her to try and get her to eat. And she'd say to me, "Wilma, you can come and see me, but don't bring me anything to eat." Anyhow, her hair fell out and she was quite a mess.'

When either Vivian or Wilma was sick, if one could not eat it was agreed that the other could have the double ration. Then, after the sick one recovered, the other reduced her own rations and increased the other's until the exact balance of food supply was struck. Every single grain of rice was counted. When vegetables or meat was part of the ration, a record was made of what was owed to the other. In this way they kept each other alive. 'I used to turn the rice into soup, with whatever weeds or vegetables we could come across. I used to take this up to her … you had to force her to eat.'

Vivian's illness spanned a period during which the nurses mourned the death of more of their colleagues. Gladys Hughes died on 31 May 1945. This was the nursing sister who, in Irenelaan, had visited the native woman Siti with Wilma and had helped to cure the elderly mother-in-law's tropical ulcer. Gladys had been living in the upper camp 'in one of the other huts with the Indonesians, and she eventually came down to the hospital with this very bad dysentery,' said Wilma, adding simply: 'She died.' During this period Veronica Clancy again fell ill. 'Veronica recovered but she used to get out of bed every night. We had little tins with red palm oil in them with a bit of a wick that we'd use for light. Veronica would hop out of bed in the middle of the night when nobody was about and eat the red palm oil.'

There was a water supply, albeit contaminated, but the women made full and grateful use of it. They collected drinking water from a well beside the river, but it had to be boiled. This was not easy because firewood was as troublesome as ever to collect.

Labour in the Belalau camp included 'chopping down trees and carrying wood into the camp, grave digging, and the women cut down the trees. Big trees. They worked very short hours because they simply could not do it. After two hours work they just had to lie down. They could not stand up,' recalled Vivian.

'We were bathing in that river,' Wilma said. 'We'd get in there to have a wash and you'd scoop up a handful of water and you'd see all this faeces floating past.' The internees were ordered not to go naked in the river to wash, 'Because we were upsetting the morals of the native guards. They could see us. Of course the Indonesians bath themselves with their sarong on, and wash themselves through it.' Again this clash of cultures occurred.

May 1945 saw Wilma receive the first batch of the correspondence so regularly despatched by her family. In 1960 she told her former nursing colleagues in Warrnambool: 'They [the letters] didn't come to us in order … Everybody knew everybody else's family, all there was to know about them.' For the first time she learned of Phyllis's wedding, of Lance's posting and his subsequent wounding. The correspondence must have reassured her to some extent, though in later years she said that sometimes it was better for internees not to be reminded of the outside world. This underlines the hurt she must have felt in 1944 when that first batch of mail arrived and there was none for her. One bundle of letters to Wilma was returned to her family, without explanation.

In July 1945 the internees were permitted to write another card home.

'My dear family and friends, early letters arrived recently,' wrote Wilma on 2 July. 'Snap wonderful. Lance looks well. Hope can walk. Hope Jack also Phyllis have families. Glad Pat is happy. Kate O'Toole has written. Longing to hear from everyone. Am still well. My love to all interested. May God keep you all safe and well. Wilma.'

On that same date Jean Ashton recorded that the daily ration had now been reduced to one small bowl of rice three times a day, vegetables (usually *kangkong*) once a day in very small amounts. 'Sometimes no vegetables for days. Meat sometimes.'

On 19 July another member of the AANS, Winnie May Davis, died in the intensive care hut and joined the others in the cemetery. One of the Charitas Sisters, Sister Olga, was critically ill with beriberi and Wilma was nursing her. 'Her arms were so swollen that she couldn't bend them to feed herself,' she said. 'You'd rub her skin and it would just rub off. I think Sister Olga was an engineer by profession, she was a very well-educated woman. She used to say to me, "Sister Vilma, you are so good, thank you so much for looking after me. I am going to my Father in Heaven and I vill pray for you." She used to say it to me every day. And eventually she did die.'

There were always tales of bravery and tenacity. 'One of the Scottish nurses, she was so swollen with beriberi that she looked like a monster. It was dreadful,' Wilma recalled. 'She used to insist on being helped every day to try and walk. She had to be hoisted up. She had an engagement ring which she wouldn't sell to get extra food. She was determined to keep her engagement ring. Well, she got out eventually and I believe she got married to her boyfriend.'

Beriberi was a relentless killer at Belalau. A cemetery was established on the hillside just above the hospital in the lower camp. It was necessarily close to the hospital. The women no longer had the strength to walk any distance, especially when carrying a coffin. Wilma was no longer involved in preparing corpses for burial, as she had been on Bangka Island, but she was in charge of a detail that would tour the hospital each morning and try to assess who was likely to die that day. She and her team would then go out and dig the graves. 'We had coffins lined up ready, leaning against the wall of the hospital. Then we had to have graves dug,' she said.

Betty Jeffrey recalled Wilma coming to the end of her bed space in the hospital and making an assessment as to whether she would last the day. Betty, although gravely ill, told Wilma to move on, that she had no intention of dying. She was to remind Wilma about this for the rest of her life. She did not know until later that Wilma did dig that grave, but it was occupied by someone else. Thereafter Betty would tease Wilma as: 'That wretched girl who dug my grave.' Sister Jeffrey kept her promise and lived into her nineties. Eventually, after Wilma had delivered a very moving eulogy at Betty's funeral in 2001, she remarked sadly to friends: 'At least, this time, I didn't have to dig her grave.'

Until her death, the missionary Margaret Dryburgh would conduct funeral services. After she died, Norah Chambers would recite a simple service based on the Anglican format. Others who might have done it were either too ill, too busy, or already dead. Anne Livingstone, the mathematician, had conducted burial services for a while. Now she was under intensive care herself, her admirable brain corrupted by disease. 'She did very much want to get out. She'd made up her mind she was going to survive. She thought, if she laid there on that bed space and didn't do anything, that she'd manage. We used to have to feed her when we were on duty.'

Wilma would climb onto the *bali bali* and feed about six patients at once, from a common container. The *bali bali* was flimsy and if she did not watch her step, her foot would go through it. 'But Anne Livingstone, she'd lie there and you'd give her a mouthful of rice, then you'd run along the rest of them to give them all a mouthful … Miss Livingstone would chew her rice, then she'd open her mouth and say "I'm ready." Of course you wouldn't be back there in time and she'd lie there, with her mouth open, saying "I'm ready." Eventually you'd get back and give it to her. But it was quite a business …' Not long before the internees were freed, Miss Livingstone died and was buried in that lonely little cemetery.

'There was always the problem of wild pigs rooting around and digging down,' Wilma said. 'You had to keep an eye next day to make sure the pigs hadn't been there.' Because of the diggers' weakness, the graves were shallow. 'Later Norah Chambers made some crosses with the names on it [sic],' Sister Catherinia revealed. Mrs Chambers etched the names of the people into their crosses by heating a nail in the kitchen fire and burning the inscription into the wood. 'She couldn't stand it that they were just there,' Sister Catherinia said. 'She wanted to have the name of the one who was under the earth.'

Although she was suffering from various diseases and injuries, including that to her spine, and she was doing night duty, Wilma remained one of the physically stronger of the Australian nurses. She refused to let anything 'knock her off her feet', no matter how serious it might be. Often Wilma, together with Jean Ashton, would do double hospital duty because somebody else in Hut 13 had been stricken. The physical and moral strength of both Wilma and Jean was phenomenal, but by now Vivian was seriously ill and was feared to be dying. The next death among the AANS, on 8 August, was that of 'Dot' Freeman,[98] a nurse from Victoria. 'Her legs stiffened up and she couldn't straighten them,' Wilma said. 'She just got worse and worse and then she died.'

Two days later, the internees were lined up by the Japanese and given a belated injection against dysentery. It is interesting to compare this sudden concern of the captors for the health of the women with the progress of the war. The first atomic bomb fell on Japan on 6 August, the second on 9 August. The High Command on Sumatra must have sensed that continued barbarism against prisoners would bring the wrath of a merciless victor against Japanese criminals after the war.

When Wilma's fourth birthday as a captive came along, on 17 August, Betty Jeffrey recorded in her diary: 'Wilma has her fourth birthday as a prisoner today. She is in her twenties, wasting the best years of her life.'[99]

Veronica Clancy described the birthday gathering and the pitiful state of the AANS sisters: 'All amusements were a thing of the past, but on August 17th Sr Wilma Oram's birthday, a noble effort was made to hold a party down in their cottage. All members of AANS who could possibly stagger were present, many starting early so they could rest on the way. It was a very happy reunion, even those curled up on the *bali balis,* in the throes of fever, enjoyed it. [Vivian Bukllwinkel was back with Wilma and Jean and was present at the party.] We had a mug of hot coffee and a tiny piece of rice bread, about half an inch square, with a tiny piece of chilli on top to add a touch of colour. Everybody had donned their freedom rags, several had even dug up a touch of lipstick. How we chatted of the day when we could really celebrate our birthdays, we all decided that we were going to ignore the last three and have them all over again in very different circumstances. Each with a secret dread in their heart: *if we can make it.* With cries of "It won't be long now", we departed to our respective huts. It won't be long now? How oblivious of that momentous date—August 17th—we were.'

For little did they know that the war against Japan had already ended. Two days previously, on 15 August 1945, the Emperor had made a radio announcement confirming Japan's unconditional surrender.

One of those mentioned above by Veronica as 'curled up on the *bali balis* in the throes of fever' was 'Mitz' Mittelheuser from Queensland.[100] She died on 18 August, not knowing that she had survived the war. 'They were just starving us,' Wilma asserted. 'They were going to exterminate all prisoners, that's a well-known fact, and we knew it at the time. And they did exterminate the ones in Borneo.'[101]

Nothing was said by the Japanese about the end of the war. The prisoners were kept in ignorance. Nothing changed until 20 August when the camp was visited by a high-ranking Japanese officer who showed an unprecedented interest in the AANS women, the *Australie kankafoos*, as they were called by their captors. Still nothing was said, and conditions did not alter, except that guard duty was taken over by local soldiers, under the supervision of Captain Seiki, and the Japanese military guards were withdrawn.

In the outside world, the main centres in Java, Borneo and Sumatra had already become sites for potential political upheaval but practical moves were being made to rescue Wilma and her nursing colleagues. The Japanese, however, would not easily give up the internees of Belalau. The visit by that high-ranking Japanese officer proves that Nippon knew the location of the women of the AANS but, for some reason, was unwilling to reveal it.

Around this time, two events occurred that would directly impact on the incarcerated nurses.

Firstly, Lord Louis Mountbatten, Supreme Allied Commander of South-East Asia, was visited at his headquarters in Ceylon (now Sri Lanka) by a war correspondent who was working for the Australian Broadcasting Commission. This man, Hayden Lennard, requested permission to enter Sumatra. His aim was not only to cover the general release of prisoners of war there, but to see if he could locate the missing Australian nurses, although it was not even certain that they were still alive. Flying Officer Ken Brown, who would accompany Lennard, said: 'He had sort of prowled around the headquarters, putting the nose in here and there.'

As a skilled war correspondent, Lennard saw this story as a scoop, should he be successful in finding the nurses. This was possibly his initial motivation for setting out on the search, though he was to maintain a close interest in the women for some years following the war. Permission was granted and Lennard hitched a ride on a plane to Singapore in preparation.

The second incident concerned a 23-year-old Royal Marine commando. His name was Major 'Jake' Jacobs.[102] Immediately after the Japanese surrender, Jacobs was called to Mountbatten's office and ordered to parachute into Sumatra with a small band of hand-picked commandos of around the same age. Their mission was to gain control of the entire Japanese army still remaining on Sumatra, around 80,000 of them, and to get the allied prisoners out.[103]

LIBERATION

On 24 August Seiki called a massed meeting of the female internees. '*Vurang sudah habis*; the war is over and now we are all friends,' he announced in Malay.

'He talked for some considerable time to say how sorry he was, [about] the way we were, and they had done the best they could for us, and that they were going to look after us, that they were going to protect us, that we still had to stay where we were. And that was it,' Wilma recalled. He also announced that the women could expect allied officials to arrive in three or four days' time.

'We are dumb,' Jean Ashton wrote. Wilma's comment was: 'But by that time, if we'd had a gun we'd have shot them.' Seiki did not reveal who had won the war, but it was not hard to work it out. 'We realised it was our victory,' Wilma said, 'because the Japs looked as though they'd been crying for several days. He said we were still under the Japanese because they had to protect us. So we still had to do what we were told, because we had to be protected from the native population. Well … we realised that,' she asserted. 'We were at the mercy of who-ever had a gun. You know, if the natives wanted to exterminate us, they could. So we co-operated with the Japs, right up.' There was no discernable unrest within the indigenous population in that part of Sumatra at the time.

Jake Jacobs and his commandos soon established headquarters at Palembang, gained the support of the Sikhs, who readily switched sides after having worked as guards for the Japanese, and secured a degree of grudging assistance from the conquered enemy. Former POWs in Palembang and other centres, who had the requisite skills, were put to work to help with the transition from Japanese rule to Allied rule. The Dutch goal was to re-establish the Dutch East Indies, but the rebel movement for an independent Republic of Indonesia was gaining strength.

At Belalau, sudden changes in routine coincided with the arrival of Jake Jacobs on Sumatra. As Mountbatten's representative, he was issuing orders that were being relayed by radio and telephone throughout the island and, to save their skins, those Japanese officers who did not commit suicide were complying.[104]

The Japanese hid the existence of the Belalau hell camp for long enough to begin to nourish their prisoners with some of the accumulated stores. 'The Japs started giving the food out of the storage hut,' Wilma said. 'They were giving us tins of Australian butter. It was obvious they'd had it all along … [now] they wanted to ingratiate themselves, they wanted us to forgive them.' Seiki said he was sorry for what had happened to the prisoners and claimed that he had done his best but, as the facts emerged, it was obvious that he and his men had done nothing of the sort.

'The clothing and medical supplies were there before peace was declared. It was the very day after they told us that peace had been declared that they gave us tins and tins of butter per person and bottles and bottles of quinine, yards and yards of material,' reported Vivian. 'It was the very next day [sic], and there was so much of it, they must have had it there all the time.' And so proof of a policy of deliberate starvation and depravation emerged.

When Wilma was asked what condition she was in at the time of liberation, she paused to consider before answering. 'I was still on my feet,' she replied carefully. 'Still working in the hospital, but I was very thin and I suffered from beriberi and dysentery, but I feel I could have survived. Without some great trauma happening to me, I could have survived.'

Within the next few days the women learned of the existence, so close by, of the men's camp. If only they had known of each other's existence, the men and women could have helped each other to survive. The Japanese themselves could have benefited from a well-planned policy of food-growing in this fertile area.

On visiting the male camp, Wilma received some sad news. 'I found out that Jock Mathieson had died, and the other men that I had known. Colonel Wynn … Out of that six, the only one to survive was a man named Kirk.' For many of the wives and children, the first indication that their husband or father was dead came when the Japanese bluntly kept them back while the other children were sent off to visit long lost fathers. The Japanese knew of the deaths but did not choose to let the women know. Similarly, the men had not been told of the deaths of wives or children. 'There were some people reunited with their families, which was good, but so many of our friends had died in the camps that it really was a very sad time,' Wilma said. 'We didn't throw our hats in the air.'

'Husbands from men's camp visit wives here and vice versa,' wrote Jean Ashton. 'Great excitement. More food given. Dutch and British men take over all heavy work. We visit the men's camp. British planes drop 38 parcels of food, cigarettes etc. We have half a slice of bread each for tea. First bread in three-and-a-half years.'

The men had to visit the women's camp in relays because they did not have any clothing. They would swap it with each other to make the trip. Wilma remembered: 'They were in tatters, the same as we were. One man came over, he was the Trade Commissioner in Singapore (I think he committed suicide soon after the war[105]), he came over and he was sitting there with his legs crossed, talking to us on the floor, and he had no fly in his trousers. But nobody took any notice of anything like that. Your body doesn't matter.'

By 6 September Hayden Lennard was already in Singapore and interviewing, among others, Huck Finlay, a former POW who was later to become a high-ranking executive with the Australian Broadcasting Commission. During this interview Lennard made a breakthrough in his search. Finlay was still in Changi at the time, although Changi had been liberated. During this interview Lennard got confirmation that some of the AANS prisoners were still alive and

on Sumatra. Finlay had been in the same camp with them until the
military prisoners were separated from the rest in 1942.

Lennard asked of Finlay: 'The group of Australian nurses in
Sumatra, did you see anything of them?'

Finlay replied: 'Yes, I was in the same camp as they were when they
were first taken prisoner. I have nothing but the profoundest admiration for them. Their cheerfulness and willingness to help was an
example to the rest of the camp … I've seen a few of them [through
the fence] since. They're looking well … but very thin. However they
still seem extremely cheerful.'

Subsequent off-air conversation with Finlay placed the women as
last sighted at Palembang.

In Australia, as soon as the Japanese surrendered, RAAF transports
from Squadrons 34 to 38 amassed at Cairns in Queensland and flew as
a group to Singapore. One crew from the 36th Squadron, flying a
DC3, consisted of two young officers: Squadron Leader Fred Madson
and 24-year-old Flying Officer Ken Brown. 'I'll never forget when we
were coming into Singapore,' Brown said. 'It was just on dusk and the
sun was magnificent. Red, rosy red. Beautiful.'

When they got there they had to find their own accommodation.
Japanese troops were everywhere. Not having been withdrawn after
the surrender, the former enemy soldiers were walking free but were
now technically prisoners. It was so soon after the cessation of hostilities that there were no RAAF camps. 'We had to borrow money from
the English people. We took over the place, made our headquarters, it
was the Sultan of Johore's palace in Singapore,' Brown said. Soon after
arrival they learned, from Hayden Lennard, that the AANS women
were on Sumatra. 'So from that time Fred Madson, who was my
"skip", decided we would go down to Palembang.'

The camp at Belalau had some unexpected visitors on 7 September.
Two 'Dutchmen' arrived with a Chinese officer called Tjoeng. One of
these officers was Jake Jacobs, who was not Dutch but South African
by birth. The other was probably Sergeant 'Happy' Plesman, who was
Dutch. Jacobs and his commandos had flown to the airstrip at Lahat

with a Japanese air crew. His other offsiders, skilled Australian radio operators called Gillam and Bates, remained in Loebok Linggau to maintain contact with Palembang while Jacobs and Plesman arrived at the camp in a requisitioned car. Jacobs recorded that conditions at Belalau were 'deplorable'[106]—and by now this young officer had already visited every other prison camp on Sumatra.

When Jacobs again visited the camp on 9 September, he ordered that another store house standing just outside the entrance should be opened. It proved to be piled high with undelivered Red Cross supplies. These vital supplies had been there during the women's entire stay at Belalau. Wilma listed some: 'Australian tinned butter, powdered milk, vitamins, mosquito nets, bandages, medicines, peanuts and other things which could have helped save lives. If we'd had them when we needed them they'd have been so beneficial to us. Sugar. So somebody beat up some butter and sugar and called it cream. I can remember Flo Trotter coming along, we'd got some coffee and Flo came along and said "Do you want some cream in your coffee?" She put in a spoon of this butter and sugar. Life took on a different complexion altogether. I think we started putting on weight almost immediately.'

On this same day, Jacobs located the AANS women and spent some time talking to them. When he returned to Loebok Linggau, he instructed Gillam and Bates to send a signal to Mountbatten's HQ which included the words: 'Have encountered among 250 repeat 250 British female internees in Loebok Linggau camp [sic] Sister Nesta James and 23 other surviving members of Australian Army Nursing Service stop Remnants of contingent AANS evacuated from Malaya in *Vyner Brooke*.'

Gillam and Bates accompanied Jacobs to Belalau on 11 September and requested immediate permission to visit the Australian nursing sisters. Gillam was from Perth, Western Australia, and Bates was from Thornbury in Victoria. Betty Jeffrey recorded: 'Viv, who is usually unmoved and very quiet, came rushing in, face positively crimson, and panted, "Australians are here!" They were about five yards behind her. To see that rising sun badge on a beret again! It did us more good than anything we have experienced so far.'

It was probably during the excited conversations that ensued—questions that ranged from whether or not Roosevelt was dead to who won the Melbourne football final—that the two Australian commandos informed the nurses about the atom bomb. 'Somebody who came into the camp to release us told us,' Wilma said. When quizzed on her feelings about the Americans dropping the bombs, her reply was definite: 'If the bomb hadn't been dropped there's no question that we would not have come home. The prisoners would not have been released … So you can make up your own mind as to whether it was a good idea or not. From my point of view it was a good idea.'

On the lighter side, Wilma remembered that during these conversations with Gillam and Bates they first heard about penicillin and Nesta James announced in a loud voice that it cured venereal disease, 'As though we were all suffering from it!' said Wilma. 'I don't know why she should have thought of that. That was something that we'd never been able to cure, and it was rather remarkable. Penicillin.' The women wanted to know everything at once.

The nurses felt let down when Gillam and Bates left the camp with Jacobs and still nothing appeared to have changed. 'We were left back in the same position as we were before, with the Japs looking after us,' Wilma said. 'We were trading with the natives by this time, getting chickens. I know Jess Doyle[107] took off her shorts and handed them over to one of the natives. He handed her a couple of chickens. It left her without any clothes, but somebody had something to give her. The natives were very short of clothing. They had none. So the little bit of clothing we had we could barter for food.'

They need not have worried. They were not being deserted, rescue was on its way. With Hayden Lennard aboard, Squadron Leader Fred Madson and Flying Officer Ken Brown had flown their DC3 to Palembang. Ken recalled, 'We were greeted there by bowing and scraping Japanese, which we know is their usual habit, and they told us that the girls were not at Palembang. They were in a camp out of Lahat.' Madson was not prepared to take the aeroplane to Lahat, because the airstrip—which as far as they knew had not been used for some time—

might not be big enough or safe enough to take a DC3. 'So he went back to Singapore,'[108] said Ken, 'left me there, with the Japanese, to go by car to Lahat to determine whether it was suitable to land the aeroplane and give him a call from there.'

With the help of a Canadian-born Japanese lieutenant, whom Ken nicknamed 'Whisky' because his name sounded like that, a team of about six Japanese soldiers assembled. A car and some trucks were requisitioned, the latter for the purpose of removing the Australian nurses.

Ken had estimated that Palembang to Lahat should have taken about two hours by car. 'There was a French boy that had parachuted in [to Palembang] ahead of us. We said we intended to go through the jungle to get to Loebok Linggau. He said, "You'll never get through. It's impossible to do it in the daytime, so you've got no hope in the night-time." And he was pretty right because we got bogged. The trucks that were following us didn't come any further.'

Meanwhile, Hayden Lennard, impatient to get moving and heeding warnings about the state of the road, opted to travel to Loebok Linggau by train. Lennard arrived before the others. 'We spent two or three hours pushing those cars out of the mud,' Ken said.

On reaching Lahat, Ken inspected of the airstrip and decided it was suitable to land the DC3. He reported this to Fred Madson by telephone, after which he telephoned the prison camp at Loebok Linggau and asked to speak to the chief Australian nurse. An amazed Nesta James was called to the phone. 'We didn't even know there was a telephone in the camp,' she recalled. 'And I went along to the guardhouse surrounded by Japs, and I was told a plane was coming for us.' Ken then proceeded by car to the railway station at Loebok Linggau, where he found that Hayden Lennard, with the help of Jake Jacobs, had commandeered the train and that the 'girls' were already on their way.

'We could hardly believe it,' said Wilma. 'We had to rouse the camp and tell everybody. The Dutch nuns next door to us boiled up the coffee. We'd never fraternised, never had coffee together, the nuns and the nurses. But we all got together and drank coffee. We were giving away things we had. I'm sorry about that now, we should have brought them home. We got together as much as we could carry because we still had to carry everything. Iole was in hospital, sick. We had to collect Iole because we couldn't leave without her. And nobody in the hospital would believe that it was true. They thought it was just a story that Jeff was putting over,[109] but eventually she convinced them, and Iole got off the bed space and we got packed up ready to go.' 'We set off in the middle of the night for Lahat. We finally got there after our trucks had broken down several times, and we wondered if we were ever going to get anywhere. Our usual trips with the Japanese ...'[110]

After a three-hour journey, during which they travelled about 12 miles (19 kilometres), the women finally arrived at the railway station. Ken Brown helped to lift them down from the trucks and get them onto the train. Ken's face contorted and he turned pale when he related this. 'The smell was unbelievable,' he said, a note of disbelief in his voice even after fifty-two years. 'The stench was just ... I can still smell it. And it was two weeks [sic] since the end of the war so they'd received a little bit of nourishment. They were in terrible condition.' For the rest of Ken's life, whenever Betty Jeffrey corresponded with him, she continued to sign herself 'Stinky'.

Jenny Greer, who had bravely led her friends 'off to see the Wizard' in 1942, had to be carried aboard the train, close to death, but everyone who could walked. Every nurse was wearing a uniform, as they had vowed to do from the very beginning. Photographs reveal that they had kept their buttons polished.

The train had a steam locomotive. It was a regular service to and from Loebok Linggau and was scheduled to leave at 8am. Because there were so many sick aboard, Haydon Lennard attempted to persuade the Sumatran train driver to leave early but the request was denied. 'Come on, let's get cracking,' Ken ordered, waving his revolver, but still the driver refused to budge. Sullen Japanese soldiers lounged aimlessly around and stared. Many were still armed.

Meanwhile, food vendors were selling their wares on the station. 'They told us not to eat anything on the train because it might be poisoned, but we took no notice of that, we ate everything we could lay hands on,' recalled Wilma. Before the train left, Jacobs' men made sure that the vendors were paid for the food.

Wilma could not recall how they got from the railway station at Lahat to the airstrip. She, like her colleagues, was in a euphoric daze, but the nurses were not out of it yet. 'They took us to Lahat and then we went to the airport, and still nothing happened. It was nearly dark, getting on late in the evening. We thought: "Oh well this is another furphy, no plane." We were about to bed ourselves down, because we were quite used to bedding down anywhere, and all of a sudden this plane came in.'

First of all there was a distant hum that could almost be imaginary, but then the hum grew louder, even though, in those abrupt few minutes of dusk between day and night in the tropics, the plane could not be seen. Fred Madson made a perfect landing in the semi-darkness, never having seen the airfield before. Ken Brown said, 'The girls didn't think he was going to arrive. Great panic. He was a great hero to put it down on that airstrip.'

'The doors opened and two people stood there,' recalled Wilma. 'They were Sage and Floyd,[111] but they were in tropical uniform and we had no idea who they were. They got out of the plane, and Major Windsor[112] got out with them as well. We were just grouped out on the ground, the twenty-four of us. Major Windsor said, "Where are the Australian nurses?" and we all fell on top of him and said "We're the Australian nurses!" Nobody recognised us though we had our uniforms on. And Miss Sage said, "Where are the rest of you?" And we said, "They're dead."'

During his appearance on Vivian's 'This Is Your Life', Major Windsor said: 'I have recollections that could have been yesterday's. Seeing you—some of you standing, some sitting, some lying in that little lean-to on the edge of that strip at Lahat. Helping to load you into the plane. One that I lifted into the plane, Jenny Greer. There were two.[113] Then standing behind the plane with Annie Sage as it took off through that long grass, and saying, "I hope it gets up", as it cut a swathe through that grass.'

Sage and Floyd stayed behind with Major Windsor to look after the sick civilians whom the AANS women, dedicated to the end, had thought to bring out with them. On the flight back to Singapore were Major G.F. 'Jake' Jacobs, Squadron Leader Fred Madson, Flying Officer Ken Brown, Hayden Lennard and Sister Chandler (RAAF), who had come in on the plane and flew back with them to take care of the sick nurses.

'The girls were very excited,' Ken Brown recalled. 'Even the ones that were ill got a new lease of life.'

'I wasn't very happy about being flown out, I didn't trust aeroplanes at all,' said Wilma. 'I went around to one of the pilots and said to him, "Do you think we're going to crash?" He assured us there was no chance of crashing. It was a troop carrying plane with seats either side, just forms. We had a couple of stretcher cases on the floor.'

Ken, who was co-pilot, confirmed that on the flight Wilma said to him: 'Ken, I hope we don't prang, I've waited three years for this!'

The flight landed in Singapore by night. 'Most of them were able to walk off the plane,' Ken Brown said, 'and they were wearing these terrible tattered uniforms. It was a very moving experience.'

The returning POWs were met by Lady Louis Mountbatten and her Red Cross helpers who greeted the nurses with a cup of tea and biscuits. 'I was looking forward to that cup of tea,' Wilma smiled. 'I hadn't had one for three-and-a-half years, but Lady Louis' aide-de-camp, dressed in his kilt, insisted on talking to me and asking me questions about the camp. Then Lady Louis wanted to know how we got on for sanitary towels. I assured her that hadn't been a problem because most of us had stopped.' Wilma gave a philosophical shrug and added, 'I never did get that cup of tea.'

On arrival in Singapore Hayden Lennard filed his story and got his 'scoop'. It was published in syndicated newspapers, including Melbourne's *Sun News-Pictorial,* as soon as it arrived on the wires. It started a feeding frenzy within the news media.

The sisters were taken to the 14th AGH in Katong, which was based at St Patrick's School where Wilma and Mona Wilton had first been billeted. 'Our cabin trunks that we'd left behind, the men had buried them but unfortunately the Japs had built on top of this, so all our trunks are still buried under the foundations of that new building,' said Wilma.

The women were admitted as patients. 'They told us we smelt terrible,' Wilma said. 'We didn't think much of that, because we had all had a wash. They bathed us and took our things from us. Burnt a lot. Then we got into these nice clean hospital beds, but at that stage we'd have much preferred to sleep on the floor. We got out of bed and got under our beds instead.' Wilma was mortified when a nursing team arrived at her bedside in the middle of the night, stripped her naked and proceeded to paint her with something in a bright colour. 'They said I had scabies,' she said with indignation. 'I didn't know.'

The women were forbidden to have visitors but people came anyway. 'It was rather fun to be called *girls* again when we all felt such toothless old hags,' reported Betty Jeffrey. 'We have also been visited by Lady Louis Mountbatten, General Callaghan, Lady Blamey and of course dozens of our own officers, troops, RAAF etc. Red Cross officials too. Colonel Black of Red Cross in Australia.'

'They tried to keep our rations down a bit,' Wilma said, 'but we wanted to eat, so we got people to bring us in eggs and when they brought us soup we'd break the egg into the hot soup and eat the egg with the soup ... The press were there interviewing us. Lady Louis came and talked to all of us. There was a Lady Park, too. Somebody said: "Come and have a look at this!" So we all peeked around the corner at this lady, and she had purple or pink hair. We were fascinated with that.[114] Matron Sage came and gave us a talk on what had been happening during the war. She tried to bring us up to date with all the news, which of course was impossible.'

Wilma's first mail home as a free woman was written from Singapore on 19 September 1945. It reveals that none of her spirit had been permanently damaged.

'Dear Mum and Everybody,' she wrote. 'Well, where to start. I have written this letter many times in [my] imagination and now I don't know where to begin. I'm a bit hazy as to the state of the family, to say nothing of the numbers. A letter arrived this morning saying 'Babies well' and I didn't know there were any, however I am somewhat more than delighted as I was hoping a few would have arrived …

'… Lady Louis Mountbatten is speaking to us individually as the survivors which, of course, is a great thrill for us. I was amazed to see how little damage had been done in Singapore—we had heard so many rumours—Lady Louis has just spoken to me—she is very charming and is doing a wonderful job here.

'Well things go at a terrific rate, I have just been having my photo taken once again and have seen some of the lads from our unit. They are all looking very fit. There is a picture show tonight and we are allowed to go. Another thrill. This is a very unsatisfactory letter but life is a whirl and I have not yet collected my thoughts.

'Mum will you please go and see Mrs Wilton. I will write to her later. Love to all the family. I will be with you very soon now. Love, Willie.'

The women were to spend a month recuperating in Singapore, during which time they had to try to readjust to army regulations. Orders were again orders. The POW nurses had been undisciplined for three-and-a-half years and had never been given much initial army training. Add to that their sheer joy at being free and it was inevitable that some would resent pressure on them to conform. There was sometimes a lack of understanding, too, from service nurses who had themselves been through the war. They had spent years under battle conditions and some disliked the attention that the media gave to the newly released POWs: movie newsreels, radio and newspaper interviews, photographic sessions.

The POW nurses were treated like film stars, they said so themselves, and felt uncomfortable about it. 'We had our hair set and our nails done,' Wilma said. 'Gracie Fields came and gave a concert to all the male and female patients. One day some of us walked into Singapore to have a look around the shops. Bought a few things.' All this attention given to severely traumatised women may not have been good for them. Betty Jeffrey recorded that on 2 October they threw a

Right: Alan in 1958. Alan had also been a POW, and by this time the effects of post-traumatic stress disorder were becoming more and more apparent in him. He was to suffer this affliction for the rest of his life.

Below: The Young family entertains Iole Harper Burkitt (seated left). This photo was taken around 1967, when Wilma and Alan's youngest daughter Christine (seated next to the twins) was aged sixteen; she was to die in a motorcycle accident just three years later.

Above: The 'girls' reunite at Sydney's Fairfield hospital, around 1978. Throughout their lives, the POW nurses maintained a strong bond and kept in close contact. Sitting, from left to right: Beryl Woodbridge, Flying Officer Ken Brown, who helped rescue the women, and Nesta James. Standing, from left to right: Wilma, Vivian Bullwinkel and Betty Jeffrey.

Above: Wilma with Betty Jeffrey and 'Weary' Dunlop. This photo was probably taken in 1988 at the dedication of the memorial seat at Duntroon Military College for the nurses who had not survived the sinking of the SS *Vyner Brooke*.

Left: Return to Mentok, Bangka Island, for the dedication of a memorial to the nurses who died, March 1993. The well was one of the only recognisable objects left from the original POW camp. Pictured are Pat Gunther Darling (at left), Flo Trotter Syer (third from right), Jean Ashton (at rear) and Wilma (far right).

Above Left: A portrait of Wilma by artist Rosemary Parrant Todman, entered in the 2002 Archibald Prize.
Above Right: Wilma with her three surviving children at Melbourne's Government House, on the occasion of her being named Anzac of the Year in 1998. From left to right: David, Elizabeth and John.

Above: Farewell–Wilma, supported by daughter Elizabeth, places a red poppy on Vivian Bullwinkel's coffin, July 2000. Of the women imprisoned together, Wilma was the closest to Vivian, and was called upon to deliver television tributes to her at the time of her death. (Courtesy *The West Australian*)

cocktail party 'To the sisters and officers of this hospital, plus a few paratroop officers, and our pilots Squadron Leader 'Fred' Madson and Flying Officer Brown. Corking party—which we had to walk out from at 6pm.'

At first it was planned to return the nurses home by plane. Then their officers reconsidered and decided instead to transport them slowly by hospital ship, along with other returning service personnel, to give them more time to adjust. On 5 October 1946, Wilma and her colleagues boarded the *Manunda*, homeward bound.

PART THREE:
PUBLIC SERVICE

HOME

The ship arrived at Fremantle on 18 October 1945. Though their reception was ecstatic, Wilma's feelings were mixed because Iole Harper and Mickey Syer would disembark there, separating them from their colleagues for the first time since the group was taken prisoner. This was to be one of the biggest adjustments to face the ex-internees and many would never quite be able to accommodate it. Not all the nurses were 'bosom buddies', such is human nature, but they were one.

'We were frightened, coming home, didn't know how we were going to react,' said Wilma. 'Afraid about getting back into life as we knew it. We hadn't lived it for so long and we were apprehensive.' Various types of psychological and physical reaction to trauma or stress were yet to be identified in 1945, but every individual was suffering.

Those who were to continue the voyage to Melbourne or Sydney, and who were healthy enough not to be hospitalised, were given two days' leave.

The *Manunda*'s next port of call was Melbourne. By the time the ship steamed through Port Phillip Heads, the nurses were distressed. 'We felt we should be together, but we knew that the girls had to go home to their families,' Wilma said. Those who came from New South Wales and Queensland sailed on with the *Manunda*. The Victorians, South Australians and Tasmanians disembarked at Port Melbourne.

The Melbourne arrival was marked by a formal welcome from Lady Dugan, wife of the Governor of Victoria,[115] after which Wilma went ashore with Vivian, Betty Jeffrey and others, including Elizabeth Simons who was to make her way home to Tasmania. The Melbourne girls were put on buses and driven to what would become the Heidelberg Repatriation Hospital, formerly the 115th AGH, where Wilma first served in the AANS. Here another gala welcome awaited— more flowers, more cakes, more speeches, more photographs—and here, at last, Wilma was reunited with her family.

Jack Oram was present at the reunion at Heidelberg. 'She was as chirpy as could be,' he recalled. 'She's very forthright. Being in the army made her that way, I think.' Wilma's sister Pat was there to meet her too. By then Pat was nursing at the Royal Melbourne hospital. 'I was supposed to be on duty, but I asked if I could go and meet her. Her legs were very skinny but her body had blossomed out, because they'd been fed up so much in Singapore. She was quite bright. They'd had time to recuperate and adjust to the difference.'

It was a happy but awkward time. The family avoided asking Wilma about her experiences, even seeming not to be interested. This shocked Wilma, who did not know until later that such reticence was the result of general advice issued at the end of the war. People were told not to ask POWs about their experiences because it was considered better for the whole population to put the war behind it and get on with normal living. 'Wake Up Australia!' was the postwar rallying call.

What Wilma had been looking forward to most, when she knew for certain that she had survived the war, was being reunited with her family and to be able to reassure them she was okay. Her thoughts were for her parents, her sisters and her brothers. 'They'd had a pretty nasty war,' she said, 'not knowing what happened to us.' To come home and find everyone apparently indifferent was hard. Wilma was not one to display her depth of feeling, but there was plenty of emotion beneath the serene exterior. 'We wanted to talk about it but people didn't, perhaps, think they ought to ask. Some people didn't want to ask and some didn't want to listen. Some didn't want to know. They could straightaway tell you what a dreadful war they'd had back here, how they couldn't get cigarettes, tea, this and that.

We suddenly realised that our experience wasn't nearly as important as we'd thought.'

The nurses were offered a bed if they wanted to stay in the hospital, or they could go out. 'Well,' Wilma recalled, 'I didn't feel like going out to confront a whole lot of emotional people, so I slept in hospital that night. The family was staying at East Brighton and I said I wouldn't come out yet. I went to East Brighton the following day.'

Wilma found the most harrowing part of getting home 'meeting the parents of the girls who had been shot, or who had died … When they actually saw us, it really hit them.' So although there were celebrations and wide newspaper coverage everywhere they went, sentiments were confused. Wilma felt guilty for having survived when so many had not.

Next came the confusion of suddenly being thrown into a social whirl and being expected to cope with it—to be bright, smiling, chatty. None of the POWs received counselling. The need for such therapy was unknown. 'The men who came back on the ship were pretty unhappy,' Wilma recalled. 'They felt people hadn't given them a very good reception. They felt, because they'd been prisoners, they were being blamed for the loss of Singapore.' The bond between the male and female prisoners was strong. Many of these men had been interned alongside the women, exchanging notes and helping them whenever an opportunity arose.

The nurses were given a small allowance for new uniforms but it took some time for these to be ready. 'Clothing was still rationed and we never got much in the way of ration tickets,' Wilma recalled. 'When Lady Dugan invited us to go to the races, we only had tropical uniforms so we had to wear those. We didn't even have anything to wear while we washed them. I remember feeling quite tatty at that race meeting.'

For the time being Wilma based herself at Heidelberg, along with Vivian Bullwinkel, Beryl Woodbridge and Betty Jeffrey. Betty had no choice. She was suffering from advanced tuberculosis and had been admitted as an in-patient. The four women clung together as a group. 'Sisters Oram, Jeffrey, Bullwinkel and Woodbridge were placed on the verandah of their pavilion ward, with Sister James, who was senior in rank to the others, in one of the inside beds.'[116] The four friends on the verandah took to playing cards—bridge. It was said that the women used the same old pack of cards that they had manufactured from a photograph album in camp and refused repeated offers of a new pack from the Red Cross. This was typical of their increasing reluctance to let go of something familiar and to step into the wider world of freedom.

POWs of both sexes gravitated towards each other inside the hospital. The more conscious they became of the outside world's perceived indifference, the more these men and women shut out the outside world. They gathered and talked quietly and exclusively. They were instinctively forming what we now know to be support groups but, without professional guidance or direction to their discussions, it is doubtful that the gatherings did much to help the members. What they did was to isolate the POWs and give them the reputation of being 'stand-offish'.

'All the POWs were in this sort of mental limbo,' said Wilma. 'Nobody wanted to go back to work and nobody knew what they were going to do with themselves. The only people we were comfortable talking to were other POWs. We seemed to have nothing in common with people who hadn't been POWs. It took us a long time to fit into the routine of the real world again. We were loath to start work, didn't know how we felt, really.'

There were things that Wilma wanted to do, if only she could release herself from her torpor. She needed to tell Mona's father and her brother Tom exactly what happened, face to face. She also wanted to go back to Warrnambool Base Hospital to see the nurses with whom she had trained, and who had trained with Mona. 'I felt that was something I had a big responsibility to do,' she said. Meanwhile, she continued to visit her own parents who were staying with their friends, the Higgins, at East Brighton.

As soon as they were deemed to be strong enough, the POW nurses were granted some leave. This was with the exception of Betty Jeffrey, who remained as an in-patient at Heidelberg for the time being.

The restless Vivian Bullwinkel and Wilma took a trip to Perth and remained there for about a month, visiting Iole Harper and Mickey Syer. 'We went to Tasmania, and Adelaide, and stayed with Viv's family. I remember going to the butcher's to get some meat, Viv and I together. Butchers used to wrap meat in newspaper in those days. We asked for the meat and the butcher slapped it 'bang' right on Viv's photo that was on the front page. He was quite oblivious to it but we thought it was hilarious.' Such are the rewards of fame and this anecdote illustrates how, even in the midst of adulation, Wilma's feet were planted squarely on the ground—as were those of Vivian Bullwinkel.

Present in the Bullwinkel house at the time were Vivian's brother and his wife. Vivian's sister-in-law recalled that during the first meal at which the family sat down, neither Wilma nor Vivian would start eating until they had compared each other's plates to make sure that both had precisely the same amount of food. This was an unconscious echo of the prison camps, and one that would remain with them for many years. When Vivian's parents pointed out that there was no bed in the house where Wilma could sleep, Vivian replied, 'Don't worry, Willie will sleep on the floor.'

The two friends went to work at Heidelberg for a while, then asked for some more leave so that they could go to Brisbane. 'We stayed at Lennon's Hotel there, then [went] to Sydney and met up with everybody,' said Wilma. 'We used to sit around in Sydney at the Australia Hotel. Beer came on at four o'clock. And as four o'clock approached there'd be a big circle of POWs. More and more of them would turn up. It was a wonderful meeting place and we'd sit there in a great circle. We'd sit till six o'clock or so. I don't know that we drank that much but it was just the company really.'

The trip with Vivian appears to have helped, as Wilma's cousin Heather James recalled: 'It was when she came back from Sydney, after they were rested and felt a lot better, and she and Vivian and I went out together. We had a wonderful time. They were so free, rehabilitated, and happy. And just wanted to do *everything*. They had so many aspirations. So good, and not a word about war or anything like that—just being home. It was a wonderful, wonderful feeling.'

Vivian joined Wilma on a visit to Jane and Alf Oram's house at Hamilton, where they stayed for a while, then Vivian left to visit other colleagues while Wilma's father drove his daughter to Murtoa to take her back to her roots.

More than fifty years later Wilma still blushed at this memory, but what happened in Murtoa was a reminder that ordinary people were interested in, and did care about, their returned prisoners of war. To her bewilderment Wilma was greeted as a hero. Men, women and children lined Murtoa's main street while Alf drove at a snail's pace, waving like the queen dowager, and the people yelled, 'Good on you!' 'You beaut!' and clapped and cheered. Gertie Jeitz recollected: 'The thing I remember most was Mr Oram sitting up in this Singer—a kind of a low slung car—and he's sitting up very proud, and all of us … we had little flags which we waved in the street as this car went by.'

Meanwhile, Wilma was sinking low in her seat and wishing she could evaporate. 'It was the longest street I've ever driven down,' she shuddered. 'It made me feel a bit of a fraud because I didn't feel that I was anything special. Yet, you see, the whole town had turned out.' Wilma begged the irrepressible Alf to drive faster, but he would do no such thing, enjoying his daughter's triumphal entry into the little town. Wilma never believed herself to be worthy of the label of 'hero'. 'I felt like a blooming wrestler, or a footballer or something! It was a marvellous welcome, there's no doubt about that, but I felt embarrassed. Then a local farmer, who had been in the First World War, put on a welcome home party for me and the other local POW, a man called Nelson Brothers. The family was overjoyed that I'd come home. I suppose they tried to help me as much as they could. I told them a bit about it but I think it was too much for them to take in. I stayed home for a fortnight or so, then I slipped quietly out of the town. I didn't tell anybody I was going.'

One of the reasons for Wilma's confusion was that her brother Lance was living at home in Murtoa at the time. Wilma felt that if anyone was a hero, it was Lance. He was persevering with adjusting to the loss of his leg, refusing to regard it as a disability, and worked at his hard-won job with the State Rivers Department, even though his heart was still on the land where he could no longer work. He remained in that job until the day of his retirement.

One of the first proactive things Wilma did, when she decided to get on with living, was to join what was then known as the Returned Sailors', Soldiers' and Airmen's Imperial League of Australia (RSSAILA), now the Returned and Services League of Australia (RSL). The first three of its aims and objectives are:

1. To perpetuate the close ties of friendship created by mutual service in the Australian Defence Force or Allied Forces; to maintain a proper standard of dignity and honour among all past and present serving members of the Defence Force; and to set an example of public spirit and noble hearted endeavour.

2. To preserve the memory and records of those who suffered and died for Australia.

3. To provide for the sick and wounded and needy among those who have served and their dependents including pensions, medical attention, homes and suitable employment.

This last aim would ultimately become a major force in Wilma's life.

MARRIAGE

On returning to Melbourne, Wilma accepted a position on one of the wards at Heidelberg Hospital; work seemed to be one effective way to put the past behind her. She maintained the serene demeanor that was her trademark, soothing with that amazing voice, but carefully hiding the restlessness that had plagued her since her return to 'normal' life. In June Wilma abruptly handed in her notice and was discharged from the AANS, on 5 July 1946, with the rank of Captain. She was a civilian again.

Wilma was offered a position at the Repatriation Department (the forerunner of the Department of Veterans' Affairs) as a charge nurse. She thought seriously about accepting the offer until one of the doctors at the Paisley Clinic—Howard Eddey, who had been a POW in Malaya—telephoned Wilma and suggested that she might find their work in the industrial suburb of Footscray interesting. The Paisley Clinic, founded in 1936 by doctors Norman Dodd and G Guthridge, was the first group practice to be established in the State of Victoria. In Wilma's time it ran a day surgery specialising in treating casualties in the workplace from the many surrounding factories. It was a consultative practice and, perhaps also of interest to Wilma, it provided services in obstetrics.

Wilma accepted the position and lived at the clinic during the week, as was the custom. At weekends she stayed with the Higgins family in East Brighton, next door to whom lived the widowed Mabel Eckersley Young and her recently returned son Alan. With jobs being difficult to find, Alan was working in a cheese factory in King Street.

Until this time Wilma and Alan hardly knew each other, but Wilma was about to forge a strong link with Alan Young. In him, she identified someone she could talk to, who understood how she felt. The understanding was mutual. Both ex-POWs were experiencing the same alienation, the same limbo. They talked and talked. Alan was eloquent and Wilma was a good listener. It was a beginning.

On Mondays Wilma started to drive Alan to King Street on her way to Footscray, dropping him off at the cheese factory. In this way she discovered more and more about him and, in particular, the remarkable parallels in their personal histories. They became mutually attracted. Wilma was particularly interested in the fact that he owned the Gippsland dairy farm and that he had gone to Longerenong College to study agriculture. 'But,' she later recounted with some amusement, 'as I once told one of my neighbours: "If you were a product of Dookie[117] and my husband was a product of Longerenong, I wouldn't give a prize to either college!"'

Following his war experiences on farms in Italy and Germany, Alan was no longer inspired by the prospect of running a dairy farm. The man who had leased the property while Alan was away refused to budge. 'There was some government regulation: having tenants on the place, you couldn't get possession,' Wilma said. The lessee had fallen behind with his rent but Alan was disinclined either to take the tenant to court over arrears, or to take over the property. He asked Wilma to marry him and she agreed, but on one condition: that he must make an effort to get the farm up and running. She saw no future for him in cheese, unless he was producing it on his own land. They shared a love of the land and Wilma saw no sense in wasting a perfectly good farm.

For the time being Wilma continued working at Footscray until eventually, early in 1947, Alan succeeded in regaining possession of the farm. He moved to Cardinia and started to get the place into some sort of order; both the land and its stock had been neglected.

Following wartime deprivations, both Alan and Wilma harboured secret fears that they might find themselves unable to have a family. They went independently to visit doctors, who could not tell what the odds might be for or against fertility. Medical opinion was that they probably would not be able to conceive. This saddened but did not deter them and, on 5 December 1947, Wilma and Alan married in the presence of their wartime colleagues, including Flo Trotter, Beryl Woodbridge, Nesta James and Margaret Anderson.[118] Vivian Bullwinkel was the bridesmaid. Also present at the ceremony was Hayden Lennard, who was now employed by the *Sun* newspaper in Melbourne. He brought a photographer along to record the event.

The newlyweds honeymooned at Mount Buffalo, a tiny mountain village back then before European immigration turned it into the spectacular ski resort that it is today. Despite their lingering fears of infertility, this interlude for Alan and Wilma was everything that a honeymoon ought to be. 'I got pregnant about a fortnight after we were married,' Wilma recalled happily.

Like so many brides before and after her, Wilma did not escape mother-in-law problems. The death of Alan's brother in the sinking of the *Hereward* 'always cast a shadow that Alan had come back and his brother hadn't,' she said. 'And it was the other brother, John, who was the social butterfly, that the mother liked. Alan was not really that type but she kept him with her when he came home from the war. She expected him to escort her to all her parties [Mabel Young was from the noted Eckersley family and her picture often appeared on the social pages of Melbourne's press]. Alan was perfect at drawing-room behaviour, wonderful … She didn't care whether he came back here to the farm or whether he didn't. She wanted him with her, to look after her. That's why she was so resentful of me.'

To Wilma's mind, it was the old story of a possessive mother dominating a guilt-tortured son. Alan's guilt would later take tangible shape and Wilma was to lock horns with her mother-in-law many times. In fairness to Mabel Young, Wilma's eldest daughter Elizabeth revealed: 'I love going to the theatre, and Dad's mother took me to a lot of things. She loved everything like that. I used to see every good movie that came out and most of the good artists that came, when I was little. But when she died that finished, I didn't do that any more.'

Wilma went with her husband to live on the broken down farm. 'Oh, the place was in such a mess!' she said. 'There were holes in the wall and the furniture was broken. We had to mend it and do it up. Then we had no proper dairy. It was falling down, so we set to and made bricks ourselves out of cement, sand and screenings. We had a mould and we used to dry the bricks in the sun.' They toiled together making anything up to a hundred bricks a day. These bricks would take about three days to dry. They were large and very heavy, especially for a pregnant woman. As soon as they had enough bricks they built a cow shed. When the shed was usable, they repaired the old machines and started milking inside it. 'And that cow shed never did get properly finished,' Wilma recalled with a smile.

They were up and milking by 6am, then carted the full cans to the front gate to meet the 'bus'—a truck that would stop around 7.45am to collect the milk and transport it to the factory. After completing their many other tasks around the farm, their normal working day ended around 7pm.

The first day's yield of milk was one single can, of which they were both very proud. Their total yield for that first week brought in a cheque for £3 ($6), which they put somewhere safe to be banked as soon as time could be found to make the trip into town. When the time came they discovered they had lost the cheque. They searched high and low for it, but to no avail. They were desolate—after all their hard work, and needing that money so badly, it had disappeared. (There was a change of luck when, in 1962, fifteen years after the event, Wilma came across the wayward cheque. With typical frugality, she presented it at the bank where it was honoured without question.)

The two ex-POWs worked side by side, trying to put everything into order. Maybe it helped that both had become accustomed to slavery— but this was slavery with a difference because it was for their own benefit. This was home. Perhaps, too, the demanding task offered an escape from memories too terrible to recall. The shabby state of the dwelling itself was something to be endured for the time being, but why worry about this when both had recently experienced so much worse?

The dwelling was a typical Australian cottage, with two bedrooms, a kitchen, a sitting room and a verandah front and back. It was in an advanced state of decay. There was no electricity, no running water and no sanitary plumbing. The toilet was the good old Aussie 'dunny'—a lean-to in which stood a removable metal container, above which was nailed a wooden plank with a hole in it and torn up sheets of newspaper hanging on a string—but this was hardly likely to bother Wilma. Besides, such facilities were common in the days before septic tanks came into use. The kitchen had only a battered wood-fire stove. On this, Wilma would heat a kerosene tin full of water, carry it to the back verandah and empty it into a bath so that they could wash. Wood for the stove was collected from the property, there still being plenty of it left over from those far-off days when Alan first cleared the scrub.

Of the years Wilma and Alan were to spend together, perhaps this period, when they worked with such dedication towards the same end, was their most fulfilling. The two were a team against the odds: they and their cattle. And the horses. 'That's really why he had a farm,' said Wilma. 'Horses. Yes, Alan wanted horses and he had horses ... He set to, amassing more, when actually it was *cows* that we should have been concentrating on.' Alan used his Clydesdales in the traditional way, for work. He may have inherited this love of horses from his grandfather, who was thought to be one of the first people to import Clydesdale horses into Australia.

Wilma's concern about the increasing numbers of horses on the property was not based on a dislike of them, but on arithmetic: horses ate too much of what little pasture was available for the cows. Cardinia can be scorching hot in summer, the sun killing off everything green, and bitterly cold in winter with severe frosts that wreak havoc on dairying land. At all times of the year winds can roar across the flat terrain, knocking down everything that stands in their way. In addition to the cruel weather were occasional insect plagues. Crickets would eat the precious grass, to be followed shortly by armies of grubs so thick that they had to be swept from the front and back verandahs before the creatures invaded the house itself. To make matters worse these grubs fed on the roots of that all-important grass. It was a tough area to farm, so it is no wonder that Wilma began to resent the horses. Alan, on the other hand, enjoyed every equestrian moment—horses made his soul sing.

On 29 September 1948, Wilma and Alan's first child, Elizabeth Anne Livingstone Young, was born. In October 1948, having just come home from visiting Wilma in hospital, Alan wrote to her: 'My darling, Viv wanted to know if we want Elizabeth reported in the POW Paper. Reported indeed? If she doesn't make the front page, there will be trouble. I am preparing a little article "How I got Elizabeth Anne" for them. There were several things I forgot to tell you. Thought they would do to write about and now I have forgotten what they were.' He ends the letter with the words 'Perhaps I had better do something advising POW how to achieve wedded bliss. What do you think, honey?' Two-and-a-half years later, on 16 June 1951, a second daughter, Christine Judith Livingstone Young, arrived. About eighteen months after the birth of Christine, Wilma was again away with the family, possibly visiting Alf and Jane who now lived with Phyllis in Tasmania. Alan's letters to her (undated) read, in part, 'I fed the hens regularly last night and gave them water also. I hope they will show their gratitude with a greatly increased egg yield. The barricade round the chook house has so far stopped Matilda getting in. I am thatching the stack now. Is it next Thursday you're coming home, honey? I see Wirth's [Circus] is in Dandenong that night. Perhaps you could get a cab to Camberwell and I will come down after milking and go? Leave Christine at Bill's. Methought you might like to do that in any case. I have plenty of company at night abed—fleas. I used some of that dog powder last night, which seemed to annoy them. We may eventually get our sleep-out.[119] I hope the kids are behaving themselves and having a good time. I have still plenty of food. I have had a nice holiday but it would have been better without fleas. They took the place of Christine, to some extent.' From the tone of his letters, Alan was coping with the farm and in a cheerful and witty frame of mind.

Alan continued to make improvements to the property. He was clever at carpentry, joinery and other crafts. Elizabeth recalled, 'Dad got a generator in the dairy. He rigged up the house with a car battery. You'd turn one light on and it was all right, but if you turned two lights on it was only half as bright. Then he rigged up a wire [to the house] from the generator down at the dairy.'

They bought a porcelain bath and hand basin to fix up a 'proper' bathroom in a shed at the back of the house. Soon Alan was connecting a shower to a cold water tank overhead. 'If we had a bath, we had to bring boiling water up from the dairy,' said Elizabeth. 'Then later we got a slow combustion stove that had a hot water service attached, so we had hot running water in the house. But we didn't have a septic tank or anything like that.' These memories were related with love and respect for a family and a home, which, though lacking material comforts, was happy and complete.

On 24 March 1954, Wilma gave birth to twin sons, John and David. There followed another confrontation with Mabel Young, who arrived at Cardinia to look after her son, Alan. '*She* was up here staying,' Wilma said. 'She wouldn't look after the girls, I had to farm them out but she came to look after Alan. And she always brought a maid with her.' Picture the socialite Mabel in that tumbledown house, with a maid in tow, looking after the 'erring son'. Wilma's doctor urged her not to return home yet, so she rested in hospital for three weeks after the arrival of the boys until her mother-in-law got tired of the rural life and quit, along with her maid. 'She didn't want me to breastfeed the boys,' Wilma said, laughing. 'I suppose she thought I looked like an old sow, sitting there with one attached to each side.'

Wilma was to find that having four infants under the age of six was, as she might say in classic understatement, no picnic. 'The year the twins were born it was impossible to get labour,' said Wilma. 'As we made silage in the spring, I had to send the twins to a friend in Dandenong for three weeks while we made it. Alan was quite well, then, and we managed by sharing the work.' Alan enjoyed helping to look after the children, but he knew how hard it was for Wilma, and the worry started to show. One night, Wilma was putting the children to bed when she discovered that Alan had vanished. 'I waited, but he just wasn't there. I said to Elizabeth, "Keep an ear open and, if the others wake up, tell them I'll be back soon."' Eventually she found him alone in the middle of one of the paddocks. This was the first of several similar incidents that began to disturb her.

Alan was experiencing bouts of insomnia. This was understandable to Wilma because both of them occasionally woke up yelling in the night, a result of recurring nightmares. Wilma's dreams often involved the *Vyner Brooke* and her struggles in the water, or sometimes she might find herself locked again waist-deep in muck and kerosene in the pitch blackness of that heaving and tossing Chinese junk at Mentok. Of all her horrifying wartime experiences, these two occasions—when circumstances were out of her control—came back to haunt her. Alan's nightmares were probably also linked to feelings of helplessness.

In her practical way Wilma summed up these phenomena as 'par for the course' or 'perfectly natural under the circumstances'. She knew she would probably go through the rest of her life with them for nocturnal company and she was prepared to put up with them. In her diaries she often made the note 'Slept badly'. Alan's struggle was more debilitating. While the pair shared so much, they were disparate personalities and the contrasts were to become more definite.

When Wilma made another trip to Tasmania in 1956, Alan wrote to her, 'My darling, Everything is going alright here … I have still plenty of food left. Have not made much impression on the first roast yet. The new can-washer is a wonder, guaranteed to wash off all the handles etc. The chooks are not responding to my treatment. They can pump their own water if they are not careful. I will walk up for the mail now. I intend to give this to the milky [the milkman] but it may be too uncertain.' The next paragraph reads: 'Ain't I a big mug. Just went up for the mail, to find it was a holiday. I will give this to the milky, honey. Love, Alan.' Then a postscript reads: 'The truck came about 8pm. I thought I had this in my pocket, but left it inside. Will give it to him in the morning.' Although this letter is in Alan's usual cheerful style, and he was working well around the farm, it contains warnings of absent-mindedness.

When life got too much for Alan, he would mount his horse and ride off. Involvement with the horses relieved his tension, but this often left Wilma to run the entire farm single-handed. The further Alan removed himself from reality, the firmer Wilma planted her feet on solid earth. Elizabeth recalled this period, even though she was so young at the time. She also remembered her mother's ability to take pleasure in little things. When asked for her earliest memory of Wilma, she smiled and replied: 'Maybe her just trying to get everything going, like milking the cows. When the twins were born, trying to cope. How pleased she was when she found someone who would help her with the washing. Simple things, like when we concreted the back door to the laundry and put a rotary hoist in. She used to work at achieving all these little things. She used to worry about Dad getting things done, because he'd never get things done. He got depressed.'

Alan's passion for horses slowly became an obsession. This might have been one of his reactions against internment. He was proud and obstinate. To find himself in a position of submission to the Germans scarred him. His time in solitary confinement was brought about by a refusal to submit to orders. Under the casual eyes of the Italians he was not too unhappy, but he hated the Germans. It made sense that he later chose to devote his life to horses. To find himself in the saddle of such a powerful animal must have been satisfying. To break it to his will, and to have it respond to the touch of his hands and heels must have helped to restore his ego. He chose the largest and most temperamental mount. 'His horse was enormous, it used to tower. Of course he had a lot of small ponies that made his horse look even larger but it was very spirited. I don't think anyone else could have ridden it,' recalled Wilma's cousin Heather James.

Family and friends brought their children to stay for weekends and Alan taught them to ride. 'They'd be sleeping around on mattresses on the floor,' said Elizabeth. 'We kids didn't get to go out very much, socially, at weekends, because we were always riding. You couldn't play tennis and you couldn't play other sports.' Wilma's interpretation of the situation was: 'Alan wanted horses, so Alan had horses!'

Riding was not a favoured pastime for Wilma. There was one memo-rable incident when the twins were only three or four. 'Alan wanted to go right up the top of this hill,' she said. 'He hadn't taken anybody else up there at this stage. Anyway, we took some feed up in the car. We dropped it off, way up in the hills. Then came the long weekend, January. On the Saturday, we set off, all of us on horseback with our food. We each had a haversack on our back and I'd cooked up various things. It was miles away—not far in the car but a terrible long way on a horse, and I hadn't ridden for years. The children were bright and cheerful, and they rode on. Here I am plodding along, so tired … It was pitch dark by now and I'm lying down on top of the horse because I couldn't sit up any longer. The children's horses would whinny and my horse would answer. Anyway, I came to a crossroad, and Alan was there waiting for me to tell me which way to go. Oh God! The chil-dren weren't that big and they'd lit a fire and got that going. When I got to this place, I got off the horse and just couldn't stand up. I col-lapsed on the ground and stayed there, and they had to cope with everything themselves.' This was an early warning of rheumatic and skeletal problems, a result of Wilma's years in the camps.

Apart from offering riding lessons, Alan had little to do with the local community at this time. He attended meetings once a month at the RSL in Pakenham, a little town not far from Cardinia, and made friends with some of the returned servicemen. Wilma was too busy to do anything other than look after the property and the children. She tried to cover this by telling Elizabeth that school fêtes were a waste of time and that, rather than bake a cake for the fête, she would send the equivalent cash to the school. Later events proved that this attitude arose not from a lack of interest but from a lack of time. To the child Elizabeth it seemed like the former.

Once or twice Alan and Wilma attended the dawn service on Anzac Day at Melbourne's Shrine of Remembrance. This was followed by the traditional annual march through the city's streets and reunions with their surviving army friends. Armistice Day, as it was then known, on 11 November was another event they consistently supported. There was again a service at the Shrine, finishing at 11am when a beam of sunlight fell on the Tomb of the Unknown Soldier, the exact time that the armistice ending World War I was signed. The Shrine—a serene building in the style of a classical Greek temple—had been erected in memory of those who had fallen in 'the war to end all wars', yet there they were honouring dead colleagues of World War II. Both of these days were important to Wilma and Alan. When Pakenham RSL started its own dawn service, around 1967, they always attended to remember colleagues who had not made it home.

OPEN HOUSE

The younger ones were unaware of problems within the household but Wilma confided in Elizabeth. 'The other kids were smaller so they didn't really have any insight into the thing. Mum couldn't talk to anybody else and I wasn't supposed to mention it at school.' Mental illness carried a stigma that could reflect on an entire family in any community, let alone in such a tiny settlement. 'It was difficult because people wouldn't do any work for us,' Elizabeth said. 'Dad was always slow paying his bills.'

Wilma had already identified Alan's problem, although there was then no name for it other than 'War Neurosis'. 'I knew exactly what was the matter,' she said. 'I recognised that he was suffering, I knew the danger signals. He wasn't concentrating, not getting on with things. Depression.' But how did Wilma explain this to a ten-year-old child?

'Just like it was,' said Elizabeth with every bit of her mother's practicality. 'Like, he was depressed from the war. I think that was more or less what it was. There were theories back then about depression, which were used to explain it, but nobody knew a lot. Explanations given to me aren't relevant now. People didn't understand and they were searching for reasons. From what I know about depression, it's much more complicated than it was presented to me as a kid.'

From available evidence it would appear that Alan was suffering from a chronic form of post-traumatic stress disorder (PTSD). *The Longman Dictionary of Psychology and Psychiatry* (Goldenson, 1984) defines PTSD as: 'An anxiety disorder produced by an uncommon, extremely stressful event (e.g. assault, rape, military combat, flood, earthquake, death camp, torture, car accident, head trauma), and characterised by (a) re-experiencing the trauma in painful recollections or recurrent dreams or nightmares, (b) diminished responsiveness (emotional anaesthesia or numbing) with disinterest in significant activities and with feelings of detachment and estrangement from others, and (c) such symptoms as exaggerated startle response, disturbed sleep, difficulty in concentrating or remembering, guilt about surviving when others did not, and avoidance of activities that call the traumatic to mind.'

According to MJ Horowitz (inter alia) '… a latency period of months or even years may intervene between the stressful event and the maximum symptomatic response … if symptoms have lasted six months or more, the disorder is considered chronic. Delayed or chronic subtypes are usually more difficult to treat.'

Wilma's wartime experiences did not have the same effect on her. She went through her shock reaction immediately after her return: the torpor; the temporary inability to get her life into gear; the repeated urges to travel long distances to see wartime buddies; sudden unpredictable impulses to walk away when additional stress was applied (this symptom stayed with her throughout life). Many of her friends attested that they had never known her to lose her temper or even to raise her voice. Therefore, to manifest the degree of reaction that she did was, by her standards, a remarkable change in her behavioural patterns. Having released some of her shock, she was able to recover relatively quickly. Her reaction was not PTSD as defined. Apart from the recurring nightmares and the initial brief period of diminished responsiveness, most of the symptoms were not present in Wilma. Likewise her brother, Lance, who had endured the shock of lying helpless on a battlefield for hours, waiting to die alone in no-man's-land after his leg had been twisted behind his head and his face slashed open. 'Lance just kept on living,' Wilma said. 'He never felt sorry for himself, just kept on doing everything that he could do. He got married and had two children, drove a car, worked right up till he was nearly 60. He had a heart attack somewhere in the early '60s, had a pacemaker put in, lived with a pacemaker all those years. He led a full life, did everything he wanted to do.'

Alan's more extreme response to wartime trauma in no way diminishes his strength of character. Put simplistically, different people respond in different ways to the same stimuli and Alan was only one of many thousands of brave men and women who, because their condition remained undiagnosed and was untreated for too long, progressed into psychosis.

Alan's symptoms continued to worsen. Apart from riding, he could not apply himself to anything. The property needed fencing but he would not do it and he would not hire anyone to do it. He could not bear to have horses destroyed when it would have been merciful to do so. He kept old animals until they dropped, feeding them by hand and attending to their every need while neglecting the farm.

The workload increased for Wilma and for the children. She tried as much as possible to make it a game for the young ones, in an effort to disguise the seriousness of their predicament. Together she and the children, in addition to the usual chores, looked after the fattening calves, sent the bull calves to market and even turned their hand to castrating the horses. Because there was no other way to force Alan into action, Wilma found herself cast in the role of nagging wife and she did not like it. She was getting no help from doctors. She would take Alan for a medical consultation but, such was his skill at appearing to be bright and articulate, nobody would listen to her. One of the last straws came when Alan began to keep a shotgun in their bedroom.

By 1959 Wilma knew that she had to get help. She wracked her brains about what to do and eventually wrote to Sir Albert Coates, who had been her Commander-in-Chief in Malaya, outlining the nature of the trouble. 'And I put on the bottom of it, *Please help me!* He wrote back straight away and said to come down to Melbourne, which we did. He took one look at Alan and he knew.' Coates recommended that Alan should be admitted to hospital without delay. 'I can't,' Alan protested,

'I've got the cows!' Coates threw a bleak look at Wilma and rasped in his abrupt way, 'She's done it before, she can do it again. Hospital!'

Alan spent six weeks in Heidelberg Hospital, where he received electric shock treatment. This was standard procedure in those days for many neurological conditions including 'War Neurosis', but it was possibly one of the worst things they could have done to a vital man like Alan Young, because shock treatment sometimes disrupts a person's mental capabilities.

While Alan was in hospital, Wilma took a chance and had a fence built. She also paid outstanding bills. 'Dad got cross with that, I think,' Elizabeth said. 'Anyway she did all that while he was in hospital.' Meanwhile Elizabeth wrote her father a letter. Until then Alan could not remember who or where he was. 'He'd been in there for a while, and suddenly he rang up and it was because of this letter I'd written to him. He suddenly remembered he had a family. He told me later that the letter was the trigger for his remembering.' Alan phoned Wilma and asked, 'What am I doing here?' Wilma told him that she would come down tomorrow to explain and that in the meantime he was not to worry about anything.'

During the period while Alan was an in-patient, Wilma travelled to the city every second day to see him. 'I couldn't go every day, it was rather too much, so I went every second day. One day I was down there and he said, "I've got no money", so I gave him what I had in my bag. When I went there next time it turned out that he'd lent it to one of the other patients and the patient had gone out and got drunk. That's why they weren't allowed to have any money. So he'd been in trouble all round and lost his money as well. I never gave him any money after that.' Fortunately for his condition, Alan never developed a habit of drinking alcohol to excess, although he enjoyed drinking.

Elizabeth's memory of those days was: 'I used to milk the cows, because Dad was in hospital a lot of the time, and I used to get dinner and wash the dishes and things after school. That was when I was in Primary School.' Intense stresses and demands were being placed on the whole family because of Alan's illness.

Elizabeth was bright and attractive with fair hair. She was very boisterous and had a tendency to talk fast, as if she wanted to get it all out before being interrupted. Christine was vivacious, headstrong like Alan, but soft-natured and physically the image of Wilma. Although Alan took pride in all of his family, he doted on Christine and she on him because they had so much in common. Like her father, she was devoted to horses.

The twins were different from each other in both looks and personality. Even at a young age it could be seen that John had inherited much of his father's cleverness with his hands and, like Alan, he had an obstinate streak. David, a born farmer, shared Alan's independence and lived for animals. 'You couldn't have done anything else with David,' Wilma said. 'He had to be a dairy farmer. From the time he was about four he was rounding up cows and calves and knew every animal on the place. If anything happened to them he used to go into the scrub and cry.'

After Alan's discharge the Youngs returned to their routine. Alan was on heavy medication but his symptoms eased. He continued with the riding lessons. At weekends, young people from the Youth Hostels Association (YHA)[120] visited regularly for riding lessons followed by excursions on horseback to local places of interest. The farm had become known as the Whinmere Stud—Alan's choice and a source of irritation for Wilma who refused to regard the place as anything other than a dairy farm. 'The people used to pay to come riding,' Wilma said, ever practical. 'It was a little help, but by the time you bought feed and, if you took into account all your expenses, you probably didn't make anything.'

Two of the people the Youngs met through the YHA, Bob and Jane Elstree, were to become lifelong friends. They recalled that Alan was never hesitant about talking of his war experiences. 'He always approached everything with a sense of humour,' Bob said. 'The Germans gave them jobs to do, and one of Alan's jobs was straightening nails. They were given thousands of nails and he had to straighten them to reuse. And he'd say, "By God, if they've got to use second-hand nails, we're really giving them a hammering!"'

'Alan was a font of knowledge,' Wilma said. 'Much more so than ever I am. The children, if they asked me questions I'd always say, "Go and ask Dad", and he could always give them the answer, and the children got on well with him. They loved him, would do anything for their father—anything, and never say a word against him.'

Alan was in his element hosting the YHA visitors, especially when entertaining city dwellers or visitors from overseas. Having made a study of local history and folklore, he was a fascinating host and guide who held his guests' attention with his stories. They kept coming back for more. This went on for many years, throughout most of the progress of his illness. Alan's imagination was fertile, his intelligence was strong and his public persona was charismatic, but he was only happy when he was riding.

'He was quite abusive towards those people,' Wilma recalled. 'How they ever put up with him I don't know. And if they fell off he blamed them, he didn't blame the horse. It's amazing they didn't pack their trunks and go.' Although it is now known that Alan's abusive outbursts were a part of his condition,[121] this was not known in the early 1960s when Alan's need was at its greatest. His outbursts never took the form of physical violence, either towards his family or anyone else, according to Wilma, who was forever loyal to him. But there always remained a danger that he might harm himself.

Wilma knew that one solution to the farm's dilemma was to try and get rid of some of the stock. 'I got an agent who had known Alan for a long time, and he came out on a Sunday afternoon and got Alan to agree to send some of the cows to the market. We had a Clydesdale stallion too and I didn't want to have that any more, so I got Alan to agree to send that in. The agent told me, "Mrs Young, any hour of the day or night, or any time, if you get Alan to agree to sell anything just send it down and put it in my yards." Anyway, we sold the stock and I took Alan to hospital again next day.'

In 1960 Alan again became an in-patient at Heidelberg for six weeks, followed by six weeks convalescence at Rockingham, a Red Cross hospital for people who needed rehabilitation after undergoing psychiatric treatment. He was not content at Heidelberg but he liked Rockingham and was happy to remain there. 'He made all those stools that you see around,' Wilma said, indicating an attractive set of high bar stools, 'and that cupboard out in the garage. He was wonderful at making things with his hands. He made the harness for the horses—bridles and things, he did a lot of that.' It was during this stint in hospital that Alan's depression was officially diagnosed, along with suicidal tendencies, although of course not as PTSD. The depressions were only apparent to those closest to him. There were two quite different Alans.

He was allowed home at weekends, so the riding school continued more or less uninterrupted although he concentrated on quiet, docile horses for learners. Elizabeth was now in her first year at the Koo Wee Rup High School and old enough to give lessons, so she took over when her father was unavailable. 'I used to take about fifteen out at a time. [I] used to spend the morning getting them accustomed to stop and start and things. In the afternoon I'd take them out for a ride.' Christine, now nine years old, was also co-opted to help. These relentless weekend duties interfered with the children's personal choices, no matter how much they appeared to enjoy them. Whether they were aware of it or not, their father's ill health impacted in many ways on their young lives. Wilma's later public speeches reveal that she knew, and that it worried her.

One weekend Alan brought home a fellow patient. 'He was just a young chap, about twenty-four,' Wilma recalled. 'I don't know what kind of a life he'd had but I don't think he'd ever been in a private home before. Anyway, he came up and some men were painting the house. I asked him to take a cup of tea out to the men, but he wouldn't. He wouldn't leave me; he was with me all the time. I stripped his bed because he was going back that night, and he ran to me and said, "I've got no bed!" He wanted to go back to bed ... He would do anything in the house with me, but not go out and mix with anybody. Alan was out with his horses, of course.'

Not long after bringing his fellow patient home from Rockingham, Alan started inviting children with intellectual disabilities to come to

Cardinia to learn to ride. This became a regular and popular break for these young people (horse riding is now a well recognised beneficial pastime for those with Down syndrome and other intellectual and physical disorders).

To try to ease the financial burden, Wilma attempted to get Alan a Totally and Permanently Incapacitated (TPI) war service pension. 'They wouldn't put him on a TPI,' she said. 'They said that would be the worst thing for him because then he'd feel that he was useless. But that was a ridiculous thing to say. I went to see another one of the doctors. He wasn't sympathetic. They all thought that I was worse than Alan was. I said to him, "How would you like it if your children had to help to castrate the horses?" He just threw his pen across the desk and said, "Oh well …" and signed the papers, and it came through.'

The castration episodes became a source of guilt for Wilma. 'I can castrate a horse,' she said, 'I've done plenty. But the children, it was bad for them. We used to put a mask on the animals with ether and we kept them down on the ground. One of the children would keep the horse under [the anaesthetic] and the children had to hold them so they didn't kick. But, anyway, it wasn't right for the children.' What effect this might have on children who loved horses is a matter for speculation. It is typical of decisions that Wilma was forced to make when Alan was not able to, and she feared that the children were too young to understand.

Wilma's experience of arguing the case in favour of a war veteran's pension was to influence her greatly. 'It's extremely difficult to get the psychiatric cases assessed to be pensionable,' according to Pakenham RSL Pensions Officer, Noel NN Webster.[122] 'It's different if you had your arm or your leg off—you've got a visible thing. But the bloke that you're talking to: it could be you talking to me and I might be quite normal in all appearances and mannerisms. But inside I might be churning around as if I'd swallowed a windmill. A lot of guys are reluctant and loath to admit it. Pride or something. They're not going to say that they're a bit around the bend, or that they drink heavily because of their stressful condition, or they belt up the wife. These things happen and it's terribly tragic.' Wilma insisted that she never experienced any such reactions from Alan. It is clear, from personal letters between them when they were away from each other, that they were in love.

The farmhouse in Wenn Road, Cardinia, soon became a gathering point for people from all walks of life. The hospitality learned by Wilma as a child within the warmth of the Oram family was automatically continued by her. The Youngs invited people to stay and, if anyone needed help, they only had to arrive on the doorstep. Nobody was turned away. The place was full of laughter at Alan's story telling, while Wilma somehow found time to lay on traditional roast lunches of a Sunday for the numerous occupants, guests, boarders and passers-by who must have sometimes caused the tumble-down cottage to groan at its joints. Bearing in mind that the home was basically now three bed-rooms and a sun room, plus the kitchen and sitting room, it must have resembled the hillbilly household of Ma and Pa Kettle when the visitors descended in droves.

Some of the guests were happy to help around the farm and Wilma probably felt that the company was good for Alan, because she encouraged it. The most welcome were those who could engage him in conversation that exercised his imagination. Apart from the horse riding fraternity, many of the young and old alike who came to stay at the house tended to be, at least for the time being, in need of some form of support.

One of the former Youth Hostellers, Jane Pittard, remembered: 'I would have been nineteen, I moved my horse to their place, so I was going down every weekend. I didn't have a driver's licence so Alan or Wilma would pick me up at the railway station. It got to the stage that I got on so well with Chrissie, and then with the family, that I'd begin to stay the night, stay the weekend. Really they just took me into their family.'

David Lording, who taught Elizabeth at Koo Wee Rup High School, got to know the Youngs through school functions. 'I met Wilma, and Alan to a lesser degree, very soon through parent–teacher gatherings. They would always help out whenever there was a school fete. I can still picture Alan coming to the school in a funny old-fashioned cart, with him standing up very high above the ground, pulled by a couple of their horses. They would provide the kids with horse rides. Then they invited us out for dinner and insisted on taking us riding. Alan, I think, regarded horses as being worthier beings than humans. Not that he was anti-social, but he revered horses and I can remember him taking us into the stables and literally introducing us to the horses.'

When Lording's wife, also a school teacher, died in tragic circumstances, he recalled: 'I met Wilma at the local shopping centre. True to form she asked, "How are you getting on? Where are you staying?" and I told her and she said, "What's it like?" and I said, "Pretty awful", and she said, "Would you like to come and stay with us?" So I was with them for probably six months.'

David Lording came into the Young household in a state of severe depression. 'Wilma was just incredibly calm, encouraging,' he said. 'At one stage I thought I might play a bit of golf, that it might help me. I remember she got out her golf clubs. I hadn't played for many years and she showed me how she did it. I don't think she was a terribly good golfer, but, you know, she didn't stop at anything. If she thought it would help me, she would do it. In the nicest way she'd always ask how I was getting on, how was school. I really owe her a lot.'

Lording was also one of the first interviewees to remark on a trait of Wilma's, a leftover from the prison camps that stayed with her. 'We always used to have porridge in the morning,' he said. 'That was a tradition. It was *expected* that you'd eat it.' If you were with Wilma, and food was in front of you, she demanded that you eat every morsel. Even the smallest leftover crumb or lump of gristle would bring the steely gaze and the pointed comment: 'Aren't you going to eat that?'

Of Alan, Lording said: 'It would be difficult for Wilma often in the morning to get him going. He seemed to lapse into periods of relative inactivity. By the time I got there, he didn't do very much on [the farm]. He had an absolute battery of pills to take. And of course she was the one who had to keep him up to the mark. Some nights you couldn't get a word out of him. A wretched condition [PTSD].'

Lording remarked that he never heard Wilma complain. 'Occasionally she'd put on a slightly wry face and say that looking after Alan was a bit of a chore,' he recalled. 'And she'd say, "Oh jolly Alan, going off to take the horses for a ride when we had the hay to cut." But no real complaints—she was very caring towards him.'

The ex-POW 'girls' would also visit, either alone or with husbands and children. They always kept in contact with each other and shared close physical contact at social gatherings, touching an arm or the hand, while they might maintain a thin invisible barrier of personal space when interacting with others. In the early sixties they communicated mainly by letter or card, but, as time passed and telephones became affordable, there were regular interstate calls. In times of trouble the group would close ranks and become 'one'. Each of Wilma's children remarked that with the 'girls' they felt that they shared an extended family of aunts and cousins.

On 29 November 1960, Wilma was invited to become an Associate (i.e. female) Member of the Sembawang Association. This is an RAAF group involving the 1st, 8th, 21st and 453rd Squadrons, which served in Singapore. They hold an annual reunion and sponsor a tree in the grounds of the Melbourne Shrine of Remembrance. Wilma was the first Army nurse to be given this honour, in recognition of her services to nursing and other organisations.

WELFARE WORK

By the time Elizabeth was in her third year at the high school, Wilma had developed into a formidable networker. A life of public service had begun.

In October 1962 she was appointed as Superintendent of the Red Cross, Pakenham Service Company. The District Commandant was a Mrs Flemming, whose position put her one step above Wilma. As new presidents often do, Wilma got a bright idea, which she put to Mrs Flemming. This was to introduce First Aid classes for children into the local schools. When she heard about it, Mrs Flemming agreed that the idea was sound. Needing no further encouragement, Wilma made a few phone calls and soon the project was under way. 'Of course, I didn't know that it had to go to Headquarters. You had to speak to the Minister for Education and see if it could fit into the school curriculum …' Here Wilma gave a wicked smile which indicated that it would not have made a scrap of difference even if she had known. 'So we got going on this. We'd found people who could do the lecturing for us. Anyway, Mrs Edwards McKay from Headquarters, the Head of the Red Cross in Melbourne, was furious! She demanded that we go down and see her. She was absolutely livid about this because she hadn't been consulted, but it was fait accompli by that time and she couldn't stop it. I found out that she herself had tried to start First Aid classes at St Catherine's before the war and it had fallen flat. Not a success. And ours was taking off like a house on fire!

All the schools around us were doing it and the kids were all interested.'

Of Wilma's other duties, Willy Kraan, a local farmer's wife who became a Red Cross member, recorded: 'Some of the responsibilities of the Branch were to assist with the Mobile Blood Bank, organise transport for people in need of medical attention, maintain a supply of medical aids for the community and, with the assistance of John McMillan, the local Ambulance Officer, she ran First Aid classes for adults.'[123]

Wilma was appointed President of the Koo Wee Rup High School Ladies' Auxiliary in 1963, an office she held for some years. She was also a member of the Parents' & Citizens' Association and did her duty in the school canteen and at working bees. Never one to do things by halves, part-way through her first presidential year she hosted a group of local parents at a meeting at her home and formed the Cardinia Auxiliary. This was the forerunner of several others formed in outlying areas served by that school '… and this made a great impact on the amount of funds raised for amenities and equipment for the school.'[124]

Willy Kraan recalled Wilma's pressuring with amusement. 'When our eldest boy was going to the Koo Wee Rup High School, she got me to join [the Ladies' Auxiliary]. They had some functions and lunch. Our son was not going to the school yet, and she said, "You must come because [the son] is going to Koo Wee Rup High School next year and Mr Hooper,[125] is coming to my Tupperware party." She was always able to draw everyone in.'

Wilma's pension in the mid-1960s amounted to only £19, three shillings and seven pence per fortnight (about $40). Alan's would presumably have been a similar amount. The family was battling to stay afloat, yet few people outside the family would have known. In 1964, Wilma approached the Assessment Appeal Tribunal regarding her service pension, but the request was disallowed and the present assessment of incapacity 'from disabilities accepted under the *Repatriation Act* as being due to war service' was to continue. This second brush with the Pensions Board probably laid the foundation of a future path that she was to follow.

Wilma remained President of the Women's Auxiliary and, in addition to fund raising, she identified a hitherto untapped talent for public speaking. Wilma might have seemed the least likely person to become an orator, especially in the presence of her eloquent husband, but the ability was there and she started to nourish it.

At the 10th Annual Report of the Henri Dunant Region of the Red Cross[126], she gave a well-researched address on the history of the Regional Divisions. She commended an increase in the training of young people, acknowledging the importance of preparing a new generation to take over from the present leaders. (Wilma never clung to a position if she felt that someone else could fill it better, and she made a point of training her own replacements.) She noted that it had been possible for her, during the year, to attend most of the regional meetings and indicated that she wanted the invitations to keep coming. Significantly, she especially mentioned those members of the Red Cross who had packed and sent parcels to wartime hospitals. Having been on the receiving end in 1941–42 she was in a position to judge the value of that area of Red Cross work:

'When one's whole conscious effort is given over to the smooth and efficient running of a small part of a large hospital, to which war casualties are being admitted in great numbers (at the time to which I refer we were fighting a retreating war) one gives little or no thought to the mechanics of how or why the Red Cross goods and services are available. There is only an awareness and a deep feeling of gratitude that all these things are at our disposal.'

She lambasted the Japanese for not distributing Red Cross parcels but mentioned the internees' appreciation of the one plundered package that they did receive: 'We were all greatly uplifted by this and, although our portion was small, the boost to our morale was great.'

Wilma could present a unique point of view. Although she never described anything in detail, she knew that the glimpses she offered of her experiences were an advantage in attracting support for worthy causes and she never hesitated to use them.

In 1965 Elizabeth qualified for a place at Melbourne University to study medicine. Wilma was still President of the Ladies Auxiliary, but in the same year she took a position on the School Advisory Board and remained in that office until 1971. She became familiar with the techniques of writing submissions to politicians and bureaucrats, for the purpose of getting financial grants for the school. This was vital knowledge, given the additional duties that she would shortly assume. During her term on this Advisory Board, she was actively fund-raising for improvements to the school, including the building of classrooms, special metalworking and woodworking rooms, a gymnasium, the canteen, tennis courts, teaching aids and many other items. She was a driving force. David Lording summed it up: 'Wilma had a lot to worry about but she always gave herself unstintingly to everything that she thought was important: obviously the kids, the community, the school were supremely important.'

When Wilma helped to establish a branch of the Red Cross at the nearby township of Officer it proved timely, for a severe bushfire swept through the area at the beginning of 1968. 'We'd had a bit of instruction on what to do in the case of bushfires, so we were able to do what we had to do,' shrugged Wilma, dismissing her role. The new branch set up its emergency headquarters in the local hall. The women sent food out to the firefighters. Those men who had to come in for treatment were put on mattresses on the floor while the women made a note of their personal details (in case of death) washed their feet for them and gave them clean pairs of socks. 'They were suffering from exhaustion and smoke inhalation,' Wilma said. 'They needed rest from fighting the fires.'

A crew of Red Cross people was sent up from Melbourne to help. 'A Mrs Fairley was in charge of that sort of thing,' Wilma explained mischievously and revealed that Mrs Fairley was the sister of the redoubtable Mrs Edwards McKay, with whom she had already crossed swords. 'They hated the sight of each other,' she chuckled. 'Mrs Fairley was a step down from Mrs Edwards McKay, and she used to tell Mrs Fairley off.' Wilma relished the memory. 'Mrs Fairley came up but *we* coped with that bushfire.' It is doubtful that the presence of Mrs Fairley was necessary, because of, as Willy Kraan recalled, 'Wilma's background in nursing and working under pressure … She organised the relief for the people who got burned out. She worked for several days.'

While she was bringing up the children, although she kept her membership of the RSL, Wilma could rarely go to its meetings. The RSL in Victoria differs from the same organisation in some other Australian states, where clubs have become huge edifices along the lines of a Las Vegas casino with flashing lights, gambling machines, crowded bars and bistros. Many of the Victorian Clubs are small and unlicensed, offering traditional RSL services in the form of personal support for members and their families. In 2001, the RSL at Pakenham was still one of those clubs and it remained that way by choice. It is situated in a residential street in a building that looks like a private house from the outside. It is used mainly for meetings of the various sections of the sub-branch, as well as a cozy place for small social gatherings. There are tea and coffee facilities, a few tables and chairs, and the main club room is largely occupied by a full-sized billiards table.

On 9 February 1968 Wilma decided to go with Alan to an ordinary general meeting. Members were asked to nominate office bearers for the coming year and, to her surprise, Wilma was nominated for President. Her own account of this unique event is casual: 'Somebody nominated me and they all voted for me,' she shrugged. 'I was President. We didn't think anything of it. None of the men seemed to want to be President, and it was just as simple as that.'

She had no idea that she was making history. At no time anywhere in Australia, within that huge and powerful organisation, had a woman ever held the office of President. The Returned and Services League was male orientated. Servicewomen were granted membership but the role of women within the RSL was confined mostly to work on the sidelines, usually through a Women's Auxiliary. For a woman during that pre-feminist period to hold any office, let alone that of President, was unheard of. The little town of Pakenham was nothing if not egalitarian—ahead of its time.

'Eventually it got into the local paper, a couple of months later,' Wilma said. 'And still nobody took any notice'—until early one morning when Chrissie came rushing into the house: '"Mum, there's somebody here from the *Sun!*" I said, "Well don't let them in." But of course they were already in—very pushy, aren't they—and they wanted a photograph. I said, "I have to get dressed." So I went in and put a dress on and they took a photo, and they put that in the *Sun.* And they wrote, "Mrs Wise—Head of the RSL" or something like that.'

At the time of Wilma's election, the Pakenham RSL did not have a Women's Auxiliary, yet its membership was 90–100 people, which was not a bad size for the district. 'I arranged for the woman who was head of Auxiliaries to visit, and I invited as many of the women around as would come. We had a good meeting and, there and then on the spot, we started a Ladies Auxiliary. You can't do anything without a Ladies Auxiliary.' Wilma did not know the meaning of the word 'no'. 'It's still going and very strong,' Rob Fox, President of Pakenham RSL, confirmed. 'The women are a great help to us and we work in very well with them. Most of our wives who are still living, they're all on it. It's great. When we have barbecues we mix in together, and the men come along and help out. We get out at the sink and wash up.'

Changes that Wilma instigated included making the place more comfortable for maturing bodies. 'The RSL was there with its cement floor and cold austerity. I said "I think we should put a carpet on the floor." Well, uproar!' Alan would accompany Wilma to board meetings. (It amused him to call himself her Prince Philip.) On this occasion he interjected, calling out, 'Don't let her spend your money!' to which Wilma promptly replied, 'If you don't keep quiet I'll spend yours!' She took no notice of objections and got a friend in Melbourne to come and deal with the carpet dilemma. 'I got a cheap quote,' she revealed, 'so they came and laid the carpet. Eventually we paid for it and they soon realised it was good. I said, "We're all getting old, and it's cold in here."' As usual, she was not easy to contradict. However, Wilma was not destined to concentrate merely on new carpets and Women's Auxiliaries, far from it. This association with the Pakenham RSL marked the beginning of her life-long involvement in welfare work on behalf of war veterans and their families.

A few months after taking office, Wilma put it to the board that the RSL should run an annual picnic for war veterans who were confined to psychiatric hospitals. Personal experience had shown a need for the inmates and their carers to take some respite, to get away from the institution and enjoy good old-fashioned country hospitality. Initially the Pakenham RSL hosted these days, but soon the event grew so popular that it was taken over by the District—a number of sub-branches combining for the purpose.

Soon to assume the main responsibility of organising those picnic days was Wilma's assistant, a fellow dairy farmer's wife named Isabel Boraston. She was a perky and practical little woman, originally from the north of England. She assured Wilma that she would be happy to help and suggested, following the success of the first picnic, that they might have the gathering at the Boraston's farm because it was safer than a public park.

'The hospitals would send us a list about six months before,' Isabel recalled. 'If some of them had been to one picnic, they gave the others a chance to come next time.' The age range of the patients was wide. 'Some were from the First World War,' Mrs Boraston said, 'and some, it was really very sad because they were quite young, they were from the Vietnam War. They'd have a game of cricket, and then I'd organise a lucky draw. They'd have a ticket and we'd give them a box of something at the end. They loved it. And I think the people that helped loved it too.'

Between sixty and eighty ex-servicemen and women took part. These days were also beneficial for Alan, who was continuing to spend time in hospital. His skills were called upon to entertain the visitors and he enjoyed it. 'He'd take people for a ride in the cart with the old horse. Some of the patients didn't want to go home when the time came,' Isabel said. Eventually, because all of the psychiatric hospitals wanted to take part in the day, the various institutions alternated year by year. 'They didn't say very much,' Isabel observed, 'but they'd sit there. One nurse told me, "You might not think that they're enjoying themselves, but they talk about it among themselves for days afterwards." And we'd have music, the old army music.'

Under the sponsorship of the 44th District Board of the RSL, and with the co-operation of many members and their wives, these gatherings continued annually until 21 February 1993, when they had to cease.[127] The reason was not that the picnics became redundant but because the government closed the institutions and it was no longer possible to organise such occasions. They were usually held on the third Sunday in February and Isabel was proud to state that they only missed one year, 1983, when another bushfire swept through the district.

The close of 1968 was marked, on New Year's Eve, by the death of Jane Oram, the mother who had mourned so deeply for her missing daughter and whose life began again when she found that Wilma was alive. It was the end of an era.

Around this time, along came another visitor who was to have a lasting effect on the Youngs. He was Alfred John Davis, known always as John Davis. Davis told Wilma that his mother, the daughter of an English peer, met his father, an Australian soldier, during World War I. The Aussie promptly got the lady pregnant and the family disowned her. Davis, the result of this *liaison dangereuse*, was to mature into a very interesting character.

His career path reveals a man who did not quite know where he was heading. During World War II Davis served in the RAAF in New Guinea as a navigator and meteorological officer. Having been brought up in the Anglican faith, he took instruction and converted to Catholicism. Following the war, he worked for some years within the Department of Civil Aviation. After doing a postgraduate course at Melbourne University in 1952, he emerged with a Bachelor of Education degree. By 1960 he was assistant headmaster at the Jewish college, Mount Scopus—an unusual position for a Catholic. He became fascinated by Judaism, particularly its history, and followed his time there by touring Lebanon, Jordan and Palestine. He then spent barely a year as a geography teacher at the University High School before coming to Koo Wee Rup High. 'He had a falling out with his local priest, packed his mother up and finally settled in a house in Pakenham,' said Wilma of his sudden arrival in the area. By that time he had published several books, all on a geographical theme, his latest in 1969 under the title *In This Our Necessity.* As a member of the School Board, Wilma met the new schoolmaster and immediately took to him. '[Headmaster] Fred Hooper said to him that his class of boys were no-hopers and all he had to do was to entertain them. Well, he was able to *teach* those boys and they all adored him! Nobody else could, nobody held their interest like he did.'

Wilma was still the President of Pakenham RSL and she persuaded Davis to become a member. 'He used to come out every weekend, then, to see us,' she said. His company was readily embraced by Alan. The two men responded to each other through conversation and Wilma's potent homemade wine.

'We decided we'd make rhubarb wine,' Jane Pittard recalled. 'I remember you only stirred it once a day. I don't know how long I had it sitting there, brewing away. Then we bottled it. It was like sparkling pink champagne and it had a real kick to it!'

'He and Alan used to have wonderful discussions,' Wilma recalled, 'and John Davis was *always right*. But he and Alan would disagree—so Alan would go off to the encyclopedia, come back and point out to John Davis where he was wrong.' Jane Pittard recalled those times: 'We'd have Sunday lunches and Wilma would put on this enormous meal, and we'd have the sun room all decked out and a lovely long table, and table cloth and those lovely big, warm, family, huge lunches. That's what she did for us every Sunday.'

Davis felt that the twins, now teenagers, were not getting the right sort of education at Koo Wee Rup. This might have been because he himself did not get on with the headmaster but, when the restless Davis transferred to Mentone Grammar School, he recommended that the twins would do much better there under his guidance. David Young took advantage of the opportunity and Davis drove him to and from school. It is safe to confirm, however, that David's true interests lay in the farm and that both boys preferred the open spaces of Cardinia to the confining walls of any Grammar School. If there were dreams of academia, they might have been Wilma's rather than the boys'.

Academic achievement for the Young family lay in the hands of the daughters. Elizabeth was already well into medical studies and was living away from home, at Janet Clarke Hall in Melbourne University. Meanwhile, Christine had finally made up her mind that she wanted to study for an arts degree. She won a place at La Trobe University. She boarded with a family at Bundoora, about two miles from the campus. 'Public transport was poor during the day and non-existent at night,' wrote Alan. Chrissie often had to go to the library at night and this lack of transport was a repeated problem. She decided to get herself a motorcycle. 'I was against this,' declared Alan, 'I know how vulnerable the rider is.'[128] Chrissie was insistent and she got the bike anyway.

On the night of 20 September 1969 Chrissie decided to ride home to Cardinia to be with her favourite foal on its first birthday, an impulse that any horse lover can understand. 'She left Bundoora for her home,' Alan wrote. 'She travelled south on Greensborough Road. At about the same time a Mr JVH[129] left the Old England Hotel, Heidelberg, where he had been drinking beer for several hours.' Subsequent enquiries revealed that JVH suddenly made a right-hand turn in front of the approaching motorcycle, without giving a signal. Christine was struck by the car and her body thrown into the air, then she was struck again, this time by a vehicle that was following JVH's car. Death was instantaneous. JVH left the scene, returning one-and-a-half hours later, on foot, to 'report' the accident to the attending police. It is possible that he was dazzled by the lights of a car that was following Chrissie, but there is no question that the man was drunk. Even three hours after the fatality, when he was eventually tested, JVH still had a blood alcohol level of 0.20.

Someone telephoned Elizabeth, who rushed to join the family. 'When I got home it was about three o'clock in the morning,' she said. 'Everyone was sitting there in front of the fire. They didn't really do anything. Even after the funeral they just sat in front of the fire. A few people came to visit, and then all the people came to the funeral. We had about 100 cars.' Chrissie was buried at the Pakenham cemetery. From that time until shortly before her death Wilma had a strong prejudice against the riding of motorcycles.

The duty of sorting everything out fell to Elizabeth because there was no-one else to do it. The boys, at fifteen, were too young to cope, even if they had known what to do. It is clear from Alan and Wilma's lack of reaction that they were deeply traumatised. Both had simultaneously and instinctively withdrawn into that state of limbo, perfected when they were prisoners of war, which had helped to protect them from pain during their years of internment. They remained in limbo until after the funeral, and Wilma never did reveal the depth of her despair to the rest of the family. She could not. She knew she must hold herself together for the sake of the children, because she also knew that this might be the brutal thrust that would tip Alan over the edge.

After the death there was silence from the authorities. Wilma attempted to confirm the date of the inquest but was given no information. Eventually, a member of the local police, one of her many influential friends, made enquiries for her and found out. Alan was horrified when the Magistrate found Christine's death to be 'death by misadventure'. He was tortured by the belief that the authorities were prejudiced against Chrissie because she was young, a university student, and that she had been licensed for only a few months.

'I got speaking to a man that worked in the courts,' Wilma said. 'He put pressure on and we got a committal hearing, out at the Ivanhoe Town Hall.' The actual findings of the court were meticulously recorded by Alan: not guilty on all counts, except for a $40 fine for driving in excess of 0.05 alcohol, a fine of $50 for careless driving, plus loss of his driving licence for six months.

Following the hearing a stunned Alan walked out of the room. 'I went out too,' Wilma said, 'One of the policemen came out and said that he'd look after him, it so devastated Alan. The fact that Chrissie was dead, that was bad enough, but for the man to get off with nothing after he was point two, it was just more than ...' Her voice trailed away, lost for words. Later she continued: 'Alan sat and wrote and wrote. Then he wrote a short story[128] for Veterans' Affairs and that got Second Prize. I don't think I've ever had a copy, I never read it. That consumed Alan's life.' He involved himself with the Victorian Temperance Alliance, the Victorian Safe Driving Association. He wrote to the press, to the Premier's Department, to relevant members of parliament, to the Chief Secretary's Office and to the Road Safety Committee. He wrote to television stations, in particular the program 'Four Corners', to judges, to lawyers, and to the Leader of the Opposition.

In his account, he wrote: 'I thought to take civil action against JVH but found my beautiful and talented daughter was worth nothing at all in the eyes of the law. I could sue for the value of the motorcycle and her clothing, but here ran into another problem. JVH's insurance would not cover him because he was under the influence.' It was senseless to him that the Court could find the man not guilty of driving under the influence of alcohol, while the driver's insurance company refused to cover him because he was under the influence of alcohol. The combination of Wilma's lobbying of politicians and Alan's letter writing did help to bring some improvements to the drink-driving laws.

One of the teachers at the Koo Wee Rup High suggested that an essay competition might make local students more aware of the dangers of drink-driving. Alan donated the first prize. This led Wilma and Alan to inaugurate the Christine Young Memorial Scholarship, awarded annually to a Koo Wee Rup student in either Years 10, 11 or 12 in memory of Christine. The prize was given for the best essay on the subject of drink-driving and was still in existence in 2001.

Wilma was afraid to leave Alan unsupervised. 'He spent a lot of time sitting in the garage, sewing harnesses,' she said. 'He was all right while he was doing that.' Her own reaction to the tragedy was to throw herself into ever more and more work. Occasionally Alan would disappear with the car, just when Wilma needed it to go to a meeting, and sometimes with amusing consequences. Neighbour and helper Janet Chandler recalled one such occasion. 'I think she was supposed to be speaking— anyway, she was all dressed up and ready to go. No vehicle! We had a young Clydesdale harnessed to the cart. It was not a proper cart, just the old carrier, and it had some chunks of wood in the back. Wilma suggested that perhaps we could drive in that. I said, "Yes, okay ..." We got half a kilometre and the horse balked and didn't want to go. I gave it a bit of a tap: "C'mon, Go!" Well, it bucked and took off, bucking up the road! The harness broke and we were losing the cart. And, as we're jolting up the road, here's Wilma bouncing around in the back with the wood. I stopped the cart, then I had to take the horse back to the house, then Alan arrived. We really didn't know whether to laugh or cry.'

After the amount of lobbying that Wilma had found herself doing in recent years, it was inevitable that she would become involved in politics. She joined the Koo Wee Rup Liberals. And, when the West Gippsland Women's Section of the Liberal Party was formed, Wilma became its first President. From then on much of her time was occupied by Liberal Party business.

Wilma's Anzac Day speech of 1971, delivered at Koo Wee Rup High, marked the beginning of a campaign for peaceful international coexistence that would typify her public addresses. It was also a strong plea for understanding of war-damaged veterans.

'Whatever you think about war and the issues involved today, do not condemn your own dead fathers and grandfathers, do not call our maimed and wounded men and women fools. Remember in sympathy and understand their motives and their sacrifices. Work with all your might to spread goodwill, understanding and appreciation among all the people of this little, vulnerable and lonely world, irrespective of race, colour and belief, so that never again will young men and women have to sacrifice themselves to preserve their way of life against the threat of those who would destroy it.'

These sentiments expressed in public did not always echo her inner feelings. She found it hard to come to terms with the post-war rise of Japan and its people to world power. In 2000 David Lording said of Wilma, 'I would describe her in principle as a wonderful role model for Christians—but there is no forgiveness towards the Japanese and she makes no secret of it. She is totally lacking in hypocrisy, she said that she can never forgive them for what they did to her and millions of others.' Remarks that she made in private confirm this. She could not forget the Japanese soldier who spat his venom on the railway station at Loebok Linggau: 'You might have won the war, but we'll get Australia anyway!'

If what she said in public sometimes did not accord with her private feelings, it was not hypocrisy but an admission to herself that her personal beliefs might be out of alignment with a modern world. In her interview publicising the film *Paradise Road*, she came close to revealing herself. The interviewer asked: 'What do you hope young people in particular will learn from seeing a movie like *Paradise Road*?'

'I hope they get an appreciation of what war does to people, the brutality that it brings out,' Wilma replied. 'Are all Japs as brutal as we found them to be? That's the point—I don't know that they are. They could be, but then we've got to bring it out and find out whether they are as brutal as they were to us. The present Japanese surely aren't as brutal as that? One would hope not, but one can't be sure.'

Usually she kept such thoughts to herself while encouraging young people to learn to live in peace. Conscious of her privilege as a spokesperson for peace, she knew that the messages themselves were more important than any leftover resentment that she might secretly feel.

In 1971 Wilma was also campaigning to open special centres in rural areas for assessment and treatment of alcoholics and drug addicts. Far ahead of its time, this campaign was in accordance with the work she was doing with war veterans, so many of whom were affected by drugs and alcohol. The Minister for Health, John Rossiter, pointed out to her that there was already an Act in existence: *The Alcoholics and Drug Dependent Persons Act* of 1968.

In a letter dated 11 October 1971, Wilma replied to the State President of the Liberal Party of Australia: 'I have your letter of 28 September and a copy of Mr Rossiter's letter of 24 September, to you. It is gratifying to note that an Act has been drafted, but I find that the Minister's attitude is quite unsatisfactory in view of the loss of time, money and effort and human personality with respect to the government effort expended on meeting this loss. The effort at present made by Mr Rossiter's Department is insignificant to the point of being practically contemptible. The ubiquitous appeal to a lack of funds is so patently a matter of cloaking indifference as to be ludicrous. This indifference on the part of Mr Rossiter is made patently manifest by his final paragraph.[130] I am abundantly dissatisfied by the attitude of the Minister and the Liberal Party in this matter and if this attitude is to be protracted from budget to budget, must seek other and more sympathetic means to press it.' Wilma was not afraid to fight the Liberals, or anyone else, if she believed in the cause.

The variety of projects with which she concerned herself seemed limitless. One day she would deal with a Minister of State and the next with a cake stall and, at the time of dealing with it, the matter would receive her undivided attention. 'Wilma was always interested,' said David Lording. 'Even if you'd told her that you'd gone to the shop to buy a packet of biscuits, she would give you as much attention as if you were telling her a fascinating story.'

Wilma retired from the presidency of Pakenham RSL in February 1972. 'She was a fantastic President, as she does with all things,' said NN Webster, who was to support Wilma in her future work. 'Her magnetism and her leadership would induce a very strong following.' Far from being the end of a phase in her life, this marked the beginning of some of the most important work that she would undertake. At the same meeting during which she relinquished the presidency, she was nominated and appointed as the sub-branch's Welfare Officer.

At RSL sub-branches, Welfare Officers are the organisation's unsung heroes. They are responsible for effecting the third Aim and Objective of the RSL: 'to provide for the sick and wounded and needy among those who have served and their dependents including pensions, medical attention, homes and suitable employment.' Their work is often voluntary and, depending on how much they become involved, it can be almost full-time. From this point on Wilma was on call virtually twenty-four hours a day. Cases were diverse. She might obtain a pension for a deserted wife who had been left by her veteran husband with six children to support. An early case involved a veteran with a wife and four children who was unable to sell his farm because, at the time, an airport was in planning to be built at Cardinia and nobody would risk buying there. The veteran had been involved in a farm accident, which left him with multiple injuries, and he could no longer work. The farmhouse had two bedrooms and their four children were sharing one of these.

For such needy people, Wilma might assist the man to apply for an increase in his Service Pension, she might also find a way to obtain labour to keep the farm operating while the man remained incapacitated. Such labour would be paid for out of various welfare funds or government grants, or a combination of both, or workers might volunteer their services. It was up to the Welfare Officer to sort through the alternatives and argue the case with the government body that is currently known as the Department of Veterans' Affairs.

Much of Wilma's work involved helping people to fill in application forms. In the last mentioned case, the farmer would probably want to apply for a Disability Pension and medical treatment. In 2001 this involved filling in a twelve-page document which included supplying full and accurate details of service in the military forces: unit, branch, countries in which the applicant served and all the applicable dates. There were questions relating to whether on not the applicant ever served under another name, or in another service. There were separate sections for mariners. These forms were as complicated and confusing as only bureaucrats can devise. Often the applicants were ill, injured and frequently suffering from the various effects of PTSD. They needed help to fill in those documents, even before they could hope to get any practical help.

Wilma attended the RSL Club Rooms on a certain day of the week, but she would also have people come to the house, or she might drive to their house. Her telephone rang constantly. Sometimes the call might be a cry for help from a spouse whose partner had come home drunk and was breaking up the house or abusing the family. Sometimes a spouse might have disappeared and a search party needed to be sent out.

Another document was the 'Lifestyle Questionnaire'. In this, apart from the usual personal details, were questions regarding inter-relationships: 'You are often tense and irritable but still get on with some people fairly well.' 'You are withdrawn and find it difficult to get on with people.' 'Does your medication affect your family life?' 'Do your disabilities affect your sexual feelings or abilities?' Many applicants might find these questions intrusive, especially if a spouse was present. Additional questions related to mobility: 'Do you have any problems walking?'; recreation: 'Are there any activities you have given up because of your disabilities?'; domestic activities: 'Can you do the washing up, house cleaning, wash the car, sewing, heavy gardening etc.?' There were questions relating to alcohol consumption and to whether or not a person had ever been a smoker.

Wilma would carefully guide the distressed applicant through these forms because they were vital in assessing whether or not the applicant's condition was due to war service. It was imperative to prove beyond reasonable doubt that the condition was caused by war service, otherwise the Department would disallow the application and months would pass before a review of the case could be scheduled.

Wilma helped ex-servicemen and their dependents in all areas of welfare, repatriation, pensions and appeals. She assisted with legacies and legatees. She dealt with war widows and prisoners of war. Some of the cases were amusing: 'I had one man who'd been to the First and Second World Wars,' she said. 'He was about 70 and he had six children (of school age). The wife had gone. He rang and said the fridge had broken down, and he wanted a new one. I was making arrangements to get a good second-hand fridge. Then he rang and said, "I've bought a new one." Which, of course, we had to help him pay for!'

Wilma occupied the position of Welfare Officer from 1972 until the day she died. She helped literally thousands of people, including many of her closest friends, the POW nurses. 'That started happening to me when I was President,' she said. 'People suddenly became aware of the RSL, so they would come to me with their problems. I even had a letter from New Zealand, asking me to start a religious sect! Cranks!' Serious again, she said: 'I didn't know much about how you got help or any-thing myself, but you gradually learn as you go along.'

An undated note in Wilma's handwriting, to be included at some future time in a speech, crystalises her personal feelings and provides a motive for her dedicated involvement in pensions and welfare: 'The wives and families needed help in handling the emotional dysfunction from which their husbands and fathers were suffering due to war service.' Wilma's own background, as the wife of a traumatised war veteran with children, inspired her to help other similar families. Meanwhile her personal life somehow continued, even though she was still taking on extra duties. In 1972 she returned to Murtoa, her hometown, which was cele-brating its centenary, to be guest speaker at their Anzac Day service.

Around this time, Jane Pittard moved into the Young house. 'Alan was often unable to do all the bits and pieces. I was just helping. There were times when he was pretty down, so I moved in, lived with them.' Jane lived there about nine months and her presence probably assisted in some ways to fill the gap left by the death of Christine. She was of a similar age and she doted on horses.

'Alan was ill [this particular day], and Wilma and I decided we'd bet-ter feed hay to the cattle. Alan always put the horse in harness, and the one we were using at the time was young. He hadn't been broken in for very long. It was a very hot summer day, and no feed. Another drought. So we piled all this hay on the back of this dray. Wilma's there in this big sun hat. I had the horse *Gee-offing* and, as his blinkers came into view of Wilma in this big straw hat, he bolted. Took off like a rocket! He came to the corner of the yard and did a U-turn, but the cart didn't. He broke the harness and the chains, and the cart tipped over. Hay went every-where and I went everywhere, and Alan was furious with us. We were only doing it to help. But that was Wilma: she decided *we* would do it.'

While Jane was staying there, Wilma revealed a little of her back-ground to the young woman. 'She gave me the book, *White Coolies,* to read. I was absolutely horrified … Then I met Vivian and a lot of the girls over the years. It was made very light of. Just that one day, she came and said: "I've got a book for you to read."'

SPEECHES AND REUNIONS

During April 1977 the television show 'This Is Your Life' was to be dedicated to Vivian Bullwinkel. For Wilma this involved a trip to Sydney, where John Davis was undertaking instruction for the priesthood. Typical of his vacillation, Davis had allowed his Catholicism to lapse. Following the move to Pakenham, he attended the Anglican Church with the Youngs and other friends. 'Then Mrs Davis [his mother] was in hospital and this priest went to see her,' said Wilma, 'and this priest got onto John. And in a few weeks John decided he was going to be a priest.' From lapsed Catholic to ordained priest was one of many giant leaps in the life of A. John Davis.

Although the show demanded that she keep the reason for her trip a secret, she knew that Davis would be hurt if she did not let him know that she was coming. 'They took us to stay in this hotel, all of us. I wrote to John. Well, I got off the plane and there he was. He'd skipped his class.' This expedition was planned to be a touching reunion between the various POW nurses and Vivian. Among the guests, apart from Wilma, were Jean Ashton, Nesta James, Betty Jeffrey, Veronica Clancy, Elizabeth Simons, Joyce Tweddell, Mickey Syer and Sylvia Muir. Also there was Ken Brown who had come to rescue them at Loebok Linggau, Dr Harry Windsor, who had flown in with the rescue team, and Dame Margot Turner who had been, as she put it herself, 'one of the Pommy nurses'.

Wilma was in an awkward position. She tried to split her time between this important reunion—one that coincided with the 75th Anniversary of the AANS—and appeasing the over-enthusiastic John Davis. Davis, who remained oblivious to Wilma's dilemma, thought he was giving her a good time. 'He dragged me all around Sydney— about three days—and he didn't go to his lectures. I didn't need it because there were cars provided [by the TV station]. He just felt in the way of an anchor, I suppose.' As usual, the feelings and needs of others rated above her own.

When his mother eventually died, Davis was left in confusion. Much of his life had been spent looking out for her welfare. Now that she was gone, with her went a large part of his incentive. Davis had already begun studying for the priesthood prior to Mrs Davis's death and, because he was looking after her, he had got permission to live away from the seminary. Meanwhile, a deep friendship had been formed with Alan. The next logical step, as Wilma saw it, after Mrs Davis's death, was to invite Davis to be part of the household in Wenn Road.

After he returned from Sydney, Davis moved in and added to the noise at Whinmere over many a long Sunday lunch. One day while Davis was away, Alan made a sign and attached it above Davis's bed. It read: 'Priest's Hole'.

At the age of fifty-eight Davis entered Corpus Christi College and in the following year he transferred to St Paul's National Seminary. He was one of a group of several men of mature age who were studying at the same time. Soon he started bringing them home and Jane Pittard remembered the little house ringing with laughter. This group of trainee priests would descend on the place and Wilma and Jane would experiment with the cooking. 'We decided we'd get out Mrs Beeton's Cookbook and we made brawn,' Jane said. 'Like potted meat. Then there was Jane and Bob Elstree ...' Jane Pittard described how Wilma's son, John, had shot a hare and Jane Elstree cooked it. 'We had jugged hare from Mrs Beeton's Cookbook. It was like a home, Wilma just took us in—Mum used to call it "lame dogs"—we were all these odd bods that had our problems and Wilma took us in.'

Davis had a pilot's licence. 'This was when my son David was working at Benalla,' said Wilma. 'My John and I flew up there with John Davis. But when we came back, landing at Berwick, I began to feel a bit iffy [i.e. air sick] and John Davis went *swish!*—like that—with a bag. He had been watching me. He jumped out of parachutes, too,' she added casually.

Davis was the only one of his fellow mature-aged students who eventually became a practising priest. Before being ordained in Sale in 1978, however, he took a trip to New Caledonia, where, while scuba diving, he suffered the first of a number of heart attacks.

When David Young decided to go to America to study farming, the Elstrees stepped in to help around the property, as did Janet Chandler and Jane Pittard. It was a way of repaying Wilma for her kindnesses. Bob and Jane Elstree had themselves recently suffered a tragedy and Alan and Wilma had been among the first to support them through this. 'David was Alan's right hand,' recalled Bob. 'That left Alan needing someone a bit younger than he was to do jobs around the place. That's when we got even closer because I helped him on the farm. We were thrown together quite a bit.'

Alan's illness stayed well hidden. 'I didn't realise that Alan wasn't well,' recalled Janet Chandler. 'He just seemed like Alan to me, always there doing what he had to do.' Her impression of Alan at this stage is intriguing: 'He didn't say anything very much,' she said. 'Alan wasn't that talkative. We just talked about what we were doing, on the day, with the horses.' It seems that to people who were not living in the house, Alan's withdrawal was seen as that of a man who was 'not talkative'. To those who had known the raconteur of earlier years, the change in Alan Young must have been sad.

When David returned after three years in America he took over the family property and made changes and improvements that incorporated many modern ideas. The methods that he had studied while he was away were destined to help Whinmere to prosper. This set him on a collision course with his father, but David persisted and his methods paid off. Wilma had no objections to David taking over. 'They'd been struggling and, when David got back from America he made a few purchasing decisions: bought a mob of cows and sold them three months later for a big profit. Wilma could see the money coming into the bank account and she was quite happy,' said David's wife, Sue.

At the end of the 1970s the family decided to divide five acres from the property to build a new house in which Alan and Wilma could live out their days in comfort. Alan was not keen to move. 'But I went to the Council,' said Wilma, 'because they were going to stop the fact that you could cut off five acres from a farm. They were going to put it down to two acres. So I, straightaway, for no reason at all, put in an application to cut off the five acres. You had to guarantee that you were going to build within two years, so I did all that.' Alan made no objection to the block being separated from the farm but was in no hurry to build. Wilma had long ago reached a point of talking things through with Alan, then following her own instincts. 'As long as you'd started the house within the two years it would be all right,' she said. This gave her a further two years to work at changing Alan's mind.

By now Wilma was so much in demand as an orator, particularly on Anzac or Remembrance Day, or Australia Day, and often to young people, that she began to draft useful paragraphs ahead of time. On 18 April 1979, she wrote a passage that she would use many times in future:

'Realising that those who lost their lives sacrificed themselves to protect Australia and the Commonwealth of Nations against oppression, we set aside one day in the year in their memory and in their gratitude. But we must do more than just set aside a day. We must do more than just remember them and their service. We must do more than just sing praises. We must see that their sacrifice is not in vain. They fought for Australia. We must see that it remains worth the saving. May we bring to our daily lives the same comradeship to our fellow men and women, give the same service to our country in the battle of goodwill, and at the same time be prepared to make sacrifices worthy of the men and women we pay tribute to today.'

Her involvement with ex-servicepeople was nonstop, especially now that her children were adults leading their own lives. Her links with the

Pakenham RSL continued strongly and her duties as a Welfare Officer escalated. On 17 February 1981, she made notes about a typical case: 'Mr X ordered injections in the shoulder and never heard any more. I rang Monday 16 March and complained, and it was to be followed up. Nothing. Wednesday 25th, nothing done and Dr Y not contacted. File gone to Entitlement Board.' By 5 December, Wilma noted that the client was receiving a Service Pension. There are hundreds of these cases, written in the same brief way in a tattered medical diary. They cover help given to servicepeople and their dependents from 1974 right through to a case that she commenced on 8 March 2001.

At the beginning of 1981 Wilma applied for an addition to her own pension. What had begun as a back injury in prison camp had progressed to severe arthritis, which had spread through most of her joints. Her body was becoming misshapen, but she refused to give in to the pain and her volume of commitment to other people intensified. By September, after applying all the processes through which she guided others, her disability pension was increased through the Department of Veterans' Affairs. (The following year, on 3 September, Wilma was classified as Totally and Permanantly Incapacitated as a result of her war experiences and her pension was adjusted accoringly.)

Then, quite suddenly, on 9 November 1981, Alan died.

'He was in coronary care in Dandenong,' Wilma said. 'I got the ambulance two or three times and sent him to hospital. They'd say he was all right.' On one occasion when Wilma and Alan were visiting the Department of Repatriation (now the Department of Veterans' Affairs), he had an attack there. 'There and then on the spot I got them to do an ECG and they said: "It doesn't show anything." He got into coronary care and I went down each day. The doctor came in while I was there and said: "We've found out what's the matter with your husband." Because, each night, his heart used to stop and they'd restart it again.'

The hospital arranged to operate on Alan the next day, but that same night, at midnight, the police came to the little house in Wenn Road to inform Wilma that Alan was dead. 'He was on medication for the depression, and I would think probably that didn't help,' she said.

'She'd been worried that something might happen to him for a while,' recalled Elizabeth. 'She had been in to see him that evening [in the hospital]. She'd only been home for an hour or so when they said that he'd died. She didn't really expect him to die just then, she thought he was all right, but she sort of accepted it. She didn't respond very much—openly.' Again, Wilma took refuge in that protective cocoon.

At the time of Alan's death, Father Davis was curate at Traralgon, a Gippsland city about an hour's drive from Cardinia. It was arranged for him to deliver Alan's eulogy. The service was held at St James's Church of England at Pakenham on Remembrance Day, 11 November. Davis paid tribute to the nurture that he had received from Alan and Wilma, who 'gave me instant and steady support and encouragement on my pilgrimage to what I have now become.' He described Alan, humorous-ly, as 'a secret intellectual' and admitted that Alan 'frequently upstaged me as I struggled with some difficult quotation.' He concluded: 'But what demonstrated for us all the proper virtues of life was the character of the home and the family over which Alan presided. Few of you here this afternoon are unaware of the fact that to their door, at the farm in Wenn Road, came a procession of those who had been dealt with harshly by life: those in any sort of need, even the need for true com-passion. Alan Young leaves behind him the pattern of a virtuous life.'

Alan had continued immovable to the end on the subject of build-ing that new house. Now Wilma checked the dates and discovered that the two-year time limit was nearly up. She phoned 'a friend' on the Council and asked if they would give her an extension. She got one, of course. Matters of house design were soon to the fore.

She did not employ an architect. Wilma 'knew a man in Pakenham' who was a draughtsman and Father Davis conferred with her on what her dream home should comprise. 'We went in and told the draughts-man what we wanted and he drew up a plan,' she said. 'We decided on alterations, then got going on it. I was the owner–builder and we were paying one of the locals as a contract builder.' If it seems that Father John was taking a close interest in Wilma's house, there was a reason. 'We were driving home from Melbourne one day. He was driving me,' said Wilma. 'He knew I was going to build, and he just said to me, "What about building a room on for me?" So I said "All right." It didn't seem to matter, there was plenty of land. So he had input into the house as well as me.' During 1983, Father Davis also contributed financially towards his wing of the house.

Built in solid brick with a large, open-plan living space, the new home gave the appearance from the outside of being a long, low ranch house. In reality it was two wings separated by a double garage. To the right were Wilma's quarters, which included accommodation for guests. To the left was what would always be known as 'John Davis's room'—a self-contained apartment with its own large bed-sitting room, fully equipped kitchenette, bathroom, and a verandah that could convert to guest accommodation.

Wilma's son John came into his own at this time. Now a qualified plumber, John Young supervised the building. 'My John was the one,' she said proudly. 'He looked at everything to make sure it was right.'

'But that took a few years,' Elizabeth revealed. 'I didn't think they'd ever finish it.'

The building program might have taken even longer had it not been for Father Davis. 'He was insistent on getting his part of it,' said Wilma, 'He went and bought his furniture, had to have it in by a certain date.' The workman who was painting Wilma's wing of the building was too busy to cope with Father Davis's demands, 'So we had to get somebody else to paint his.' Davis was agitating because the process was taking too long. The poor priest had cut through a lot of church bureaucracy to get permission to live outside. 'He kept wanting to come in,' Wilma said, 'but you can never tie builders down to a certain date—and everybody was rushing through to get it ready—and we didn't have a proper fence around.' Being part of a dairy farm, it is to be expected that one or two cows might wander. This proved to be the case before Davis's occupation. 'I came over [from the old house] one morning,' Wilma said, giving a guilty laugh, 'and there was a cow in John Davis's side, and it had made a mess. That had to be cleaned up. We got a fence around the place, then, and kept them out.'

Davis moved in before Wilma because she kept putting off her own day of upheaval. 'I went up there the week she moved in, helped her to unpack all the things that she had in boxes,' Elizabeth recalled. 'Threw some out. A lot of it was stuff that Dad had even before the Second World War. I don't think he ever cleaned anything out.'

While the house was in the lengthy process of construction, Wilma received a letter from the Australian War Memorial asking if she would donate some of her POW souvenirs to its collection. The timing could not have been better because Wilma still had just about everything she had been able to salvage on that day when Nesta James got news that the 'girls' were about to be rescued. Considering the women's haste at the time, and the fact that so much of their property was subsequently seized and destroyed when they arrived in Singapore,[131] Wilma had kept quite a collection. It included the clothes that she inherited from Valda Godley, plus the hat that she knitted from string, the purse given to her by Vivian Bullwinkel, the 'trompers' that she made and many other items. Much of this memorabilia found its way into the museum, where it remains.

The whole family was so relieved when the house was finally ready that they picked Wilma up along with her belongings and transported them en masse from the battered old farmhouse to the new abode. By 21 May 1984, she was able to record that everything was 'warm and comfortable.' Her change of address cards were posted on 1 July. Meanwhile, on 12 February that year, Father Davis suffered another mild heart attack.

That Wilma was apparently sharing her home with a priest raised a few eyebrows. Wilma, however, regarded the situation as straightforward and those who knew how her household had always operated would find nothing remarkable about it either: Father Davis needed somewhere to live, so Father Davis got somewhere to live.

Around this time Davis was appointed to work on the Tribunal of the Catholic Church. It was a stressful job that involved investigating marriage breakdown, possibly leading to annulment. Although his hours covered only a three-day week, there was a volume of paperwork to be covered outside of those hours. The good Father would study papers in his apartment while Wilma pursued her Welfare Officer work in the main house. At 5.30 every evening, if Wilma was at home, came the booming announcement of 'happy hour!' from Father Davis, whereupon Wilma joined him for a pre-dinner drink. In Davis's case, 'happy hour' usually amounted to more than one drink. Sometimes it was tricky for Wilma to get away, but there was never a dull moment in the company of A. John Davis.

At Christmas that year, while Davis was away on a study retreat, he sent Wilma a card that read, 'I have never been happier in my life.'

'He was just so content,' she said, 'He had everything he wanted.' But his health was unstable and, on 4 February 1985, Wilma recorded that he was again ill. She called the doctor, but by the next day he was improving. One morning, later in the year, Wilma noticed that he had not emerged in time to go to work. She let herself into the apartment and found Davis dead on the floor having suffered a heart attack.

The 'girls' continued to stay in touch and, at the Ex-POW Association's reunion on 20 September 1984, Wilma was reunited with Jenny Greer, Beryl Woodbridge, Mickey Syer, Joyce Tweddell, Flo Trotter, and 'Del' Delforce. This 1984 reunion was marked by a public exhibition of World War II memorabilia in the Myer Mural Hall in Melbourne. Wilma's contributions to the Australian War Memorial were among the exhibits, and she attended a formal dinner on opening night, where she was guest speaker. In the audience sat the 'girls' and many dignitaries, including the legendary 'Weary' Dunlop.

The exhibition ran until 20 October, during which time, on 10 October, Wilma attended the dedication of a Memorial Tree at the Shrine of Remembrance, in the presence of the Governor of Victoria, Rear Admiral Sir Brian Murray. This tree was dedicated to the Totally and Permanently Disabled Soldiers' Association of Victoria.

On 18 March the following year, she received a letter from Sir Edward 'Weary' Dunlop regarding the application of another of her Pakenham veterans for a TPI pension. Weary was working, along with many other commitments, as an advocate. When a case became too hard, too complicated, or it seemed to have been unfairly rejected, the RSL's Welfare Officer could contact an advocate to argue the case more fully in front of the tribunal at the Department of Repatriation.

In his note to Wilma, Weary summed up the dedication of welfare officers and advocates in getting a 'fair go' for veterans. 'I am afraid that the Delegates' letter to the unfortunate JMA reflects a change in policy which will lock out most future applications for TPI. It is very inequitable in that the self reliant and independent people who have carried their disabilities for many years will not get the same consideration as those who caved in early. However, please get Mr A. to appeal, stressing his disabilities which seem likely to have had him out of the workforce for a long time now. I would like to have a copy of his appeal statement. He certainly need not fear any loss of pension as a result of the appeal. I would be quite happy to make a comment on the file précis if it were got to me. It seems to me that it is the sort of principle that should eventually be taken to the courts for clarification. By the way, Wilma,' he added, 'do you have a copy of that excellent Address that you gave at the opening of the Memorabilia? I would love to have it and it should be in the ex-POW Records.'

On 21 April 1985, at the Nurses Memorial Centre, Wilma spoke on the 150th Anniversary of the State of Victoria:

'Everywhere we see infidelity sullying many callings and traditions in our country, and we look with dismay as we discern selfishness, greed, indifference and obstruction white-anting the structure of our society. Let us hope profoundly that our profession remains free from such influences and that young men and women will see it as something more than a profession, a true vocation in which they will persevere with fidelity and true charity, holding fast to the principles of life that do not change.'

Wilma remained adamant that, no matter what changes took place in nursing education, the basic principles of nursing should never alter.

On 10 November that year, in anticipation of the following day's Remembrance Day services, another speech she gave made some pithy points while purporting to deal with the history of Armistice Day:

'But let us not be self-centred and think only of our own. Let us remember the millions of innocent men, women and children who played no part in the fighting, or for that matter the war machine, but lost their lives because of the fighting and perhaps, more particularly, the atrocities that were committed against them.'

Wilma's concerns were not confined to the allies, but included all people who suffer as a result of war.

By 1986, Wilma's constant exposure to publicity and her reputation as a speaker meant that she was being approached for her opinion on all manner of subjects. During this year the television series 'Tenko' was shown, a BBC series depicting the fall of Singapore and the subsequent internment of a group of women. Based on fact, the program's stories were supposed to be fictitious. Wilma was canvassed for her opinion of it. 'Our behaviour through-out our time in prison camp was dignified and ladylike, so it appeared to me that some scenes were "over-played"', she stated. 'Some parts were fairly realistic, others not as accurate as we remember our conditions and, as far as I know, at no stage was an abortion performed in our camp. When one has lived under those conditions, it is not erased from memory by the effluxion of time and TV programs have little effect.' Wilma always chose her words with care. Her use of 'effluxion' was deliberate.

In September 1986 Wilma was made a Life Member of the RSL. The plaque reads: 'Life Membership of the Returned Services League of Australia has been awarded to Wilma EF Young by the National Executive in appreciation of services rendered as a member of the Pakenham Sub-branch. Dated at Canberra, 11th September 1986.'

This, along with many other awards and plaques, was permanently displayed in the sitting room of her new home.

A few days later she was at a ceremony at the Heidelberg Hospital, to re-dedicate a plaque to nursing sisters who lost their lives on the AHS *Centaur* and in Malaya. Although the main speaker was Major General AL (Alby) Morrison AO, DSO, MBE,[132] Wilma also spoke and the Major General afterwards joked, 'You upstaged me!'

The plaque stood in a new rose garden. The original had been planted in the hospital grounds in 1944, but was re-located because of extensions to the buildings. After laying a wreath, Wilma commented to the *Age* newspaper: 'In those camps we found out that life is pretty precious.'

Ever conscious of her responsibility to pass on the message to the young, the following day Wilma was up at the tiny timber town of Swifts Creek, not far from Omeo, where she spoke of her POW experiences and played a videotape for the school children. She was immediately invited to speak early in the coming year to schools at Ensay, Omeo and Benambra—all, except Omeo, tiny settlements, but all given Wilma's total attention.

She took up the cause of ex-servicewomen's pensions in June 1987. It was at a reunion of ex-POWs to which Wilma habitually went. On this occasion the function was attended by Tom Uren, a Minister in Prime Minister Bob Hawke's government, and Wilma lobbied him. She pointed out that, until then, ex-servicewomen had always been granted the service pension under the same terms and conditions as those of ex-servicemen. 'Recently the pension for ex-servicewomen who are also war widows has been frozen. Why?' she demanded.

In a follow-up letter to the Minister, dated 20 June, she continued her argument: 'If the financial position of a war widow alters for the better, her service pension may be reduced and if her position worsens, her service pension cannot be brought up to her original rate. If her financial position improves, she may lose the service pension completely and, subsequently, if her position as regards her finances once again worsens, she can never be granted the service pension ...' Wilma concluded her letter with the plea: 'These women have given many years of their young lives to overseas service.'

The breadth of her interests is impressive. A letter to her from the State Library of Victoria, dated 27 July 1987, indicates that Wilma was researching the works of the 13th century Japanese poet Kamo-no-chomei. A pencil written note accompanies it in Wilma's handwriting: '... inter-subjectivity ... inner feelings ... metaphysics ... speculations on the nature of being, truth and knowledge ... abstract or subtle talk … mere <u>theory</u> … Japanese scholar Hojoki or ten square hut … Tales of the Heiski … Kamo no chomei … amoral, no moral, immoral, morally wrong or evil, dissolute …' These are notes taken from the *New Encyclopedia Britannica* Vol. 6, Chicago, 1985, and the research was evidently for a speech to be delivered on the following Remembrance Day, when she addressed the RSL on the subject of love:

'It may seem strange in the present selfish and materialistic world that to sacrifice oneself constitutes an act of love, for love has come to mean a sort of possession, a gratification and a satisfaction. But love relates to the inter-subjectivity of people, to that which in metaphysics is called the "I—you" [and] relates to many.'

Lest it be imagined that Wilma's whole life was taken up by matters of ex-service personnel, it is worth knowing that her hobbies included a keen interest in horse racing. Her home town of Murtoa has a well-known race track that she regularly visited with Alf Oram in the old days; she was a familiar face at the Pakenham race course and was also a member at Moonee Valley. Generally she backed horses for small amounts, but she was a dedicated follower of form and thoroughly enjoyed the pageantry and thrill of the sport. It was one favoured pastime that she had been able to share with Alan.

For the ex-AANS 'girls', there was a get-together each year in one of the capital cities. In 1988 it was at the Nurses' Memorial Centre in Melbourne, a 'living memorial' to those who had lost their lives. The numbers of their survivor colleagues were beginning to dwindle. Nesta James had died in 1984, and Beryl Woodbridge in 1986. On 21 April 1988, the reunion was attended by Wilma, with her ex-POW escort Wally Sheldon, a Changi survivor. Elizabeth Simons usually made the round trip from Tasmania in a day, especially to attend. Jean Ashton, Betty Jeffrey and Viv were regulars and, on this occasion, Veronica Clancy was also able to be present. She stayed overnight at Wilma's then they went together to a reunion for the 4th Motor Transport. Immediately following that they attended the reunion for the 13th AGH. Wally was again with Wilma and they returned to Pakenham by train, arriving around 11pm.

On Sunday 24 April, Wally drove Wilma to Ballan RSL, where she was the Anzac Sunday guest speaker, after which she marched with the men for the traditional celebrations. On the following morning, Anzac Day, she was back in Pakenham, where she attended the dawn service. From there she went to the Brunswick RSL for her usual reunion with the Sembawang Association. This list of events shows the strength of Wilma's commitment to keeping alive the memory of her friends.

By now Wilma was 72 and, although she allowed herself no respite, there were those who considered that she needed a little help to meet the demands that she placed on herself. NN Webster was one of those people. 'I first became involved, more or less as a sympathy reaction to Wilma's involvement, in assisting veterans with pension applications. In the first instance, I was assisting her with her transport. She used to then go into St Kilda Road to the Repatriation Department, where they made a room available for her. She was interviewing principally ex-POW personnel, with whom she had a great affinity. I started helping her to get backwards and forwards, because she had disabilities, but I'm sure that people with less handicaps wouldn't have endeavoured to do what she did for her fellow veterans.'

Everyone who came into contact with Wilma confirmed that she had an abundance of feeling for the work. Each year she would record the anniversary of Alan's death in her diary. She never forgot him, she never stopped loving him, and she never forgot his torment. The memory of this was her main motive for trying to ease it in others.

Apart from NN, another supporter appeared to help Wilma to continue with her work despite her waning health. This time the knight came in the shape of a pugnacious little survivor of the Malayan campaign. A former Judo teacher with muscles of iron and a mouth which cannot keep up with a brain that works at lightning speed, Andrew 'Shorty' Ware serves as an advocate and is one of the most sought-after in his field. 'An advocate,' explained Shorty, 'takes on the case of anybody who's not getting a fair go. You're a veteran, you go before the Department and you say: "I believe I am entitled to …" The Department will give you a hundred reasons as to why you aren't. An advocate's job is to prove otherwise.' Without an advocate to help them to plead the trickier cases, many Welfare Officers would not be able to untangle the red tape that ties some veterans to the bottom of the pensions ladder. Shorty is an independent, an unpaid volunteer. He may accept payment if it is offered but he does not ask for it. He is typical of the amazing people who work in this field.

Wilma first met Shorty when he was employed as the driver of Sir Edward 'Weary' Dunlop. It was Weary who persuaded Shorty to take on the challenges of advocacy. After the usual thrust and parry at the Department, it was Shorty who succeeded in getting Weary's own pension increased. Wilma first used Shorty's talents in 1988. Her diary entry of 2 August records: 'To POW rooms. Shorty Ware came to help us and he is very dynamic with a lot of knowledge.'

From then on the collaboration was regular. 'That little girl [Wilma], she used to have a handbag, and she used to be stooped over. And she'd be looking into why some old digger wasn't getting justice. I don't deny she gave me many a case. She'd ring me in the middle of the bloody night and she'd say to me [here Shorty impersonated Wilma's ladylike inflection]: "Oh Shorteee … could you do me a favour? Bet hasn't got the right pension …" So I said I'll do it!' The 'Bet' he refers to was Betty Jeffrey, whom he usually called 'Young Jeff' and for whom Wilma also pleaded the case. With Shorty as advocate, Wilma eventually managed to secure a better pension for Betty Jeffrey.

On 14 August 1988 Wilma travelled to Canberra for the dedication of Changi Chapel. The little makeshift corrugated iron chapel once stood within Changi prison camp in Singapore and was dismantled and shipped to Australia at the end of World War II. It lay in storage for more than forty years until it was restored and re-erected, this time in the grounds of Duntroon Military College, where it was re-consecrated. Wilma noted that she travelled first class on the same plane as Weary Dunlop, and that she sat next to politician Ros Kelly[133] at the ceremony. She reported that the dedication ceremony was 'very beautiful', then off she went to the headquarters of the RSL for a party, and from there to a dinner at Anzac House.

Wilma attended pensions hearings at the Department most Tuesdays, often in the company of NN or Shorty, or both. Liberal Party functions were consistently supported by her, and she campaigned during the referendum of 3 September of that year, standing in the rain at Cardinia and giving out how-to-vote cards on the day. In October she visited Brisbane and made a point of meeting her former POW mate, Val Smith.

While touring the World Expo in Brisbane, an extravagant exhibition commemorating Australia's bicentennary, she collapsed. 'A disastrous day,' she recorded. 'Very hot and I became unconscious and was taken to hospital at the Expo.' Next morning she was well enough to continue her schedule and, by the end of the week, was at a dinner for all ex-POWs at Jupiter's Convention Centre and Casino.

The episode at the Expo was the first of a series of fainting spells, but she paid no attention, refusing to interrupt her routine or make concessions to her age. Nothing, she was determined, would knock her off her feet.

The picnics for mentally ill war veterans were still in full swing. At the 1989 picnic, Wilma was interviewed by the *Cranbourne Sun*, in which she stressed the need for these functions and for her interest in veterans' welfare in general: 'A lot of Veterans are suffering and they don't get much of a go. Many have carried illnesses since the war. They're not complainers but their disabilities get worse as they get older. Many are told it's their old age, not war disabilities. I think every veteran has some sort of mental or nervous disorder stemming from service.' The last sentence is telling, because more than once Wilma admitted that she, herself, carried residual psychological damage.

This damage manifested itself in her compulsive hoarding, in her inability to waste anything, especially food, and her sudden fury when she witnessed waste of any kind. She would buy leftover vegetables from the greengrocer, to salvage the last pea, bean or slice of tired old pumpkin. She could afford the best these days but she just could not bear to see anything thrown away. She even bought many of her clothes at the charity shop. She kept the same clothes for decades, and would continue to wear them unless someone pointed out to her that they were long out of fashion.

On one occasion she almost verbally attacked an unfortunate newspaper reporter who was visiting her. The reporter attempted to help by throwing out the coffee grounds. Wilma saw red and her other visitor, who knew of her obsession, restrained her and quietly asked later, after the reporter had left; 'How long would you have made those last in prison camp?'

'For a week,' Wilma replied, then berated herself for being a 'silly old woman' and promised herself that she would try to change her ways. She did not succeed.

During May 1989, Wilma went to Perth to stay with Vivian and her husband Frank Statham.[134] Since Viv's move to Perth following her marriage, the two friends had to rely on contact by telephone—long conversations that usually took place once a week. The friendship survived prolonged separation while Wilma was busy raising her family and while Vivian was fundraising for the Nurses' Memorial Centre and, later, when she spent some years living abroad. Their bond was unbreakable. They had been through too much together.

Wilma and Viv attended various functions together in Perth. On 4 May they went to a meeting of the Returned Nurses Association and, on the following day, to dinner at the Naval Officers' Mess at Sterling Base. On 17 May they went to the graduation ceremony of the College of Nursing and, the day after, they were off to a meeting at the War Museum, followed by dinner at the College of Nursing. On 19 May they went to Probus, on 20 May to a conference, and the following day to a TPI service at the War Memorial followed by a church service at St George's Chapel. Such a schedule was normal for both of them and they thrived on it.

At around this time, Wilma was attempting to get Vivian's pension increased through the Department, which rejected the application until Wilma enlisted the formidable services of Shorty Ware. Even then it was some months before Wilma managed to get Vivian's pension adjusted. Wilma's diary entry for 1 July, when she was attending the annual reunion of the Murray–Goulburn POW Association, noted: 'Two people approached me about wanting to go public about Viv's pension but I asked them not to do that.' This approach was in response to Weary Dunlop's speech that night, where he spoke of the difficulties that veterans were encountering in getting pension adjustments, and he cited Vivian Bullwinkel's rejection. Wilma's own needs were greater now, too, and she had to make an application to the Department for authority to undergo regular podiatry. Her feet were deformed by rheumatoid arthritis, which was invading her entire body.

National politics again loomed when Wilma was approached by a student who was researching the nurses' wartime experiences. One of Wilma's replies to the questionnaire was significant: 'As for now, it seems to me to be an error that we are selling our country to the Japanese, who maintained throughout the war that, whatever happened, whoever won the war, they would control Australia. They had no doubt they would be successful. A better decision would be to allow the Japanese to lease land rather than buy it outright. In the not too distant future we will all be forced to learn the intricacies of Japanese bowing and their culture.'

Notwithstanding the sarcasm of the final sentence, Wilma had given a lot of thought to the trend of the Australian government, under Bob Hawke, to sell off the country's major assets. Although she had no ambition to be a politician, she did not hesitate to inform politicians what she thought they should do. By now she had access to a large number of them and she used this access to achieve her ends.

Wilma visited Jean Ashton in Adelaide during August 1989, where she also caught up with Flo Trotter and Joyce Tweddell. Wilma was staying with Jean but they moved into the Ambassadors Hotel where it was easier to be close to the action. Here the former internees, including Vivian Bullwinkel and Veronica Clancy, found themselves being kept awake by the hotel disco, which did not end until 3am. The next day they were off to a banquet to celebrate the 75th anniversary of the Red Cross, then to a POW dinner and reunion. Following this convivial day, Viv, Jean and Wilma decided that, rather than be kept awake again by the disco, they would go to it. There they sat, three elderly ladies, watching and thoroughly enjoying themselves. The hotel staff was pleased to see them and sent over a bottle of champagne, which Viv and Wilma promptly drank.

Even after such a late night they were well enough to go to church in the morning, then to The Snooty Fox for lunch, then to the Elizabeth Hospital to view the memorial window. After that they went to Red Cross House where they bought souvenirs. Wilma then went to the casino, played Keno and came out square. Is it any wonder that these women survived the prison camps of World War II?

At the beginning of September Wilma was in Sydney attending a book launch, after which she went to visit Pat Gunther. By 12 September she was back home, speaking to students at Hastings High School about her war experiences. Four days later, Shorty escorted her to dinner at the Beverley Crest Hotel in St Kilda where, again, she was guest speaker. On this particular night, however, she noted that she was not feeling well.

The following morning Wilma collapsed on the floor while she was trying to get out of bed. David and Sue came over from their farmhouse and David drove her to Pakenham hospital. For the next two days she remained in hospital 'feeling awful', with David and Sue visiting her daily and John each night after work. On Wednesday 20 September she suffered a severe attack of angina. By Friday Elizabeth had arrived from her home in New South Wales, accompanied by her daughter. From this sudden influx of family Wilma could be in no doubt that she was seriously ill. The following week Shorty turned up with Betty Jeffrey, and 'Jeff' again visited Wilma the following Friday. Jack arrived with his wife, Pat Oram telephoned from Swifts Creek and, a day or so later, Lance and Kayla arrived. Wilma knew that everyone had been given a fright, so she must have determined that it was time to get better.

On 8 October she returned home, and David and Sue and their children moved in to look after her. It would, however, take more than a severe heart attack to knock that lady off her feet. A cheery letter to

Wilma from Jean Ashton, dated 14 October, urged Wilma to think about going to the POW reunion in Tasmania, organised by Elizabeth Simons, to be held the following year. She closed the letter by signing herself 'Your old sleeping mate, Jean.'

Wilma persevered with her healing and by 18 October David and Sue were able to go home. On 27 October, following a series of tests, Wilma reported succinctly to her diary: 'Front artery blocked—the other two are working'—the implication being that she would get along without the services of her 'front artery'.

By 9 November her schedule returned to normal and so it continued, regardless of being told, on 5 December, that a gastric ulcer had now been added to her list of disabilities. So the 1980s ended, and during the last year of that decade, Wilma was awarded the Red Cross Long Service Medal. She was also appointed, as a Member, to the Divisional Regional Planning Committee of the Red Cross.

Anniversaries
and Memorials

Nineteen-ninety opened as an auspicious year. Wilma received an invitation to attend Government House on 2 February to be presented with an Advance Australia Award. Only thirteen groups or individuals from the State of Victoria are chosen each year to receive this award, given for outstanding contribution towards the enrichment or advancement of Australia. Wilma's statuette was presented to her by His Excellency the Governor of Victoria, Dr Davis McCaughey.

On Anzac Day Wilma was guest speaker at Werribee, where she urged her audience: 'Let us remember that we live in a country that has not known the ravages of war fought on its soil; let us value our freedom of speech, our homes, our jobs, our holidays, our churches.'

For the annual POW reunion, Elizabeth Simons again made the trip from Tasmania, and the event was attended by Veronica Clancy and Betty Jeffrey, among others. Veronica went to the Anzac Day march with Wilma, who noted that this year they both rode in a jeep—the long walk now beyond them.

Meanwhile, interest was increasing in the music of the prison camp's voice orchestra. In August Vivian hosted a large choral concert in Perth, featuring the music arranged so long ago by Margaret Dryburgh and transcribed by Norah Chambers. After attending the concert, a spectacular success, Wilma visited Iole Harper[135] who was in poor health.

Visiting each other interstate remained a regular activity for the 'girls' and, in October that year, Wilma again called on Elizabeth Simons. This time she stayed several days and Elizabeth hosted sightseeing excursions. Later that month Wilma was again re-united with Elizabeth Simons when they shared a dinner at the Hyatt Hotel in Melbourne with Vivian Bullwinkel, Betty Jeffrey, Shorty Ware, Veronica Clancy, Weary Dunlop and, over from England especially for the occasion, Mavis Hannah. Having put her heart attack behind her, Wilma was on her feet non-stop, though supported by weekly trips to the podiatrist. She was on medication for her heart and also for the arthritis, but she still drove her car and was out and about most of the time.

The following year, in February, Isabel Boraston drove Wilma to the picnic at Badgers Creek for the POW Association. February is often one of the hottest months in that part of Australia and, suddenly, Wilma collapsed and had to be taken by ambulance to the hospital at Healsville. She had an ECG and was given oxygen, but was discharged later that afternoon and driven home. Immediately Wilma was on the telephone to NN Webster, arranging for him to go with her to the Department the following Tuesday, so that she could be present for the POW panel hearings.

Three days later she asked Shorty to visit her at home, so that they could hold the Veterans' Review Board meeting by teleconference. With that business out of the way, Shorty drove her to Epworth hospital where she got the results of the ECG and was satisfied that: 'The heart condition has improved—one artery affected.' After ascertaining that she was, by her standards, in robust health, Wilma lunched with Shorty at the hospital before returning home. That night she was in the Liberal Party office at Cranbourne, doing several hours of telephone canvassing for a coming election.

During April some of the wind was taken out of Wilma's sails when she ran her car into a deep ditch at the side of the Cardinia Road. She was uninjured but there was a lot of damage to the car and she suffered a shock. From then on she stopped driving at night. That same month she was also saddened by the death of Mickey Syer, thinning still further the ranks of that brave bunch of women.

In July, during a physical check-up, Wilma learnt to her astonishment that she had been deaf in her left ear ever since the sinking of the *Vyner Brooke*, when she was hit on the head by the rafts. Such had been her trauma that she did not acknowledge the deafness for fifty years. There was no treatment. She decided, as she had put up with it thus far, that she would endure it for the remainder of her days, although she was eventually fitted with a hearing aid.

Remembrance Day 1991 was special. Ten of the surviving POW nurses attended a ceremony at Changi Chapel to dedicate a memorial to those of their profession who had perished in war, with special emphasis on the nurses who died during World War II. There was nothing in the Australian Capital Territory dedicated to nurses who had given their lives, though the nurses were mentioned briefly during the chapel's re-consecration in 1988. The Ex-POW Association spearheaded a movement to rectify this. A plaque was unveiled and a seat, located directly in front of the chapel to facilitate quiet contemplation by visitors, was dedicated. The plaque, which is in the lawn on the west side of the chapel, reads: 'In memory of Australian Army Nursing Sisters who became prisoners of war and especially those who did not return. We will remember them.'

The ex-POW nurses present were Wilma, Betty Jeffrey, Vivian Bullwinkel, Jean Ashton, Pat Gunther, Sylvia Muir, Flo Trotter, Veronica Clancy, Joyce Tweddell and, journeying especially from the UK, Mavis Hannah. The sight of them being escorted onto the lawn with Wilma leading the file, bent but not bowed, was very moving. They were given a respectful reception by an audience of several hundred. Relatives of some of the nurses who died, including Mona Wilton's brother, Tom, also attended.

During the dedication speeches, Colonel Jan McCarthy[136] quoted Annie Sage: 'With these women it was a different kind of war. They fought against anything which threatened to destroy life. Theirs was courage not stimulated by the lust of battle but born of a woman's natural instinct to tend the sick, the helpless and care for people.'[137]

In her own words, Colonel McCarthy continued: 'The forty-one nurses who died were never allowed to enjoy the reunion with family and friends, return to communities and the nursing profession to which, I am sure, they would have contributed magnificently over the ensuing years. Nor were they allowed to enjoy marriage, families, or even to grow old. They were denied all these privileges. Instead they lie in foreign lands and seas.'

The following day everyone went again to the War Memorial to be shown the collection. They appreciated their own POW exhibit, though Wilma recorded afterwards that she did not sleep well during this trip to Canberra. There were too many 'absent friends', in the words of Vivian Bullwinkel, and the nightmares returned.

At the end of the same year, by now needing a walking stick, Wilma gave in and applied for a home help to come to the house once a week and do the heavy housework. She continued to do as much as she could, including window cleaning, and was surprised if sometimes she felt a little dizzy afterwards.

On 30 December, a letter from Pakenham Shire informed Wilma that she had been granted the Citizen of the Year Award. She was also invited to go to Melbourne and take part in the Australia Day Parade. She rang and refused the Australia Day Parade, opting instead to attend Pakenham Council's Australia Day barbecue. She was immediately invited to be its guest speaker, an invitation that she accepted.

Because of publicity attached to receiving the Citizen of the Year Award, Wilma was interviewed many times during the week leading up to Australia Day, particularly about the sinking of the *Vyner Brooke*. She told the *Age* newspaper: 'The memories stay with you forever. And since everybody's been talking to me about it, I suppose I have been shipwrecked every night.'

February 1992 marked the fiftieth anniversary of the fall of Singapore, and Wilma arranged to be part of a large contingent to visit Singapore. She had to be able to produce medical certificates to justify transporting so many drugs, her essential medication. These certificates reveal that Wilma was suffering from ischaemic heart disease, peptic ulceration, arthritis and lumbar spondylitis. She was approved fit to travel, however—wild horses would not have kept her away—and left Melbourne on 12 February, fifty years to the day that the *Vyner Brooke* sailed with her and Mona aboard.

The tourists visited Changi prison and the Changi museum, then Selarang barracks to view the square. On the second morning, Wilma and Joyce Tweddell made a special trip to the Methodist Girls' School to present the students with some books on Australia, after which they rejoined the main group at St Andrews Cathedral, scene of the former hospital and their last desperate stand in Singapore in 1942. A service was conducted by the Archdeacon of Singapore and the Dean of St Andrews. Wilma described it as 'a very moving service.' Many photographs were taken and they laid a wreath at the plaque where they paid solemn tribute to their fallen friends.

The next day she and the others went to Kranji War Cemetery for a dawn service. Then they were off to the ANA Hotel for luncheon as guests of the members of the AIF Scholarship Board, whose Patron was Weary Dunlop. Wilma recorded that she: 'met Weary and many others. All 8th Division Sisters came.' Wilma's friend Wally Sheldon was also part of the contingent—Wally had survived his sojourn in Changi by growing vegetables to supply to the camp. At this luncheon it was moved by the ex-POWs that they should lay the foundations of a scholarship in Changi 'as an act of gratitude to the Chinese community who risked so much to help the members of the AIF.'

Acquaintance was renewed with some of the Dutch and Eurasian women with whom Wilma had been imprisoned, people she had not seen since those terrible days and who had prospered since.

Three months later Wilma was off on another trip, this time with daughter Elizabeth to Europe. Their first destination was Paris. They visited Versailles and Fontainbleu and, on the following day, Disneyland Paris. Then, while her daughter attended a conference, Wilma joined a tour to the Normandy beaches and other battle sites. One of the women on the bus asked: 'Are we all Americans?' to which Wilma replied that she was Australian. The American wanted to know what Wilma was doing on the tour, to which she replied simply: 'I am interested, too.'

The next stop was Amsterdam, again for a conference, but Wilma went on the usual bus tours and, when she was free, Elizabeth wheeled her mother. Food, and its quality or otherwise, featured often in Wilma's diaries. Peptic ulcer regardless, she retained a healthy interest in good food. One restaurant they visited was owned by an Indian woman whose father was a prisoner in Palembang during the war. Elizabeth recalled this particular night: 'Mum, when she had a lot of her friends over, used to enjoy cooking fried rice. It was a big dish and she'd put all sorts of things in it. She'd serve that dish but she'd keep a little bit over and she'd always put heaps of chillies in that because she thought she liked it hotter than everybody else. Every time she'd go out to a restaurant, she'd ask for it hot. She always complained that it wasn't hot enough. But when we were in Amsterdam we went to this restaurant just near the centre and she said she wanted it *hot*—and she was happy with that. It was *hot HOT!*'

Wilma got on so well with the proprietor of the restaurant that she was invited back for afternoon tea the next day while Elizabeth was at the conference. Wilma wrote: 'I then went and had afternoon tea with the lady who owns the Asian restaurant. She was very welcoming and we had tea and hot chicken legs, which were delicious. They had been marinated for two days.'

The trip continued through conferences in Brussels and London, and Wilma lived every moment, except that without Elizabeth and a wheelchair she often could not keep up with the tours. 'I was left behind as usual, but a lady from Greece stayed and helped me to the bus. In Brussels she went with her daughter to the hotel gymnasium for a 'work-out'. Her diary entry for 27 May reads: 'Elizabeth up about 9am and went to the gym. I went too. Elizabeth had a swim and I went on the exercise bike, with great difficulty. We then had a shower— there was a walk-in shower at the gym—then to breakfast.' Wilma on an exercise bike would have been a sight to behold.

In England she caught up with Mavis Hannah and her family, who were her hosts for a few days. Mavis was an excited host to Wilma and Elizabeth and, after a day or so, they all set off to visit Jenny Greer at Chichester. Wilma's diary entries for this period tell a number of anecdotes: 'After a drink and some discussion, we went to the Bedford Hotel, where we were to stay for two nights,' wrote Wilma. Her room had a shower and toilet but Mavis's, which was opposite, did not. They decided that Wilma would leave her door ajar so that Mavis could have easy access to the toilet. Mavis tottered back and forth as often as necessary until she grew tired of the journey and used a container in her own room, which Elizabeth had to surreptitiously empty for her into Wilma's toilet.

After a bibulous meal with Jenny at the pub that night, next morning they expected Mavis to come down for breakfast but she opted to dine in her room. After breakfast they all went to see Jenny and her brother again, then off to the Fox and Hounds for lunch, after which they returned to Jenny's flat, where 'Jenny and Mavis drank and dozed, and I dozed,' noted Wilma. 'We went to a Pizza Express for our evening meal. Mavis and Jenny had their usual drinks.'

'We got a taxi and went back to the Bedford Hotel,' Wilma continued. 'Mavis was the worse for wear and it took Elizabeth all her time to get her into the hotel to her room.' Once this was achieved, Wilma and Elizabeth had to undress Mavis and put her to bed. It seems that her old pals were overjoyed to see Wilma, but somewhat to excess. On her return to Melbourne, Wilma noted indignantly that it took her two weeks to recover from the 'jet lag'. After her heavy touring schedule, she experienced another couple of collapses.

Vivian's husband telephoned Wilma on 16 November, to let her know that Viv was in hospital in Perth with chest pains, following a stressful journey to Bangka Island. Viv had been helping to plan a memorial to be erected on Radji Beach near the site of the massacre.

By the New Year Vivian was very ill and there was doubt, after her work in setting it up, that she would be well enough to unveil the Bangka Island memorial. Wilma took some of the strain, negotiating with the Department on her friend's behalf. She kept in close touch with

Viv, suggesting that perhaps Jean Ashton might unveil the memorial in Viv's absence. After giving the matter some consideration, Vivian suggested that it might be diplomatic for a government representative to perform the ceremony. On 16 January Wilma noted that she had spoken to Vivian by phone and that her friend sounded weak. During the next four days, as Vivian's deputy, Wilma was inundated by the media, which swooped in force for interviews and photographs. She bore it with her usual serenity and answered the same old questions over and over again.

The following day, *The Australian* newspaper broke the news that Vivian was gravely ill with cardiac complications and would not attend the pilgrimage to Bangka Island. Meanwhile Wilma liaised with the Department on the Order of Service and all the other formalities.

On 23 February 1993, Wilma took on yet another responsibility when what was then called the Combined Hospital Representatives (now the Combined Forces Medical Personnel) was formed. Jean Parry explained why the organisation came into being so long after World War II: 'The idea of the luncheon was that so many were old, and so many of the men and women belonged to a small unit, and these, because of age and distance, were beginning to fold up. At that stage it was only the hospitals. We formed that so that they could perhaps meet together as a combined thing—but not to take the place of their own units … Wilma came along to that very first luncheon. The next year one of our members thought it would be rather nice, give it a bit of prestige, if we had a Patron. All the names were thrown into the ring and we chose Wilma because she was a POW, and she was the youngest. She's been our Patron ever since.' So another annual event was added to Wilma's calendar. 'And now it's getting bigger and bigger,' Mrs Parry continued, 'because at first we had the Army hospitals who served overseas, including the CCS and the hospital ships. We put out a questionnaire at the first luncheon. Someone suggested that perhaps we should widen it to people who served at home, the Base Hospitals, so that was included. Then we included the Air Force and the Navy—so now it's combined.'

At the same time Wilma was involved in Liberal Party business for the coming Federal elections on 13 March 1993, the zeal of her campaigning in no way diminished by her years.

The pilgrimage to Bangka began on 27 February that year. Wilma told one of the interviewers, 'It'll hurt like hell,' but she said she was returning to Bangka Island for her best friend Mona Wilton: 'Even after fifty years, I never for one day forget her.'

Vivian had rallied enough to attend and the large group included politicians, members of the Department, military personnel, Indonesian dignitaries, relatives of the women who had perished on the *Vyner Brooke*, on Bangka Island and Sumatra and, probably most poignantly of all, relatives of their fellow POWs who had died since. After the group met at their Jakarta hotel, Wilma wrote: 'We then proceeded to have a magnificent dinner which was smorgasbord. Elizabeth waited on me. [Her daughter accompanied her on the trip.] We were also presented with a beautiful bunch of orchids each. To bed finally about 10.30pm. I met the Indonesian General in charge of the Army.' The official dinner was also attended by Indonesian war veterans.

The next day everyone went to visit the British War Cemetery 'where our girls are buried'. The known remains of all the AANS women had been recovered and now rest in the War Cemetery at Jakarta. 'We had a short service conducted by Jim Molan, Military Attaché,' Wilma's diary records, 'and Jean and Mavis laid a large wreath. We then laid flowers on the graves of our girls and talked to the Molan children and they helped to find the graves. We returned to the bus and I felt sick and sat quietly while we toured around Jakarta.' They stopped for lunch at a Chinese restaurant, where the medical staff for the tour insisted that Wilma should get out of the bus and have some lunch. To help to relieve physical demands on her, they afterwards made sure that a wheelchair was available.

On Monday 1 March the pilgrims were flown to Bangka Island. 'Arrived Bangka, after travelling in a small plane, to a wonderful welcome,' Wilma wrote. 'Leis around our necks and some young people in beautiful costumes and music, of course. Cameras popping and then in bus and a four hour drive across Bangka to our hotel. A lot of steps at the front. We were welcomed again with a drink and then walked to our bungalow down a lot more steps. We were put into a two-roomed bungalow with a bathroom. Jean, Elizabeth and self.'

Wilma did not reveal what emotions she felt on that first day, but it must have been a stressful 'homecoming' for all of the women, especially those, like Wilma, who had not set foot on the island since the nightmare voyage across to Palembang in April 1945.

The dedication of the Army Nurses' Memorial took place on Radji Beach the following day. 'Up at 5am,' wrote Wilma, 'breakfast 6am and to bus 7am. I was sent in a car as it was more comfortable. Mavis too. We set off to Mentok. We stopped after about two hours for a drink and the toilet and then on to Mentok. The road we were travelling [was] pot-holed and unbelievably rough. The people in the buses had a much worse trip than we in cars. We had a police escort all the way there and all the way back for our four to five hour journey. It was a long convoy of vehicles. We arrived at the lighthouse for our dedication ceremony. There were comfortable couches for us to sit on. And a tape of our music was played. There was a fairly large crowd of us and all the Officials. The service was very dignified and emotionally sad. Viv and Coralee Gerard[138] performed the unveiling and after prayers the ceremony was over. Wreaths were laid.'

The visitors were taken to view the site of the camp at Mentok where so much disease had struck them down and they had experienced their first AANS deaths. 'The only recognisable object was the old well which is still in existence,' Wilma recorded, although there was also a section of the concrete floor of the kitchen. 'We then went to the Customs House but it is so changed that it is hard to recognise.' This was a restricted area and the women were not permitted to look over it. A video recorded on the day reveals that Wilma stood on the Mentok jetty, staring along its length, her face stony and herself totally under control. She later said that she had wanted to stop there a while longer, quietly looking out to where the *Vyner Brooke* had gone down, but it had been a long day and the guides were anxious to get the women back across the island. 'At 5pm we started our journey home to Parai Beach Hotel over that dreadful road. After stopping once more at the tin mine our journey came to an end about 10pm or 11, I am not sure which.'

Regardless of occasion, Wilma was always on the alert to lobby a politician or a public servant. This time she collared Lionel Woodward, who was representing the Department on the pilgrimage, regarding a client of hers who was terminally ill. A return letter signed by him, and dated 16 March, reads: 'I have followed up the matter. And understand that Mr X's lung cancer has been determined to be war caused and that pension is payable at the rate of the Extreme Disablement Adjustment. Formal notification of the decision will be despatched this week.' Wilma the Welfare Officer had struck again.

On Wednesday morning they were up early and set off for the airport where they boarded a small plane to fly them back to Jakarta to connect with a flight to Singapore. Elizabeth left to return to Sydney while Wilma continued with the tour. 'Must say that our carers are doing a wonderful job of looking after us,' she wrote. Thursday saw her and the other POW nurses laying wreaths at the Kranji War Cemetery in Singapore. 'I found Mona's name on stone and in the book of names,' she wrote, adding, 'I nearly broke up when I saw Mona's Number.' This was followed by another visit to Changi jail and the Selarang Barracks. Then came a tour of the north-west battlefields of Singapore Island.

The tour continued until 6 March when Wilma flew home. On 11 March, at a Ladies Auxiliary meeting at Pakenham RSL, she reported: 'For those of you who receive *Chin Up* [the official magazine of the RSL] I want to clear up a mistake in the last issue on page 5. I quote: The memorial stone was flown to the island as were the nurses and thanks to an appreciative government. End of quote. This is quite wrong. The piece of granite used for the memorial was mined on the island and put in place by the local tin mine management. As for the nurses, we all except Vivian paid our own fare and, for the record, it cost me nearly $3000.' Our stickler for accuracy often wrote to newspapers, magazines or other media to correct information that was wrongly reported.

Wilma was back in time for the federal election and went to Cardinia to vote. Despite another overall win for the Labor Party—one which the controversial leader Paul Keating described as 'the sweetest victory of all'—Wilma's local constituency remained staunchly Liberal, with a slightly increased majority, which must have given her some satisfaction. On 14 March she recorded: 'Election won by Labor. What a disaster!'

On 18 April she was guest speaker at the Nurses' Memorial Centre, where she first delivered one of her most effective speeches. Preceding it with an account of her trip to Bangka Island, she inserted a passage that was to become part of many future addresses:

'When the chips are down, what do we hang on to? We value life itself, the ability to live with very little in the material sense, to maintain our emotional and mental capacity, the friendship, support and dedication to each other. We all need each other and should love our neighbour. True friendship is when you will give your little to help a friend in need. War is an abomination and there are no winners. The result of war is there for all to see—broken minds and bodies, broken families and a lifetime of grief. I urge you all to cherish and nourish your friendships.'[139]

FUNDRAISING

By May 1994, Wilma was part of the movement known as Australians for Constitutional Monarchy and she spoke at a meeting in Ballarat where, she noted with satisfaction, there was an attendance of more than 350 people. In her address she said:

'It is a myth that we would identify more closely with our Asian neighbours if we gave up our allegiance to the Queen. Our Asian neighbours Japan, Thailand and Malaysia all have monarchs, so why not Australia? Constitutional monarchy, when one looks around the world, seems to bring the most stable government ... We fought under the flag, we kept the flag at all times—even as prisoners, if possible. It gives us identity and we still drape the coffin of an ex-service man or woman with our flag. Let us keep our constitution, our flag and our Queen. Our heritage is fragile and, when we are afraid of losing something, we realise how precious it is. We still, ladies and gentlemen, have one power—the power of the free and secret vote. Let us use it wisely.'

On 29 June 1994, Wilma became a Life Member of the RSL with Gold Badge. The plaque reads: 'Life Membership of the Returned Services League of Australia awarded to Wilma Young by the National Executive in appreciation of services rendered as a member of the Pakenham Sub-branch. Dated, Canberra, 29th June 1994.'

During August of that year Wilma finally gave in to the demands of her body and took command of a four-pronged walking stick, which became her trademark for a number of years. She was still able to drive in daylight, but confined herself to short distances.

On Sunday 16 October Betty Jeffrey telephoned to let Wilma know that Vivian had suffered a stroke in Perth. The 'girls' all rallied, with telephone calls to and from Perth, and Wilma kept in especially close touch, relaying Viv's progress to the others. A card to Wilma from Jean Ashton, dated 9 December 1994, reads: 'Had a card from Tweddie who had been in touch with Frank Statham about how Vivian is slowly improving. Vivian has had such a busy life with a demand for her presence at many functions. Although last few years not so busy. Frank would help her in those times. We three were solid friends long ago, Wilma—and that precious friendship has continued over the years.'

By December Vivian had recovered enough to walk with the aid of a frame. On 17 January 1995 Jean Ashton suffered a slight stroke but recovered from it and, by 22 January, Vivian was able to talk to Wilma by phone. By the beginning of March Viv was again in hospital. Again she recovered.

On Anzac Day, at the Anglican Church in Pakenham, Wilma delivered a variation on her 'friendship theme':

'We must teach our young people the value of love, understanding and toleration. Show them that freedom not only has privileges but also obligations. Let us look at our neighbour and see in his eyes a friend, a responsibility and a support.'

Later in the year Jean Ashton turned ninety and Wilma was in touch with the Department in Adelaide to make sure that her old 'sleeping mate' was being well taken care of. By October, Lance had been diagnosed with cancer of the bowel and underwent a major operation, to be followed by chemotherapy. On 14 November 'Tweddie' died.

Wilma kept on going and, that year in her Christmas newsletter, Patsy Adam-Smith[140] recorded: 'Lovely gentle Wilma Young 3.5 years in prison camp, she and I at the Pakenham races yesterday laughing and punting with nothing over fifty cents.'

In March 1996, Wilma wrote to Helen Colijn, a former child of the same prison camps as Wilma and author of the book and video *Song of*

Survival: '[Your book] is so real that sleep has been eluding me these last few nights. We all lived together in such cramped conditions but never talked about what had happened to us to bring about our fate. Your shipwreck was horrific, mine was a pleasure cruise in comparison, a mere sixteen hours in the water and taken prisoner immediately on landing and my head wound gave no trouble. I remember well your arrival in our camp on our second trip to Mentok when you were refused access to your rice which we had ready—Vivian Bullwinkel and I stood guard over it all night so that it was not touched.'

On 17 August 1996, Wilma turned eighty and the family threw her a party in a local hall, which was attended by more than sixty guests. She told them: 'I have reached eighty after many ups and downs. I never expected to get this far, the general opinion in 1945 was that we might reach forty.'

During her eighty-first year, Wilma's diary entries became unusually sparse and her writing feeble. She was apparently depressed—certainly she had not been feeling well. All this began to change in November 1996 when the Commonwealth Government approved a submission to establish a Canberra memorial to service nurses. Wilma summarised the history of this project in a speech delivered during 1998:

'Over the years several attempts were made (unsuccessfully) to establish a national memorial to service nurses. Finally a new submission spearheaded by the Royal College of Nursing, Australia, and supported by the Australian Nursing Federation, the Returned and Services Nurses, branches of the RSL, the Corps Association of the Royal Australian Army Nurses Corps as well as all the peak nursing organisations across the nation, was approved by the Commonwealth Government in November 1996.'

It had always been a sore point for nurses in general, and especially service nurses, that no official memorial existed in the nation's capital. There was the small seat and plaque at Changi Chapel but nothing else, and that was in the secure grounds of the Duntroon Military College. Both sides of Anzac Parade were lined with extravagant memorials to men who had fought in almost every campaign in which Australia had been involved. Still more were planned but the nurses had, until now, no official place there. This would redress the balance.

On 14 February 1997 a ceremony was held to dedicate the site on Anzac Parade. Wilma was present as a guest of honour along with the POW nurses and other service nurses of that generation who were well enough to attend. The site was marked, for the time being, by a plain white cross and a small plaque. The day was warm and sunny and a marquee was set up under which the guests of honour sat. Before the ceremony, to the accompaniment of muted drums, four representatives of the women's services—army, navy, air force and nursing—marched to the site and formed a guard of honour around the cross with bowed heads and reversed arms. The service was moving, but perhaps the most moving sight of all was to see those elderly women representing the nurses who had died. Not only the Sumatra nurses were represented but also those who had been taken prisoner in Rabaul and transported to Japan. Nurses who had served in all the various theatres of war, from World War II to the present day, were present.

Afterwards, a fund-raising lunch, attended by more than four hundred people, was held in the Convention Centre. A fundraising campaign was launched, though the amount needed to build the memorial had not yet been finalised, but Wilma was inspired.

Until now Wilma had never charged a fee as a public speaker, but she began to put a price on her services to raise money for the Nurses' Memorial, which meant so much to her. She threw herself into the campaign. When a national raffle was launched to raise funds, she took tickets with her wherever she went and persuaded anyone and everyone to buy some.

Dr Dot Angell, who was the original chairperson of the Memorial Committee, formed a close friendship with Wilma. 'There was a natural link between our POW nurses and the fundraising for the Nurses' Memorial,' said Dot, who spoke in particular of Wilma's involvement with the raffle. 'She probably sold more raffle books than anybody else. No matter where she went, she had her raffle books. I had terrible trouble keeping her supplied with raffle books, she raised so much money. She used her connections with her RSL work and her POW work and any of the functions that the State Committee [for the memorial] ran. At all of her speech making activities, she used to sell raffle tickets or raise money in some way for the Nurses' Memorial.'

It is estimated that, of her own accord, Wilma raised around $10,000. 'Which,' Dot pointed out, 'is a lot of money for an old lady.' She described how it almost became an embarrassment because now Wilma would say, 'Yes, I'll speak, as long as you make a donation.'

By coincidence, the timing of the launch of the appeal for funds was shortly followed by the release of Bruce Beresford's film, *Paradise Road*. On 2 March 1997, Wilma attended a private preview after which she lunched with the producer Sue Milliken. Pat Gunther was also there and, on the following day, she and Wilma were interviewed on film for publicity purposes. In her interview Wilma returned to the psychological damage suffered by war veterans.

'A great many of the men that went through the war have carried those injuries all these years. Been brushed off as being drunkards, or no-hopers, but they've been sick. And I think we want to get through to people that the war did terrible things to people's minds. Made them so they couldn't cope with living. People didn't understand that they were having difficulties. And they just need a little bit of help … There's a lot of men still suffering from anxiety neurosis. A lot of women and children have suffered over the years because of their husband's inability to communicate with them. Communication is the breath of life and people can't communicate. So many men I talk to will say—they'll come out and tell you all about what happened to them during the war, and then after they've done that, they'll say— 'I've never told anybody that before.' That's what they need. They need a catharsis … I would like the young people to be more tolerant of the men who went to the war. And the women … you see such horrific things. It's no good saying, "Forget it," because it's quite impossible to do that. Men who come back from war need debriefing, and they didn't get it. Vietnam veterans didn't get it either. But I know, from working with the World War II veterans, how a lot of them are still suffering. I know that.'

With the sudden additional publicity that she commanded, Wilma lost no opportunity to promote the appeal for the Nurses' Memorial. She turned down no invitation to talk about the movie. In doing this, she would close her presentation with an appeal for funds or a sale of raffle tickets. On 12 March she was at Warburton for a reunion with the POW Association and a couple of weeks later she went to the last reunion for her fellow nurses who had trained at the Warrnambool Base Hospital. These reunions were reducing in number, as were the participants.

The Nurses' Memorial was not the only project in which Wilma was currently involved. She was also supporting the Sir Edward Dunlop Medical Research Foundation (SEDMRF). On 12 April she attended a lunch at Valda's in Warburton. Valda Street, owner of Valda's, was formerly the secretary to Weary Dunlop. Also present were Veterans' Affairs Minister Bruce Scott, Dino de Marchi, who was Chairman SEDMRF, and Jack Fitzgerald, Secretary of the ex-POW and Relatives Association. Wilma sold raffle tickets that day and at the same time lobbied the Minister on behalf of her current welfare cases.

On 20 April, she was called upon, without notice, to give the speech at the Anzac Day service at the Nurses' Memorial Centre. She spoke about *Paradise Road*:

'It was shown in America early this month and has received some acclaim and some criticism,' she told her audience. 'The positive response in the USA said that they related to the feeling of the film and what it conveyed to them. It is a story of courage and the overcoming of adversity against great odds. That is the positive response. The more negative was that some were offended by the violence and took the view that it was exaggerated and should not be shown. It has also been said that it never happened and has been made up.'

Wilma and some of her colleagues were bothered that certain episodes in the film, which did not happen in their camp, were portrayed as if they did. The 'girls' reluctantly conceded that this might be necessary for dramatic impact, but it was disappointing to them that the film was not more successful. Wilma continued to support it at its various state-wide releases, and the sceptical attitude of some of her interviewers angered her.

Shortly after attending the official premiere in Sydney and taking part in a spate of interviews and photographic sessions, she was interviewed by the Melbourne radio station 3AW. By this time she was irritated enough to speak more frankly than ever before. During this interview she was asked, 'What do you think of the Japanese?'

'They are a brutal, untrustworthy race of people,' she replied.

There was an astonished pause from the interviewer. 'You still believe that?'

'I still believe that,' said Wilma. 'The truth about their atrocities has never really been told. They exterminated thousands and thousands of helpless people, bayoneting them and beheading them.'

'So you're not one of those people who is prepared to say, perhaps, that was sixty years ago, perhaps we shouldn't carry that grudge, that there's a new generation of Japanese?' asked the interviewer.

'I don't think there'll ever be a new generation of Japanese,' Wilma replied. 'We've always got to be alert to the fact that they are untrustworthy.'

Her muted though sensational outburst during that radio interview caught the attention of some of the media. On 12 June, *Herald Sun* reporter Jill Singer headed her critique of *Paradise Road* as 'silly road to racism'. 'One of the survivors took to our airwaves recently to defend the film. "It's not racist," she said, "because it portrayed what really happened." Fair enough. After all, we didn't hear the American critics, or anyone else for that matter, damning *Schindler's List* for picking on the Germans. If we accept that a supposedly accurate, if one-sided, portrayal of past atrocities is in itself not racist, what is? The interviewer went on to ask the survivor if she still "hated the Japanese" *Quelle surprise*! She did.'[141]

The film was well intentioned, and the ex-POWs were unanimous in their praise of Bruce Beresford's depiction of certain aspects, in particular the evacuation of Singapore and the *Vyner Brooke* sinking.

However a number of the women remarked that no film and no actors could ever accurately depict the squalor and degradation of the camps. Wilma is on record in this book as saying so, as did Elizabeth Simons, Pat Gunther and Betty Jeffrey.

In a speech delivered shortly afterwards, Wilma said:

'We endured three-and-a-half years in the most sordid and squalid conditions when malaria, dysentery, beriberi and other diseases were rampant. I trust you will view this film as part of our history and work with all your might that it will never be repeated. Remember we are all human beings and should love our neighbour. The voice orchestra was a cultural experience which lifted us out of our camp. The film is simply part of our history and must be told accurately to keep faith with our friends and colleagues who suffered torture and death at the hands of the Japanese. We must tell it so it will never again be repeated. We must try to love and understand our neighbours.'

During July at Wangaratta hospital, she focused on two of its graduates who did not come back: Sister CM Ennis, who was 'lost at sea' when the *Vyner Brooke* sank, and Sister DGH Elmes, who was shot on Radji Beach.

'War feeds on hate, greed and jealousy,' she said. 'We must hand the task of finding a way of spreading goodwill, toleration and love of our fellow man and woman to your generation. The solution has eluded mine.'

She attended the Royal College of Nursing's fundraising dinner at the Indonesian consulate on 5 September. Four days later she was selling raffle tickets at the Naval and Military Club reunion. On 15 September she was guest speaker and raffle ticket seller at the Rosebud Women's Section of the Liberal Party. She collected a fee for this speech and donated it to the Memorial. On 9 October Veronica Clancy died.

On 31 October, Wilma granted her life-patronage to the Combined Forces Medical Services Committee, Army, Navy, Air Force. In that speech she was able to announce the launch of the appeal to raise funds for the Service Nurses' National Memorial. 'Today in Canberra there is an official launch of our appeal for funds of $2,000,000.' Until this date the funding goal had not been officially revealed.

Wilma noted her fiftieth wedding anniversary in her diary on Friday, 5 December: 'Married on a Friday at 5.30pm, 50 years ago today.' Alan was never forgotten.

On the following Wednesday she was aboard a plane to Tasmania to visit Elizabeth Simons. Elizabeth, then in her eighties, met her at Burnie airport and took her on a sightseeing trip in her car. Wilma noted: 'The fields look green and the gardens beautiful. The poppies are a sight to see and the beeches are lovely, and the views. We had a lovely lunch after Elizabeth had given us morning tea. Then a rest and conversation before Elizabeth drove us back to airport at 4.15. Sue met me at Camberwell and we were at home at 8.30pm with honey, carrots and strawberries. Tired but happy.'

A year that had begun with Wilma in a depressed state gathered momentum until the speed was again breakneck. As the year picked up and she became involved in the memorial fund raising, her hand-writing got stronger and her attitude returned to normal. She was back on her feet.

The beginning of the following year, 1998, was marked by the death of Lance. It was not unexpected. The brother and sister had continued to be close. In later years Lance and Kayla moved to Frankston and both Wilma and Lance belonged to the Frankston RSL, where they would meet about once a month for lunch. Wilma spoke at the funeral, as did Lance's daughter and grand-daughter, but it is from his mate, Nevil Campbell, that this quote is taken: 'Lance was indeed a wonderful, cheery, optimistic soldier. Never a worrier, calm under stress, very brave when things were tough. So he was in his life.'

Interviews and personal appearances continued for Wilma, but she commented in her diary on 11 February, 'It is getting more difficult to have interviews.' On 13 February she was interviewed on the ABC's 3LO. Of the Nurses' Memorial, she said: 'It means everything to us—all our friends that died and were killed, ill treated … I also know what it means to the families. Just think of the families who had daughters shot and killed over there, and they've had no focus for their grief, something public where they feel that it's recognised by the country … that their daughters gave their lives, so that people like us are able to sit here in peace and security.'

In April came another turning point for Wilma. She and Dot Angell went to the Noble Park RSL where the Vietnam veterans were holding a reunion. The beer was flowing; the language was as torrid as the atmosphere inside the club room. Wilma spoke about the Nurses' Memorial and made a big impact on the men.

One of them, known as 'Bilko', described how he saw this bent old lady pulling herself to her feet out of a wheelchair and thought to himself, 'What the hell is this?' He impersonated Wilma's movements, showing how she pulled herself cautiously to the podium, then how she immediately straightened her body and read clearly from her notes without a stumble. 'When she got to the bit about, "When I was shipwrecked …" I said to myself, "Hey, I never got shipwrecked!" Then she went on to say, "When I got taken prisoner …" And I said to myself, "Hey I never got taken prisoner …" Then she finishes up with, "And I was a captive for three-and-a-half years." I said to myself, "Hey, I was only in Vietnam for one year!" What the hell have I got to complain about?!'

The Vietnam veterans took Wilma to their hearts. She sold raffle tickets as usual and accepted a donation towards the project, but this was more than a fund-raising exercise—it became a catharsis for many damaged men and was to be the first of a number of visits during which she spoke privately to them. Who she spoke to and what she said was never divulged, but she is known to have helped many Vietnam veterans to hold their devils at bay, if not to expel them.

The following week Wilma delivered the Anzac Day address at Frankston RSL. She used the 'Do not condemn your fathers or grandfathers' speech (see p. 241) and made an appeal for funds for the Nurses' Memorial.

'Fear and hatred are but one side of the coin of human contact—the dark side—the other side being co-operation and tolerance. A mere turning of the coin will affect the conversion, and enemies of yester-day can become the friends of today. There is a new generation in Europe and Asia. Let us be realistic and admit that many of our children have suffered from our traumatic experiences and the effect on our lives.' Again that emphasis on the sufferings of veterans' families, the vicarious traumatisation.

This same year Wilma received the Anzac of the Year Award. The wording on the plaque reads: 'RSL Anzac of the Year award for 1998, Mrs Wilma Elizabeth Forster Young in recognition of outstanding services to fellow Australians and to the community in a positive, self-less and compassionate manner, in accordance with the best traditions exemplified by Anzac. For and on behalf of the National Executive, dated Canberra 25 April 1998.'

On 8 June Wilma was listed in the Queen's Birthday Honours as a Member in the General Division of the Order of Australia, 'For service to the welfare of ex-service personnel, particularly ex-service women, and to the community.' She attended Government House on 2 October to officially accept her Order of Australia (AM), accompanied by her three children.

NN Webster said: 'We used to feel bitter about somebody who got a recognition that we felt came nowhere near the qualification criteria of Wilma Young, with her service—not only to the RSL and veterans but also to community. She was a leader. The person being interviewed [for pensions or welfare] would have no idea of what pain she was in.'

Shorty Ware put it pithily: 'She should have had a DBE and the whole bloody lot! She was an angel in disguise, she was the best woman I'll ever know.'

Each year without fail Wilma had made the trip to Numurkah for the reunion of the Murray–Goulburn branch of the Ex-POW Association. This year only seven of the original POW men were present, plus Wilma. The guest speakers were Ray Wheeler, President of the Ex-POW Association of Victoria; Sharman Stone, who was the Federal Member of Parliament for Murray Valley; and Alex Murphy, Senior Vice-President of the Victorian Ex-POW Relatives

Association. This was the fiftieth and last of those reunions. Another door closed on the past.

On 31 July Wilma spoke at the Australian Nursing Federation, which was one of the moving forces behind the establishment of the Nurses' Memorial. She thanked them for raising monies, then added: 'We must thank God that we are still in possession of this wonderful country of ours, that we so nearly lost in World War II, and may we always pay our tribute to the brave nurses who have served in war. As members of this great nursing profession, may each and every one of us gathered here today continue to work towards the unveiling, in October 1999, of a fitting memorial.' She drew the tickets for the raffle, then added a significant post script to her speech: 'As war is all pervasive, let us also not forget those dedicated nurses who so selflessly have looked after all the civilian casualties of bombs and landmines. For they too have grieved alone.' This remark foreshadowed a cause that she would embrace during the coming year—that of the civilian surgical teams who volunteered to go to Vietnam from Australian hospitals between 1964 and 1972.

Wilma's good friend Wal Sheldon died on 22 August, and early September saw the death of Iole Harper. During June, Ken Brown, the young Flying Officer who had risked so much to get the nurses out of Loebok Linggau, had also died.

Wilma was at La Trobe University on 10 September, where she delivered a lecture outlining her POW experience, and this was followed by a question and answer session with the students. A letter of thanks from Katie Holmes of the School of History, Faculty of Humanities, said, in part: 'I have never seen a group of students so engaged and so moved. Both immediately after your talk, in the tutorial following and the tutes next day, they could hardly stop talking about how impressive you were as a speaker, how affected they had been by the experiences you shared with them and to answer questions …' Subsequently the students volunteered to take up a collection for the Service Nurses' National Memorial.

On 24 September Wilma was again at the Noble Park RSL with the Vietnam vets. She had a profound effect on these men, many of whom still suffer symptoms of post-traumatic stress and most of whom are on TPI pensions. John Meehan, the Pensions Officer at Noble Park, is a Vietnam veteran who has served both the RSL and the Vietnam Veterans' Association of Australia for some time. He keeps a large photographic portrait of Wilma and copies of her obituaries on the wall of his office, as a calming influence and to remind himself of some of the good advice she gave him. 'We've all been damaged,' he said, referring to RSL Pensions Officers with backgrounds like his and Wilma's. 'We've all been knocked about a bit, so we're suffering from a lot of these problems, and we're helping people in similar situations. And it's very important that we don't become too subjective.'

Meehan described his personal experience of wisdom received from Wilma, regarding welfare or pensions cases: 'She used to tell me that you've got to take your time and get the lot,' he said. 'You'll lose it if you don't. And she was one who really pushed me to start, late last year, a Burn-out Course. We got a professional lady to come in and lecture to us on Burn-out. Wilma also told me how to close cases down. Some of us were leaving cases open and, by doing that, our emotions were still open. She told me a few of these things and she gave me wonderful advice. She told me to slow down and not be so aggressive towards people at the Department of Veterans' Affairs. She said, "John, you can get the lot if you just take your time." She could see that sometimes the hairs stick up on my neck with some of these people, when I perceive an insult, or that a poor decision has been made. She used to say, "There's more than one way to skin the cat."'

On 10 October, at the Pascoe Vale RSL, Wilma spoke about the Nurses' Memorial and the history of service nursing, those killed and those decorated. She covered Vietnam too, again including the civilian nurses, and also the Philippine Islands.

'Since the Boer War in South Africa in 1899, Australian nurses, more often than not paying their own way, have cared for casualties in every conflict to which Australia has committed troops. In the Boer War, sixty-five nurses were deployed and one died at Bulawayo. In World War I, 2500 nurses served at Gallipoli on the hospital ships, on the island of Lemnos, in Egypt, and on the Western Front. Twenty-five died. In World War II, 4000 nurses operated alongside our troops in all theatres of war. Many died, whilst others suffered terribly as prisoners of war. Since then, our nurses have served in Japan, Korea, Malaya, Vietnam and the Gulf War, and United Nations peacekeeping missions in Somalia, Cambodia and Rwanda. In all, ninety-eight nurses have given their lives in the service of their country, but there are many of our nursing colleagues who suffer still from their wartime experiences. This memorial will also honour their service.'

Though still so active, Wilma was making arrangements for the period following her death. Her diary entry for 13 October reads: 'I rang War Graves Commission—they will do a headstone for me if I am put in Chris's grave. Her plaque will have to be removed and then, when the headstone is finished, it can be placed either at the foot or in the middle.' Christine's grave lies beside Alan's in the cemetery at Pakenham. Wilma kept a brochure from the War Graves Commission which listed those who were eligible for a war grave: 'All VC winners, those on T&PI pension at the time of death or who are granted T&PI status subsequent to their deaths and those whose deaths have been accepted as service related.'

Notwithstanding the staunch efforts of people like Wilma, fundraising for the Nurses' Memorial was not progressing as well as expected. On 16 October, the Memorial Committee's spokeswoman Ita Buttrose told the press that the committee was disappointed by the response to the appeal thus far from the corporate sector.

However, 1998 did seem to spearhead a revival of interest by the public in Australian values, including the Anzac tradition, and on 11 November Wilma told the _Pakenham Gazette_ that the Remembrance Day ceremony was one of the largest that she had seen in the main street. 'There used to be about half a dozen of us that gathered on the corner but today there was a good crowd,' she said. That evening, at the Berwick RSL, she delivered the address, again appealing for the Memorial fund.

Following a worldwide competition, the winning design, from Sydney-based sculptor Robin Moorhouse, was selected in November:

'Horizontal in form, it will feature a pair of curvilinear, low-sculpted glass walls, raised slightly on an elliptically shaped platform. The surfaces of the glass walls will display images representing important events in the history of Australian service nursing.'[142]

On 3 December Wilma was at the Westbourne and Williamstown Grammar School, speaking to the children. She gave Year 10 her speech on her POW experience after which she sat in the library and answered the students' questions. Immediately following that session, her diary records that she: 'Went to speak to Grade 4 children and received a Star and also a pencil from the teacher. Had lunch and then spoke and answered questions from about 40 teachers and pupils from about Year 10. Was given a book about the school and $300 for the Nurses' Memorial.' Three full-length lectures, followed by three question and answer sessions, for a woman of eighty-two.

During February 1999, Wilma was helping Betty Jeffrey to find somewhere to live where she could receive the daily care that she now needed. Betty's mind was as sharp as ever but, although she knew that she ought to move from her home, she remained reluctant to make that final break. With the help of friends, Wilma took Betty to view various care facilities.

Wilma was attending her usual luncheon at the Frankston RSL, on 3 March, when she suddenly collapsed and was taken to hospital. 'I was there about 4 hours, had CT scan of head and an X-ray and an ECG, all normal and no reason could be found for sudden collapse. Had an injection of stemital to stop vomiting and had a blood test,' her diary entry states, but a week later she was again doing the rounds and making speeches.

By the end of the month, with the help of Colonel Jan McCarthy, Wilma was contacting everyone she could think of who would be interested in attending the unveiling on 30 April of a memorial in Perth to the nurses who perished on the *Vyner Brooke* and subsequently. This memorial took the form of an avenue of trees, one for each of the nurses, each with its own plaque. Red flowering gums were planted in parkland on the banks of the Swan River. This project also marked 100 years of women's suffrage in Western Australia. The memorial was jointly unveiled by Vivian and Wilma, both of them in wheelchairs.

By August Wilma was forced to discard the four-pronged walking stick and graduate to a mobile walking frame. Her right leg was mis-shapen sideways and almost L-shaped from the knee, she was bent forward and leaning heavily on the walking frame, not because she was fused into that position but for reasons that will be revealed. Still she did not let up. Constantly she made notes of ideas for future speeches. On the back of an envelope she jotted the words: 'War that has bedevilled my generation is driven by hate, greed and envy. We must look with hope to your generation to provide the leadership needed to take us out of this morass.'

On 12 August she spoke at the Shrine of Remembrance on the fiftieth anniversary of the Geneva Conventions. 'Even Wars Have Limits' was the theme of the day, it being 136 years ago since, in 1863, Henri Dunant, 'who was so horrified by the destruction and suffering of war, called for an international agreement on how war was to be waged. His action led to the establishment of the first Geneva Convention of 1864. Following this, a further three Conventions or laws were struck to guide International practices in wartime. The four conventions are as follows: The first provides protection for the sick and wounded members of the armed forces on land; The second convention provides protection for the wounded, sick and/or shipwrecked members of the armed forces at sea; The third convention provides protection to the prisoners-of-war, whilst … the fourth Convention provides protection to the civilians caught up in the fighting. To disregard these Conventions can render a Nation guilty of war crimes against humanity.'[143]

Journalist Ross Brundrett of Melbourne's *Herald Sun*, who was present at the ceremony, noted: 'Without Mrs Young the day's meaning would have been diminished, lost in a swirl of noble words expressed by politicians … and the precision of military ceremony. Under a sea of grey clouds, only slightly warmed by the eternal flame, Mrs Young hauled herself out of her wheelchair, hunched over the lectern, and spoke from prepared notes. Seven pages of text she spoke, never stumbling, as she recounted her days as a World War II nurse in Malaya … At the Shrine, Mrs Young told her audience, "We pointed out to our captors that, as prisoners of war, we should be treated under the Geneva Convention, but were told that Japan had not signed the Convention and were therefore not bound by it.'"

The social side of Wilma's life was never ignored. On 21 September she was granted Honorary Membership of Mooney Valley Racing Club 'which reflected the long association you and your late husband had with [the club].' The horses were still running for her with her fifty-cent bets.

On 20 October Wilma flew to Canberra to be at the unveiling of the Australian Service Nurses' National Memorial. This was the culmination of everything that she had worked towards during the past couple of years and she was pleased to be there with those of her old POW friends who were able to make it. These included Vivian, who was very frail but enjoying every moment, Jean Ashton, Pat Gunther, Flo Trotter and, from the surviving nurses who had been imprisoned in Japan, Lorna 'Whytie' Johnston. During most of those few days in Canberra, because Vivian's husband was unwell, Vivian came to sleep in Wilma's room—the two old mates were together again.

The day of the dedication was warm and sunny and the attendance was huge, around 4000 people. Arriving in support of the nurses came more than 100 members of the Vietnam Veterans' Motorcycle Club. When the police sighted this mass arrival of bikies, their first instinct was to move them on, but there was nearly a riot among the many elderly and respectable nurses and members of other medical services. 'Let them stay!' was the cry, 'Leave them be, they're here for us!' The bikies stayed. They put themselves on duty beside every set of steps, so that they could help the elderly up and down, and their language was as faultless as their manners. They looked impressive in their black leathers with the emblems and badges and those bushy beards, and their arrival on more than one hundred Harley-Davidsons was almost, if not quite, as impressive as the RAAF flypast. There are no prizes for guessing how the Vietnam bikies came to be involved.

From Wilma's point of view the day was perfect. 'We were seated at the Memorial ready for 10am,' she wrote. 'The memorial is stunning and will inspire the profession for generations. It needs a lot of time to know it and appreciate it.'

Following the dedication, far from returning wearily to their various home states, most of the POW nurses flew to Melbourne to attend the National reunion of the Ex-POW Association of Australia, arranged by the Victorian government, and to be held in the Melbourne Park Function Centre. Some who had not been able to make it to Canberra were here, including Betty Jeffrey and Elizabeth Simons. Wilma's diary entry for that day is typical of her routine whenever she was a part of one of these happenings: 'Up early. At 10am to Viv's room to meet the hairdresser and have a comb up. At 11.30am caught a taxi to Melbourne Park where we met up with many POW and their wives. Drinks in the VIP room and then to the main function room where we had a very nice lunch and spoke to many people.'

October also heralded another turning point in Wilma's eventful life. Her carer during this reunion week had been her friend Dot Angell, who served in Vietnam as a member of one of the civilian nursing teams. Through her acquaintance with Dot, Wilma became aware of some perceived injustices, and these got her fighting spirit up.

She had learned of Dot's experiences as a member of a civilian surgical team in Vietnam during 1966–67. Having seen photographs, Wilma likened the conditions under which these teams were working to those she had experienced in prison camp. 'Of course it was nowhere near as bad as they experienced but that's the way she describes it,' Dot said. During the Vietnam War, many teams of civilian aid workers were sent into Vietnam to help the civilian population. Among these were Australian surgical teams, which served in such areas as Bien Hoa, Long Xuyen, Vung Tau and Ba Ria. Health personnel included doctors, radiographers, laboratory technicians and administrators who served along with the nurses.[144]

The experiences of the naïve young nurses who volunteered to go into the war zone are harrowing.[145] When they returned to Australia after fulfilling their tours of duty, many were suffering physical and psychological symptoms of post-traumatic stress. It was the same old story. No counselling was provided, nor was there any official medical follow-up. As the years passed it became apparent that other physical and psychological problems were being added to these symptoms. These were probably the result of exposure to certain elements of the war, such as defoliant sprays. What made Wilma's blood boil, and got her so deeply involved, was that these people were receiving no government help with ongoing medical and other expenses which arose from these illnesses. There is a sad irony in the fact that government allowances and pensions are granted, through the Department of Veterans' Affairs, to people who immigrated from Vietnam and who served in the Vietnamese Army. Some of these are the same people that the civilian surgical teams had treated in Vietnam.

Wilma and Dot had been talking about this for some months when, on 15 October 1999, during the reunion of the Ex-POW Association of Australia, they got together to form what would become the CN–ASTV (Civilian Nurses–Australian Surgical Teams, Vietnam). Wilma's diary entry for that day reads: 'Dot and I dressed for dinner at 7pm and waited for Maureen[146] and Elaine[147] to arrive. We then formed a committee for the Civilian Nurses Surgical Teams who saw service in Vietnam. Dot is President and Maureen Secretary–Treasurer. Elaine and I are outside members and there are to be other members as permission is received.' The aims of the committee are to promote and support the development of government structures that recognise the veteran status of the group membership; to act as a lobby group; to co-operate with similar organisations throughout the world.

In due course the group was officially registered, a trust fund was set up and Wilma agreed to be part of the CN–ASTV committee. In doing this she faced perhaps the biggest political challenge of her career. The cause is controversial and, to attain its goals, would involve major changes in future government policies wherever and whenever civilian aid teams are sent into war zones or areas of conflict. Because the case is ongoing and may involve litigation, it cannot be reported here in detail. However, at the age of eighty-three, as an experienced Welfare Officer and advocate for the rights of war veterans, Wilma launched herself into this cause, knowing that she would come into conflict with many acquaintances in political and military circles. She lobbied state and federal politicians, she talked to everyone she met who might help, she raised money for the trust fund, and she appeared in the media. Some people in high places tried to silence her. Letters were written, warning her not to get involved but nothing could deter her because it was a cause for which she wanted to fight.

Meanwhile the POW nurses reunion continued, everyone having a whale of a time. Vivian spent hours in front of the poker machines, complete with wheelchair, and sometimes did not get to bed until after midnight. Wilma's diary entry for the Saturday is amusing: 'Up early and Viv and I had our hair set, Viv had a rest. Dot and I checked wheelchair for Elizabeth (Simons) and waited in foyer for Elizabeth to arrive. We then took her to our room where she had a small lunch. We rang Betty J. who had earlier said she would not attend the afternoon tea I had arranged in a private room. Elizabeth was very persuasive and I spoke to Betty who finally agreed to come, under protest, so Dot went in the car to bring her in.'

The challenge of 'bringing in' Betty Jeffrey was ongoing and something that the 'girls' were used to. In her later years Betty refused to go to nearly every function, claiming that she was not well enough, which was probably true but then none of the women were performing handsprings these days. The 'girls', who were like a group of sisters in a large family, would bicker with her and cajole her, usually managing to persuade her to take part. Once she got there, Betty always enjoyed herself but would never admit it.

That night the group attended a dinner at the Convention Centre where astronaut Dr Andrew Thomas was guest of honour. 'He showed us a film of his journey into space,' Wilma wrote, 'where they joined the Russian Space Station and lived up there for 20 weeks. A most fascinating and enlightening film.' Vivian posed for a photograph with Thomas. It would be hard to know which of these two modest people was more impressed by the other.

On the Sunday everyone attended a service at the Shrine of Remembrance, followed by a barbecue at the Melbourne Park Centre. 'A very large crowd at the BBQ,' Wilma recorded, 'but we procured a table and some food and we were able to spend our last hour together, Viv, Elizabeth and myself. After Elizabeth left, we rang for a taxi for Viv, and Dot and I set off home … I unpacked a few things and then to bed.' Another, smaller diary entry for the same day reads: 'Returned home, tired but happy to have been at the reunion.'

By the end of October the house at Cardinia was being fitted with special aids so that Wilma could negotiate it with her wheeled walking frame and the wheelchair. There was a special toilet seat and a bar for the bed, and the back and front doors were also measured for ramps, but that is not to say that Wilma was less active. On 5 November she was guest speaker at the Cardinia Primary School. She addressed the children on the Geneva Conventions, showed them part of *Paradise Road*, then stayed to take part in question and answer sessions. Far from slowing down, she was accepting bookings months in advance.

Remembrance Day that year was special. Wilma was up early to attend the ceremony at Noble Park RSL. 'It was attended by a large crowd,' her diary records, 'and John Meehan conducted a moving service. We then went on to the unveiling of a memorial to nurses who have served in war. It was my privilege to unveil the plaque and to make a speech, which was well received.' This is a self-effacing description of what was an important day in many ways and especially for many of the Vietnam veterans. She focused on the 123 Vietnam civilian nurses 'some of whom are present here today, who so selflessly volunteered to nurse the horrific civilian casualties of the Vietnam population during that conflict … They too must eventually take their place in the annals of nursing history.'

The men had raised the money themselves for this special memorial. It reads: 'This monument commemorates 100 years of service given by Australian nurses in all wars, from the Boer War through the two

World Wars and all other conflicts to the year 2000. This memorial is dedicated to nurses both military and civilian who suffered and died whilst representing Australia in times of conflict. This monument was officially opened by Mrs Wilma Young, AM, née Sister Oram, a former POW of the Japanese. 11/11/1999.'

Wilma adjourned to the Club for a barbecue with the Vietnam veterans. 'Rambo took Maureen and I for a ride on his motorbike, which was different but very enjoyable,' Wilma wrote. This simple diary entry covers a huge emotional step that Wilma took that day. 'Until probably three years ago, she had this thing about motorbikes and death and all that sort of thing,' said 'Tombstone' Kinkade. 'We were here for a day with Wilma and one of the boys from the bike club had his trike.' Wilma was persuaded to put on a crash helmet and get on the back of Rambo's trike. 'She went for a roar up and down Heatherton Road, and did everything,' Tombstone said. 'That exorcised the demons about her daughter being killed on a motorbike. She'd never been near them and, all of a sudden, she felt good about motorbikes and people that ride motorbikes.'

On Thursday 18 November, despite the reservations of certain associates and organisations, Wilma accepted patronship of the CN–ASTV and for the remainder of her life continued to lobby for its cause in the face of hefty opposition. Out of respect for her memory, the CN–ASTV has not sought another patron. Wilma's name still appears on its official paperwork.

During November she finally conceded that something must be done about her hips. She was bent double from the pain. On 2 December she collected the results of her X-rays. 'Not good,' she wrote. 'The hip bone is eating into the pelvis, and the back is not good either.'

Dot Angell described it: 'There was the stage when this hip, she literally was walking around on a hip where the top of the femur had gone through the pelvic bone. Most people would be lying out flat in excruciating pain and she was still walking on it. I think that sums up the stoicism of this woman. She was absolutely grey and yet refusing to not keep walking.'

On 15 December Wilma recorded, after seeing her doctor, 'There is a 25 per cent risk of it not being successful. Bone has come right through socket. Risk of fracture of hip and will require a bone graft. And there is no pulse in my ankles. If there is no operation I will be in a wheelchair. If I am operated on I will be off leg for six weeks.'

Immediately following Christmas, Dr Elaine Duffy played hostess to Wilma for a couple of days at her house near Traralgon. She related with amusement the sight of Wilma returning naked from the shower to her bedroom first thing in the morning, bent double and pushing her walking frame. Prison camp had eliminated modesty, although it should be explained that, considering her disabilities, it was easier for Wilma to get dressed in the bedroom than the bathroom and she did not expect to meet her hostess so early in the morning.

Later that year Wilma herself recorded a similar incident. Her house stood by itself in the centre of that five-acre block of land and there were no close neighbouring houses. She wrote: 'Marie Thomson [Vivian's carer] rang just as I was ready for the shower, so I sat without clothes, talking on the phone. The mailman came early, and there was I at the window!' She thought it was hilarious. The mailman's thoughts are not known.

Wilma kept in contact with Marie and others close to Viv, monitoring her health. Viv's husband, Frank Statham, had recently died and Wilma was keen to settle her friend close to her, in a nursing home in Melbourne where they could see each other regularly. Vivian was amenable to the idea and Wilma had been inspecting possible locations on her behalf. Viv's health was rapidly worsening and, as the weeks went by, it seemed less likely that she would be fit enough to be moved.

Meanwhile, Wilma was undergoing tests prior to having the hip replacement. In addition to the state of Viv's health, this was a source of stress for her because she was aware of the risks. Then, suddenly, one of her grandchildren was in a serious car accident and lay in a coma. Frantic for him, and with memories of her daughter Chrissie etched permanently in her mind, she visited the hospital every day to be with him.

She was herself admitted to hospital on 22 February 2000, and the operation was performed the following day. During the procedure there was a sudden drop in blood pressure and they very nearly lost her. Her diary entry for that day, obviously filled in some days later, reads: 'Blood pressure dropped to 70 and oxygen level down. Given blood and a drip and dopramine to raise the BP.' Never daunted, by 1 March she was sitting out of bed and two days later was able to get herself to and from the toilet. By Monday 6 March she 'went for a walk' and no longer needed help in the shower.

At first everything seemed to be going well, but by the end of March she felt abnormal pain in her hip and restricted movement. Her doctor immediately called her in for a check-up and X-ray. '[Perhaps] a tendon was split during the operation and is probably bleeding,' she guessed. She had already been prescribed 4mg of warfarin per day, for her heart, and now painkillers were prescribed, but the pain intensified. Ignoring this, she went to the Noble Park RSL for the Vietnam Veterans' Anzac Day service, and throughout the month of April she fulfilled more speaking engagements and attended the annual reunion of the 13th AGH. 'Getting down in numbers,' she commented. Again she attended the dawn service at Pakenham, and again she attended the Sembawang Association reunion. She seemed determined to fit everything in. No interruption to her schedule was to be tolerated.

On 10 May she made an appointment to see Peter Reith, who was her Federal MP as well as Minister for Defence at the time, to lobby him about the Vietnam civilian nurses, the government having just made a decision not to recognise the civilian surgical teams for repatriation benefits. Three days later she drove to Ballarat with David and Sue and their three children. The occasion was the unveiling of a memorial to Sir Albert Coates, who had been her commanding officer in the 13th AGH, and who had helped her so much during Alan's illness. 'A large crowd present and I met a lot of POW. Many tributes were paid to Sir A. I spoke a short tribute and met the sculptor of the statue.' On the Sunday she recorded that a 'devout and sincere service of remembrance for Sir Albert' was held at the Mount Pleasant

Uniting Church hall. 'Then to the unveiling of the statue. It is a statue that brings Sir Albert to life and has great meaning.'

Many tests were made that month on her hip and, on 6 June they opened up the operation site and found that part of the prosthesis had trapped the sciatic nerve. Again Wilma's blood pressure dropped dangerously during the procedure and she was put on a saline drip and received two bags of blood. Yet, while she was in hospital, she published an article 'War is an Abomination' in *Care News and Views*, July 2000 edition. For this she was interviewed from her bed: 'Try to understand that freedom is a privilege that can never be taken for granted; make a conscious effort to render the world a better place,' she said. Soon she was up and walking with the aid of a crutch and was released.

She was at the Department of Veterans' Affairs by Tuesday 20 June, giving a speech aimed at drumming up support for the CN–ASTV. 'Speech well received and I was given a donation of $250 for the Civilian Vietnam Nurses,' she recorded. Two days later, the Minister for Veterans' Affairs, Bruce Scott, replied to her comments by mail: 'Successive Government policy on Repatriation benefits for civilians has consistently required that they be attached to Australia's Defence Force. Only members of approved philanthropic organisations such as Australian Red Cross Society and Salvation Army who provided welfare services to Australia's Defence Force during specific conflicts have been deemed to have been attached to the Defence Force. In line with established policy, the Government has decided not to extend repatriation benefits to members of Australian civilian surgical and medical teams who worked in Vietnam as no clear evidence of their attachment to the Defence Force was provided in support of the Review's recommendation.' It went on to say that the Department was willing to review individual cases under certain circumstances.

During all this Wilma was being kept informed about Vivian Bullwinkel, who was desperately ill. On Monday 3 July 2000, Viv died. The media, the military, the Department, knew that Wilma was closest to Viv so they immediately contacted her. Putting aside her own feelings of bereavement, Wilma delivered tributes to Viv on television and other media. She arranged to go to the funeral in Perth, at the same time helping to organise proposed services of tribute in both Melbourne and Canberra. She flew to Perth for the State Funeral, which took place on 10 July, and put a single red poppy on her dear friend's coffin.

'At 3pm we went to Crematorium for private cremation,' recorded Wilma in her diary. 'A lovely lot of flowers. After the service we all had dinner at the hotel with staff from Vet Affairs,' she wrote. Also attending the funeral were Flo Trotter, Pat Gunther and Elizabeth Simons.

Willy Kraan, Wilma's friend, said of this period: 'On the Friday we went to a 'do' with the Liberal Party and then, on Sunday morning, she flew out to Perth for Vivian's funeral. She was back on the Tuesday night, about 7 o'clock, and on the Wednesday morning there was [a service] for Weary Dunlop. She went to Melbourne to that memorial, and in the afternoon I thought I'd better go down and see how she is. I rang her and said, "Are you all right? I've got a paper I'll give you. If you feel up to it I'll come and bring it over." "Oh yeah, yeah, come," she says. Well, while I was there, a friend rang and asked if she was going to this meeting in Melbourne. And Wilma said, "Yes." So they went to Melbourne that night. A few days later I saw her and asked her, "How did you go?" "Oh all right," she said, "but it went quite late and I got so tired." I said, "Wilma, no wonder you were tired—anyone else would have been exhausted!"' What Mrs Kraan did not know was that, as well as attending Sir Edward Dunlop's tribute on 12 July, immediately following it Wilma went to a meeting of the CN–ASTV.

Of Wilma herself and her involvement with the CN–ASTV, Dot Angell said, just eight weeks before Wilma's death: 'She is a woman who loves life, and will live it to its utmost for however long that she has to live. And she will be involved in any cause where she believes that she can help. I really admire her greatly for the way she's taken up the cause of the Vietnam veterans—particularly from the point of view of the civilian nurses. She will go out of her way. The politicking that she's been doing is quite incredible. She wrote letters to Bruce Scott and Bruce Ruxton [then head of the RSL] and made very clear her views on what was happening. And she likened the situation to what happened to them when they came back from World War II.'

Wilma noted during August: 'I sat on the bed this morning and dislocated my right hip—it was very painful when I stood up, so I sat down to think and fortunately it clicked back into place, so I was alright again.' Ten days later she went to see her specialist about it. 'He said the angle of my knee helped to dislocate my hip. He sent me to Victoria House for injections into my spine to help my back. Taxi took me to Victoria House where Dr B injected cortisone into my back. My back is a little better and I can stand straighter but my hip still painful.'

On 20 August, in Melbourne, Wilma went to the service of thanksgiving for the life of Vivian Bullwinkel, which she had helped to organise. She read the second lesson: 1 John 3:1–23. Eulogies were delivered by Colonel Jan McCarthy and Professor Olga Kanitsaki.[148]

By September Wilma's life was so busy, and her need for quick communication so great, that she entered the age of technology and bought herself a computer. She took lessons and was soon using the email system and accessing the Internet—at eighty-four years old.

Wilma was getting ready to attend her local RSL meeting on 14 September, when the telephone rang and she was informed that Betty Jeffrey had died the previous evening. Wilma had worked very hard to persuade Betty to go into care and, eventually, her old friend made the move to a nursing home not far from where she had lived. She was only resident there for a few weeks before she died, quite suddenly. 'I was shocked,' Wilma wrote. 'When my taxi came I did not go to RSL. I rang Sue [Young] and Dot [Angell]. Sue thought it better that I stay home. There is to be a private funeral … Dot came to be with me. I rang Sara, Jeff's niece, the funeral is to be private and probably not until Wednesday.'

This death, coming so close to that of Vivian, affected Wilma. She attended the private funeral on 20 September and delivered the eulogy, in which she said: 'Betty's wonderful sense of humour and her adjustment to our situation helped us all. During our imprisonment she never lost hope of eventually finding Matron Paschke and her friends.

During our three-and-a-half years of incarceration she was ever help-ful and inspiring—full of fun when things were grim. I recall on one Melbourne Cup day in the camp, Betty found an old bag, slung it over her shoulder and called the odds. A lovely light-hearted moment when we were all hungry.'

In the same month, Wilma attended a birthday party at Melbourne University in a room on the top floor where there was no way up but by the stairs. University staff carried her up, wheelchair and all to the top floor, her sudden appearance resembling the triumphal entrance of a Cleopatra being borne aloft by slaves. She remained there enjoying herself until after midnight.

On 18 October, she addressed a luncheon in honour of Victorian ex-POWs at 'Gumbarwil' the home of Dr Alexander and Mrs Amanda Dunlop at Smith's Gully. She spoke to help to raise funds for the Sir Edward Dunlop Medical Research Foundation, 'the aim of which is to raise funds for medical research which will benefit veter-ans and their families.'

This same year, thanks to Wilma, seven members of CN–ASTV were invited to attend the luncheon of the Combined Forces Medical Personnel (CFMP) in the Dallas Brookes Convention Centre. By this action, the CFMP officially recognised the CN–ASTV. This was a sig-nificant step in the right direction for the civilian surgical teams.

Wilma's health was visibly deteriorating. She was losing a lot of weight. Another hip replacement was scheduled but she was reluctant to go through the experience again. Dot Angell said at the time: 'She's now facing a decision, which is going to be quite a big one—she needs the other hip done. And this one that's been done will never be any good unless she has the knee done on that side. Because of the way her knee is, it's throwing the hip out. That's half the problem, but she reacted very badly to the anaesthetic—that frightens her terribly.'

On 11 November Wilma flew to Sydney where she delivered the oration for the fourth annual Fiaschi Oration[149] at the Director of Health Services Dinner. Dot Angell again accompanied her as carer. 'Wilma was asked, but she insisted—and this is the nature of the woman—because Pat Gunther lived in Sydney, that she should be asked as well, otherwise it would have hurt Pat's feelings. So they did a joint oration,' said Dot.

'Pat came 5.45pm,' Wilma's diary recorded, 'and we had a chat in our room until 6.45pm. When we went downstairs to attend the Medical Symposium Military Dinner, where there were about 310 in attendance. A long night, with toasts and presentations. Pat and I eventually gave our speeches about 10pm and finally to bed 12.30am. Our speeches were well received and recorded.'

Wilma spoke of the devastating effects on the women and children left at home. 'And, in some cases it is even more devastating when soldier husbands return from the war. At the time of World War I, World War II, Korea and Vietnam, the needs of these men and also women were not adequately met. The health and emotional damage was not recognised by the medical profession, the Australian government, nor by the community at large. Consequently some wives and children have suffered vicariously, all have been deprived and have had to face these hardships alone. Men who could not assimilate back into society were regarded as derelicts, for whom there was no hope. Some were to end up in mental institutions, in divorce, or as suicides. Wives and families were given no help in the emotional dysfunction of their loved one, and were at a loss to understand their own feelings of trauma. This lack of counselling has resulted in great social loss and tragedy. Let us never repeat this monumental disaster.'

Present among the guests were Gordon Samuels, AC, Governor of New South Wales; Bruce Scott MP; Lieutenant General Peter Cosgrove, Chief of the Army; and Major General Peter Abigail, AO, Land Commander Australia. No concession was made to the age of Wilma and Pat. Both were exhausted after it was over. People had become so accustomed to thinking of the POW nurses as indestructible that they forgot they were octogenarians. After not getting to bed until after midnight, Wilma had to be back in Melbourne the next day.

A few weeks later she again made a trip north, this time to be with her daughter, Elizabeth, who had suffered a serious accident to her spine. Wilma found herself again making daily trips to a hospital to be with someone she loved. She was frantic that Elizabeth might be left paralysed. This turned out not to be the case but, at the time, it must have seemed to Wilma that this treadmill of accident, emergency and crisis would go on forever.

VALE

On 20 March 2001 I stayed with Wilma for a couple of days at Cardinia. She was in good spirits but looked unwell. When she opened the door, she said: 'I've done myself in, Barb!' What she had done was to try and sweep the garage between the main house and John Davis's wing, preparing for my arrival, and it was too much for her. She looked as if she might collapse. Nevertheless, she and I worked on the biography. However I noticed that she was content to let me cook and serve dinner. When I left two days later, she was sitting in that wheely walking frame and I said goodbye. Then, on impulse, I hurried back and gave her a kiss on the cheek, saying, 'That's because you're lovely ...' and she blushed with pleasure, unaccustomed to overt displays of affection. It was the last time I saw her, though we stayed in regular contact by phone.

On 3 May she had another heart attack. The following week she sounded almost like her old self. She was laughing and looking forward to getting home. I made arrangements to visit again as soon as she was strong enough. She had been told that they would be doing an angioplasty the following day, on 11 May. That operation failed and the doctors decided that the only option was to attempt heart bypass surgery. Wilma knew that this was a matter of 'kill or cure' and was resigned to it. 'There's no alternative, Barb,' she stated with conviction. 'If I don't have it I'm dead anyway.' The operation was set for 24 May. I telephoned her that morning and was in time to have a few words with her before they wheeled her away for the operation. She thanked me and I said, 'Bye bye, Wilma …'

'Bye bye, Barb,' she replied, and it sounded final. It was.

When they opened Wilma's chest for the heart bypass operation they found enlarged lymph glands, which indicated that she also had some form of cancer. Although they performed the surgery the prognosis was critical. On the third day she sank into a deep coma. She died shortly afterwards on 28 May with members of her family around her.

The following poem was found among Wilma's papers after she died. She accredited its authorship to an anonymous poet in the American Legion. It epitomises her philosophy and her sense of humour.

When I quit this mortal shore
And mosey around this earth no more
Don't weep, don't sigh, don't grieve, don't sob,
I may have found a better job.

Don't go and buy a large bouquet
For which you'll find it hard to pay
Don't hang around me looking blue
I may be better off than you.

Don't tell folks I was a saint
Or anything you know I ain't;
If you have stuff like that to spread
Please hand it out before I'm dead.

If you have roses, bless your soul,
Just pin one on my buttonhole
But do it while I'm at my best
Instead of when I'm safe at rest.

Hers was the funeral of a hero. A eulogy was delivered by the RSL; and the Last Post and Reveille were sounded by a military bugler. The Civilian Surgical Teams from Vietnam were there, making a bright splash in their red jackets. Perhaps the most touching representation came with the attendance, from the Vietnam Veterans' Association, of the bikies.

'Tombstone' Kinkade relished the moment. 'Before she died,' he explained, 'she asked that the boys from the Vietnam Veterans Motorcycle Club carry her out. And it was the greatest honour to do that. Then, at the funeral, the whole service was held in the church and only the bikies led her through Pakenham. She had all the bikies take the hearse, just the hearse, and we took her right through everywhere.'

The Vietnam veterans were well represented, some in their best suits mingled with other mourners, but no-one could miss the bikies on their roaring Harley-Davidsons. Dressed in their leathers with bold and brash emblems, they escorted Wilma along Pakenham's main street. Some may have wondered at the presence of the single Harley tricycle positioned immediately behind the hearse—it symbolised the time when she had ridden with 'Rambo' and laid her demons to rest.

John Meehan always summed up Wilma as 'a class act' but let us grant the final word to Shorty Ware. This is appropriate, because he is used to having it.

'She did it in such a meek and angelic way. So, I'm the advocate that *she* made for all the POWs. If it hadn't been for her, I wouldn't have done the POWs. I've done over 1500 cases and *all* that is Wilma Young, because I'm just mirroring her work. They call me Rumpole, Ratbag, Motor-Bloody-Bigmouth … that's me. But Wilma, she's more than that. She's Angel, Carer, Server … all those things. She was a silent angel, the exact opposite of me. If I were as quiet as her, it wouldn't get done. But Wilma? Wilma was silk.'

ACKNOWLEDGMENTS

This book received some financial assistance from the Department of Veterans' Affairs, under its *Their Service—Our Heritage* program. I would like to thank Bruce Scott, MP, who was Minister for Veterans' Affairs at the time.

I would like to thank the following friends and colleagues of Wilma Young who consented to be interviewed and people who contributed otherwise to this biography: Dot Angell; Jean Ashton; Beryl Beaurepaire; Isabel Boraston; Ita Buttrose; Janet Chandler; Barry Clugston; Helen Colijn; Robin Collins; Kathleen Crouch (née Smith); Pat Darling (née Gunther); Midge Donelly; Elaine Duffy; Ken 'Bilko' Earney; Jessie 'Blanchie' Eaton Lee; Jane and Bob Elstree; Vincent Foo; Rob Fox; Gwen Friend; Lenore Frost; Pat Gaye; June Gibson; Katie Holmes; Elizabeth Hookway (née Simons); Colleen Huston; Mrs MK Jacobs (for the late GF Jacobs); Heather James; Betty Jeffrey; Lorna 'Whytie' Johnston; Brendan 'Tombstone' Kinkade; Henk and Willy Kraan; Betty C Lawson; Elizabeth Livingstone; David Lording; Jan McCarthy; Ray McCarthy; Peter Mann; John Meehan; Gertie Miller (née Jeitz); Sue Milliken; Jack Oram; Pat Oram; Sylvia 'Kayla' Oram; Jean Parry; Rosemary Parrant-Todman; Jane Pittard; Harry Sassé; Trish Starr; Vivian Bullwinkel Statham; Sheilah Timms (née Jenkin); Margaret Turner (for the late Veronica Clancy Turner); Andrew 'Shorty' Ware; Noel 'NN' Webster;

David Whatley; Paul Willis; Phyllis Wilson; Tom and Phyllis Wilton; David and Sue Young; John Young. NB: To save embarrassment, lest I should commit an error, I have opted not to mention any applicable titles, gongs, ranks, awards or letters after names in the above list. I hope those who are entitled to them will forgive me this omission.

Thanks also to the following organisations: the staff, officers and volunteers of the Australian War Memorial, for their always courteous cooperation; the Australian Broadcasting Commission; the Department of Veterans' Affairs; Channel 9; Channel 7; Pakenham RSL, Victoria; Noble Park RSL, Victoria; the *Gazette*, Pakenham (South Eastern Newspapers); the Vietnam Veterans' Association, Noble Park branch; the Civilian Nurses–Australian Surgical Teams, Vietnam (CN–ASTV); the Returned and Service Nurses' Club of Victoria; the Nurses' Memorial Centre, Melbourne.

Special thanks to literary agent, Selwa Anthony, who believed in this book, offered me valuable advice and guidance, and brought the work to publication.

Thank you, dear Wilma, for patiently continuing to answer 'the same old questions' as well as a lot of new ones. It was an honour to know you.

NOTES

1. Later Gertie Miller.
2. Later Kath Crouch.
3. Later Sheilah Timms.
4. $50,000; a considerable sum in those days.
5. Vivian Bullwinkel Statham, AO, MBE, ARRC, ED, FNM, FRNCA, 13/12/1915–3/7/2000, a national heroine of Australia.
6. John Livingstone Young, VX20341, 3rd Lt AA.
7. Wilma's army number was VFX58783.
8. This information was not revealed to them until after they left Perth.
9. Matron IM Drummond was killed on Radji Beach 16 February 1942.
10. Sister K Kinsella, VFX61126, 2/4th CCS, died at sea 14 February 1942.
11. Sister VJ Clancy, NFX76282, 13th AGH, survived the POW camps.
12. Sister JE (Elizabeth) Simons (later Hookway), TFX6023, 13th AGH, author of *While History Passed*.
13. Sister Kerr was shot on Radji Beach.
14. Later Thelma McEachern.
15. Later Sir Albert Coates.
16. Source: Thelma (Bell) McEachern.
17. J Bassett, *Guns and Brooches*, p. 137.
18. ibid.
19. See www.angellpro.com.au/wahsui.htm for details.
20. Matron OD Paschke, VFX33812, lost at sea 14 February 1942.
21. Nurses of both the 13th AGH and the 2/10th AGH were aboard the *Empire Star*. Two of them were decorated for bravery: Margaret Anderson was awarded the George Medal, and Veronica Torney became a Member of the Order of the British Empire.
22. *While History Passed*, p. 7.
23. Sister CJ Ashton, SFX13548, 13th AGH, survived the POW camps.
24. Sister AB 'Betty' Jeffrey, VFX53059, 2/10th AGH, survived the POW camps.
25. Sister JJ 'Blanchie' Blanch (later Jessie Eaton Lee), QFX19074, 2/10th AGH, survived the POW camps.
26. Captain RE Borton, OBE, became a POW and survived the war.
27. Sister KM Neuss, NFX75027, 2/10th AGH, was killed on Radji Beach 16 February 1942.
28. Sister PB Hempsted, QFX22714, 13th AGH, did not survive the POW camps.
29. Sister JK Greer (later Jean Pemberton), NFX70937, 2/10th AGH, survived the

POW camps.

30. See Goldenson, *The Longman Dictionary of Psychology and Psychiatry,* 1984, for a concise definition of post-traumatic stress disorder (PTSD).
31. Sister JM Muir (later McGregor), QFX22816, 13th AGH, survived the POW camps.
32. Sister EM 'Shortie' Short, QFX22911, 13th AGH, survived the POW camps.
33. This afflicted those who slid down the ropes of the *Vyner Brooke* when abandoning ship.
34. J Ashton, diary.
35. Brigadeer Dame Margot Turner was appointed DBE in 1965. Soon after her retirement in 1968 she was appointed Colonel Commandant of the Queen Alexandra Royal Army Nursing Corps.
36. Sister J Tweddell, QFX19070, 2/10th AGH, survived the POW camps.
37. Sister B Woodbridge, VFX53060, 2/10th AGH, survived the POW camps.
38. Sister FE Trotter (later Syer), QFX19077, 2/10th AGH, survived the POW camps.
39. Of Kingsley, the soldier whom Vivian had tried so hard to save, Wilma reported, 'He was very sick. We had him in the hospital, or what we called the hospital, but there was really no hope of saving him.'
40. Sister FR Casson, SFX13418, 13th AGH.
41. Sister RJ Wright, VFX61329, 13th AGH.
42. Preservation work done since on the uniform, which is in the collection of the Australian War Memorial, has all but obliterated the blood stains.
43. Sister CM 'Del' Delforce, QFX19071, 2/10th AGH, survived the POW camps.
44. Group Captain Rice did not survive the POW camps, but Modin did and was able to make the pilgrimage to Bangka Island in 1993 with the survivors and relatives of the massacre victims.
45. Sister EM Hannah (later Allgrove), SFX19595, 2/4th CCS, survived the POW camps.
46. Sister GL Hughes, VFX61331, 13th AGH, did not survive the POW camps.
47. Sister WM Davis, NFX70498, 2/10th AGH, did not survive the POW camps.
48. anon, *Bushido: Code of the Warrior, Soul of Japan,* www.geocities.com/Tokyo/9151/bushido.htm
49. Sister DS Gardam, TFX2183, 2/4th CCS, did not survive the POW camps.
50. Sister AC Syer, WFX11105, 2/10th AGH, survived the POW camps.
51. Sister VE Smith, QFX22819, 13th AGH, survived the POW camps.
52. E Hookway (née Simons), letter to the author, 8 January 2003.
53. This statement conflicts with Betty Jeffrey's diary, which states: 'The next week was just too awful to write about—we didn't go near the place again but I really think the mental strain was far worse than even being shipwrecked or bombed.' This discrepancy may have arisen because Jeffrey was in the other cottage with the 2/10th AGH. It is possible that some of the 13th AGH or 2/4th CCS took the cleaning job as a way to earn a little much needed money. We will never know, because Wilma died before the author could question her about this. However, she twice edited the Hooper transcripts and never altered this sentence. When questioned in 2003, Elizabeth Simons neither confirmed nor denied this.
54. One of the female doctors, an Englishwoman.
55. W Young, interview with Margaret Evans, ABC Radio, 20 January 1983.
56. Kayla Oram's given name is Sylvia, but she prefers Kayla and is called by that name throughout this book.
57. This was not the vocal orchestra that was later the focus of the film *Paradise Road*, but a choir that gave occasional concerts or sang hymns at church services.
58. Sir Alexander Godley, GCB, KCMG, 1867–1957 (Governor of Gibraltar 1928–1933).
59. It was from the Indian trader Milwani's shop that Wilma bought the knitting cotton

from which she made the items now in the collection of the Australian War Memorial.

60. Sister WR 'Ray' Raymont, TFX6012, 13th AGH, did not survive the POW camps.

61. On 20 August 1942, alleged exchange ships (displaying a white cross) were sighted in Yokohama harbour by the Australian POW nurses who had been sent to Japan from Rabaul. See *Not Now Tomorrow*, p. 116, and *We Band of Angels*, p. 94, regarding repatriation of American POW nurses during World War II.

62. B Jeffrey, diary.

63. A combination of facts gleaned from Betty Jeffrey's and Jean Ashton's diaries supplies this fuller version. The reason it is related here, in detail, is to show just how degrading some incidents could be—as Wilma put it, 'the sordidness of the camps'.

64. Nor was this the end of the sorry tale, because it has a postscript. After the war was over, Betty Jeffrey and Vivian Bullwinkel were walking along a street in London, England, when they heard a delighted cry: 'Sister Jeff! Sister Jeff!' On turning around they were confronted by Mrs Close and her two daughters, all smiles and full of delight at this unexpected reunion with old 'friends' from the prison camp days.

65. This alludes to Wilma's expectation that Pat would still be studying nursing.

66. Later Kath Donald.

67. Sister K Kinsella, VFX61126, sister in charge 2/4th CCS, drowned at sea 14 February 1942.

68. This would have been ingeniously concocted out of ground rice and anything else available.

69. *On Target* see Bibliography.

70. A thatch of palm leaves.

71. Sister Catherinia, a Dutch Charitas Sister, survived the POW camps.

72. They started out with 27 inches (68.5cm) but as the huts became more crowded this space decreased. This accounts for the differences in the reported measurements.

73. *Women Beyond the Wire* see Bibliography.

74. *While History Passed*, p. 67.

75. Unidentified POW's statement; extract from *In The Face of Adversity* see Bibliography.

76. Lance knew that the Japanese could not speak Arabic, but he hoped his mate Nev would know it was him and not a Japanese ambush.

77. They fought at Sattelberg.

78. The subject of the film *Paradise Road*.

79. Nora Chambers, a British woman, graduate of the Royal Academy of Music in London and wife of a government civil engineer. Prior to the war, apart from her studies, she lived much of her life in Malaya.

80. Lines from the popular wartime song *Bless 'em all*.

81. A similar promotion had been granted to all the POW nurses but none of them knew about it and, at the time, would rather have had the paper itself than what was written on it. There had been a period when promotion would have helped. It could have enabled them to be interned with the other military prisoners, where the food was only slightly better, but, most importantly, where the personnel were receiving regular pay.

82. The dress is now in the collection of the Australian War Memorial.

83. Translated from the Japanese (source: *Chin Up*, June 1996). The original document is now in the United States National Archives, Washington DC.

84. *White Coolies*, p. 122.

85. It is likely that Nesta James was part of the advance party, along with Wilma, Jean Ashton, Betty Jeffrey, Veronica Clancy and Vivian Bullwinkel. Even though there are slight differences in detail, these can be accounted for if Nesta was in a different part of the group and also by the fact that all of the reports, apart from Jean

Ashton's, were given some time after the event. In every account what followed was a horrifying and degrading experience, and it came to be recognised as one of the many war crimes associated with the internment of these women.
86. To date, the Japanese have not apologised.
87. *White Coolies*, p. 136.
88. Audrey Owen was a New Zealand civilian who came to Singapore in 1939. Before internment she had been a dedicated worker for the YWCA in both New Zealand and Malaysia.
89. Every term such as 'hospital', 'convalescent ward', or even 'kitchen' or 'church' is used in the context of the squalor and inadequacies of the prison camps.
90. Sister IA Singleton, VFX48842, 2/10th AGH.
91. Sister Catherinia, interview for *Song of Survival*.
92. *White Coolies*, p. 151.
93. *Women Beyond the Wire*, p. 234.
94. Sister KC Blake, NFX70528, 2/10th AGH survived the POW camps.
95. Sister CSM Oxley, QFX19073, 2/10th AGH survived the POW camps.
96. *Women Beyond the Wire*, p. 244.
97. The names Ishimara and Shigemura refer to the same man, the spelling being based on the witnesses' interpretation of how the Japanese name sounded and the transcriber's of how to spell it.
98. Sister RD Freeman, VFX39351, 2/10th AGH.
99. *White Coolies*, p. 179.
100.Sister PB Mittelheuser, QFX19068, 2/10th AGH.
101.*Prelude to the Monsoon*, p. 187.
102.Major Gideon François Jacobs, author of *Prelude to the Monsoon*.
103.For the full story, see *Prelude to the Monsoon*.
104.A small number of Japanese officers followed the traditional code by taking their own lives. Compared with the number of Japanese officers on Sumatra, the suicide rate is insignificant.
105.This is hearsay.
106.*Prelude to the Monsoon*, p. 134.
107.Sister JG Doyle, NFX70449, 2/10th AGH.
108.Madson flew a plane load of gravely ill Palembang POWs to Singapore.
109.Betty Jeffrey was known to be a great prankster.
110.Wilma explained that the prisoners needed all the protection they could get. 'It was more dangerous getting out than getting in,' she said. 'As he'll tell you in his book [GF 'Jake' Jacobs] he went to one camp where there were Swiss people and they'd all been exterminated. The whole camp. So there was great danger.' This massacre, which occurred at Brastagi on Sumatra, was attributed to Indonesian rebels, but Jacobs opined that Japanese were also implicated.
111.Matron AM 'Annie' Sage (Matron-in-Chief, AANS) and Sister Floyd (of the original 2/10th AGH, who had been evacuated aboard the *Empire Star*).
112.Major Harry Windsor would later perform Australia's first heart transplant operation.
113.The other nurse was probably Beryl 'Woodie' Woodbridge.
114.The 'purple or pink' hair that Wilma described was probably the fashion for using henna that was popular immediately after the war ended. The culture gap was wide between the nurses and their contemporaries. So much had happened in the outside world, there was so much to learn. Towards the end of her life, Wilma told the author that she was still hearing about events or happenings that she had missed when she was in the prison camps.
115.Major-General Sir Winston Joseph Dugan, GCMG, CB, DO (Governor of Victoria 17/7/39–20/2/49).

116. *On the Duckboards* see Bibliography.
117. Another agricultural college in the same department of the University of Melbourne.
118. Sister Margaret Anderson (later O'Bryan) was awarded the George Medal for bravery aboard the *Empire Star.*
119. Australian slang for a closed-in verandah.
120. The YHA is a long-established non-profit organisation. It helps travellers with low-cost accommodation and has no age limit on membership.
121. 'Sporadic and unpredictable explosions of aggressive behaviour may also be associated with PTSD.' CR Figley, *Trauma and its wake*, vol. I, Sunner/Mazel, New York, 1985.
122. Noel Webster prefers to be called 'NN' and is referred to as NN throughout this book.
123. W Kraan, letter of support for Wilma's AM award.
124. KR Doherty, submission for Wilma's Anzac of the Year award.
125. Fred Hooper was then Principal of Koo Wee Rup High School.
126. Named after Henri Dunant, a Swiss, who founded the Red Cross in Italy in 1859.
127. Mrs Boraston still had cupboards full of crockery and cutlery when the author interviewed her in March 2001. She had only recently asked Wilma what she should do with the equipment. Wilma's instruction, only a few weeks before her death, was 'Hang onto it, we might need it again.'
128. A Young, *An Account of an Accident* see Bibliography.
129. The man is probably still living at the time of writing, thus the author has chosen not to reveal his identity.
130. The final paragraph reads: 'Once sufficient funds are available for adequate facilities to be provided, the Act will be proclaimed and developments will determine the degree to which the Assessment Centres should be provided for country areas.'
131. Much was seized to be either destroyed or fumigated for health reasons.
132. Major General Morrison was at the time Honorary Colonel Commandant of the Royal Australian Regiment.
133. Ros Kelly was Minister for the Environment in Bob Hawke's Labor government.
134. Lieutenant-Colonel F Statham predeceased Vivian.
135. Married name Iole Burkitt.
136. Colonel J McCarthy ARRC (retired), Honorary Colonel and Representative Honorary Colonel RAANC.
137. Colonel AM Sage, CBE, RRC, foreword to *White Coolies.*
138. Colonel C Gerard, RAANC, Matron-in-Chief and Director of Army Nursing.
139. *This War Never Ends: the pain of separation and return*, see Bibliography.
140. Patsy Adam-Smith, AO, OBE; respected Australian author.
141. J Singer, *Herald Sun*, 12 June 1997, p. 19.
142. Department of Veterans' Affairs, *Vetaffairs*, vol. 14, no. 3, November 1998.
143. W Young, 12 August 1999.
144. See www. angellpro.com.au/cnastv.htm
145. See Dr D Angell, *Breaking the Silence: the meaning of the experience for the civilian nurses in Vietnam,* PhD thesis, La Trobe University, Melbourne.
146. Maureen (McLeod) Spicer, Research Co-ordinator, Department of Emergency Medicine, Royal Children's Hospital, Melbourne.
147. Dr Elaine Duffy, Dean Professor of Nursing, Windsor University, Ontario.
148. Professor Olga Kanitsaki, Head of Department, School of Nursing, RMIT University, Melbourne.
149. Fiaschi was the first Surgeon General of Military Medicine.

BIBLIOGRAPHY

BOOKS AND PERIODICALS

The official newsletter of the Sembawang Association, *Apa Khabar*, March 2001.

Bassett, J, *Guns and Brooches,* Oxford University Press, 1992.

Bowman, AM, *Not Now Tomorrow*, Daisy Press, 1996.

Bryant, RK, Harris, AL and Rae, CJE, *On Target*, 2nd/3rd Light Ant-Aircraft Regiment (self-published), 1987.

Hall, ER, *Glory in Chaos—RAAF in the Far East, 1940–1942*, The Sembawang Association (self-published), 1989.

Hamilton, T, *Soldier Surgeon in Malaya*, Angus & Robertson, 1957.

Hunter-Payne, G, *On the Duckboards*, Allen & Unwin, 1995.

Jacobs, GF, *Prelude to the Monsoon,* George Mann Books, 1979.

Jeffrey, B, *White Coolies*, Angus and Robertson, 1954.

Kenny, C, *Captives,* University of Queensland Press, 1986.

McKernan, M, *This War Never Ends: the pain of separation and return*, University of Queensland Press, 2001.

Norman, E, *We Band of Angels*, Random House, New York, 1999.

Sandilands, J and Warner, L, *Women Beyond The Wire*, Michael Joseph, London, 1982.

Simons, JE, *While History Passed*, William Heinemann, 1954 (also published as *In Japanese Hands*).

DOCUMENTS IN THE COLLECTION OF THE AUSTRALIAN WAR MEMORIAL

Australian War Crimes Board of Inquiry (ref. AWM54–553/6/2).

Australian War Crimes Board of Inquiry (ref. AWM54–1010/6/126).

Australian War Crimes Board of Inquiry, Vivian Bullwinkel testimony (ref. AWM54–1010/4/24).

Australian War Crimes Board of Inquiry, Nesta James testimony (ref. AWM54–1010/4/78).

Bullwinkel, V, personal papers (ref. PR1216 AWM).

Clancy, V, memoirs (ref. MSS1086 AWM).

Jeffrey, AM 'Betty', diaries (ref. 3DRL/1857 AWM).

Mathieson, J, letter to Wilma Oram (ref. AWM PR88/163).

Oram family, wartime letters to Wilma Oram (ref. AWM PR84/345).

UNPUBLISHED PAPERS

Angell, D, *Breaking the Silence; the meaning of the experience of the civilian nurses in Vietnam*, PhD thesis, La Trobe University, Melbourne, 2002.

Ashton, J, wartime diary, courtesy of Jean Ashton.

Davis, AJ, speeches, courtesy of Wilma Oram Young.

Friend, G and Jeffrey, B, interview notes for the radio series *White Coolies*, 1956, courtesy of Gwen Friend.

Hookway, E (née Simons), letter to the author, 8 January 2003.

Jeffrey, B, personal letters to Gwen Friend, courtesy of Gwen Friend.

Mann, Lieutenant AJ, memoirs, courtesy of his family.

Oram family, wartime letters, courtesy of Wilma Oram Young.

Oram Young, W, speeches, courtesy of Wilma Oram Young.

Oram Young, W, personal diaries and papers, courtesy of her family and Dot Angell.★

Wilson PR (Hon. librarian, RAANCA & R&SNC, Victoria), *Nomination for an Award in The Order of Australia*, by permission of Phyllis R Wilson.

Wilton, M, wartime letters, courtesy of the Wilton family.

Young, A, letters, courtesy of Wilma Oram Young.

Young, A, *An Account of an Accident*, courtesy of Wilma Oram Young.

★At the time of writing, the personal papers of Wilma Oram Young had not yet been catalogued.

AUDIOVISUAL SOURCES

Amateur audio tape, Barry Clugston interview with Nevil Campbell, 1 June 1998, by permission of Barry Clugston.

Amateur audio tape, Wilma Young speech to colleagues, Warrnambool, 1960.

In the Face of Adversity, motion picture, Kestrel Films (for the Department of Veterans' Affairs).

Paradise Road promotional interviews, video, 3 March 1997, by permission of Sue Milliken.

Song of Survival, motion picture, Veriation Films, California, USA, 1985, by permission of Helen Colijn

Survivor, television program, Crawford Productions, Melbourne, November 1986.

Talking History: the survival series, episode 5, television program, Australian Broadcasting Corporation, 8 August 1987.

This Is Your Life, Vivian Bullwinkel episode, television program, Channel 7, Sydney, 24 April 1977.

Roger Penny interview with Wilma Oram Young, radio program, Australian Broadcasting Corporation, 11 April 1989.

Unveiling of the nursing memorial plaque at Changi Chapel, amateur video recording, Canberra, 11 November 1991

Amateur audio tape, Barbara Angell interviews with: Dot Angell, 21/3/01; Isabel Boraston, 21/3/01; Ken Brown, 18/9/97; Janet Chandler, 7/9/00; Kathleen (Smith) Crouch, 14/3/01; Midge Donelly, 24/3/01; Bob and Jane Elstree, 6/9/00; Rob Fox, 21/3/01; Pat Gunther Darling, 6/2/03; Heather James, 4/9/00; Betty Jeffrey, 7/6/97; Lorna 'Whytie' Johnston, 5/5/98; Brendan 'Tombstone' Kinkade, 13/9/01; Willy and Henk Kraan, 6/9/00; Jessie 'Blanchie' Eaton Lee, 6/5/98; Elizabeth Livingstone, 11/1/01; David Lording, 8/9/00; Gertie (Jeitz) Miller, 14/3/01; John Meehan, 13/9/01; Jack Oram, 10/9/00; Kayla Oram, 18/3/01; Pat Oram, 24/3/01; Jean Parry, 5/9/00; Jane Pittard, 7/9/00; Harry Sassé, 4/9/00; Sheilah (Jenkin) Timms, 16/3/01; Andrew 'Shorty' Ware, 13/9/01; Noel 'NN' Webster, 7/9/00; Tom Wilton, 16/3/01; John Young, 6/9/00; David Young, 6/9/00; Sue Young, 21/3/01; Wilma Oram Young, 6/6/97, 9/2/00, 6/6/00, 11/1/01, 20/3/01.

THE HOOPER TRANSCRIPTS

Mr Fred Hooper was headmaster of Koo Wee Rup High School in Gippsland, Victoria. During 1992 he interviewed Wilma for a biography for which, eventually, no publisher could be found. These interview tapes remained in Wilma's copyright and, during 1999, Wilma edited and updated the transcripts for the author (see Wilma's diary entry for Monday 25 October 1999). These edited and updated transcripts are used with her permission. The writer acknowledges the extent of the original work done by Mr Fred Hooper, but has used none of it apart from Wilma's edited transcripts of the interviews. The tapes, from which these transcripts were taken, are only one of many acknowledged sources of information for this current work. The author wishes to thank the Hooper family for releasing the unedited tapes. They are now in the personal collection of Wilma Oram Young.

INDEX